AVICENNA

Of all the philosophers in the West, none, perhaps, is better known by name and less familiar in the actual content of his ideas than the medieval Muslim philosopher, physician, princely minister and naturalist, Abu Ali Ibn Sina, known since the days of the scholastics as Avicenna. In this lucid and witty book, Lenn E. Goodman, himself a philosopher, and long known for his studies of Arabic thought, presents a factual, pithy and engaging account of Avicenna's philosophy. Setting the thinker in the context of his often turbulent times and tracing the roots and influences of Avicenna's ideas, Goodman offers a factual and credible philosophical portrait of one of the world's greatest metaphysicians.

This book details Avicenna's account of being as a synthesis between the seemingly irreconcilable extremes of Aristotelian eternalism and the creationism of monotheistic scripture. It examines Avicenna's distinctive theory of knowledge, his ideas about immortality and individuality, including the famous Floating Man argument, his contributions to logic, and his probing thoughts on rhetoric and poetics. Taking advantage of the latest scholarship, Goodman's book is more than a philosophical appreciation. In every section, it considers the abiding value of Avicenna's contributions, assaying his thought against the responses of his contemporaries and successors but also against our current philosophical understanding.

Avicenna will have considerable appeal for all Arabists and Islamicists and also students and scholars of philosophy.

L. E. Goodman is Professor of Philosophy at the University of Hawaii.

ARABIC THOUGHT AND CULTURE

This new series is designed to provide straightforward introductions for the western reader to some of the major figures and movements of Arabic thought. Philosophers, historians, and geographers are all seminal figures in the history of thought, and some names, such as Averroes and Avicenna, are already part of the western tradition. Mathematicians, linguistic theorists, and astronomers have as significant a part to play as groups of thinkers such as the Illuminationists. With the growing importance of the Arab world on the international scene, these succinct and authoritative works will be welcomed not only by teachers and students of Arab history and of philosophy, but by journalists, travellers, teachers of English as a second language, and business people – in fact any who have to come to an understanding of this non-western culture in the course of their daily work.

Also available in this series:

AL-FĀRĀBĪ *Ian Richard Netton*
IBN KHALDUN *Aziz Al-Azmeh*
IBN RUSHD (*Averroes*) *Dominique Urvoy*
MOSES MAIMONIDES *Oliver Leaman*
THE ARABIC LINGUISTIC TRADITION
Georges Bohas, Jean-Patrick Guillaume, Djamel Eddine Kouloughli
THE CLASSICAL HERITAGE IN ISLAM *Franz Rosenthal*

Forthcoming:
IBN ARABI *Ronald Nettler*
NAGUIB MAHFOUZ *Rasheed El-Enany*

AVICENNA

Lenn E. Goodman

ROUTLEDGE

London and New York

First published 1992
by Routledge
11 New Fetter Lane, London EC4P 4EE

Simultaneously published in the USA and Canada
by Routledge
a division of Routledge, Chapman and Hall Inc.
29 West 35th Street, New York, NY 10001

Typeset in 10 on 12 point Bembo by
Leaper & Gard Ltd, Bristol, England
Printed in Great Britain by
TJ Press (Padstow) Ltd, Padstow, Cornwall

British Library Cataloguing in Publication Data
Goodman, L.E. (Lenn Evan)
Avicenna. – (Arabic thought and culture)
I. Title II. Series
181.5

Library of Congress Cataloging-in-Publication Data
Goodman, Lenn Evan,
Avicenna/Lenn E. Goodman.
p. cm. – (Arabic thought and culture)
Includes bibliographical references and index.
1. Avicenna, 980–1037. I. Title. II. Series.
B751.27G66 1992
181′.5-dc20 91-40142

ISBN 0-415-01929-X
ISBN 0-415-07409-6 pbk

CONTENTS

PREFACE

The name of Avicenna is well known in the west. His ideas, less so. Many readers of philosophy know that philosophical inquiry and exploration were nourished and sustained in Arabic and Hebrew texts and discussions during the long period between the closure of Plato's Academy a thousand years after the birth of Socrates and the first light of the Renaissance, sparked in part by translations of philosophical works from Arabic into Latin in late twelfth-century Toledo. But few are aware of the exact nature of the philosophical contributions, if any, of "the Arabs." Fewer still, even among specialists in philosophy and philosophical history, are aware of the abiding philosophical interest of the ideas and arguments of the great Muslim and Jewish philosophers who wrote in Arabic, of whom, at least in the area of metaphysics, Avicenna was the outstanding example.

The great names in the Islamic philosophical tradition, which flourished in the ninth to fourteenth centuries, are al-Kindī (c. 801–66), al-Rāzī (d. 925 or 932), al-Fārābī (c. 870–950), Ibn Miskawayh (936–1030), Avicenna (980–1037), al-Ghazālī (1058–1111), Ibn Ṭufayl (c. 1100–85), Ibn Rushd (1126–98), and Ibn Khaldūn (1332–1406). Al-Kindī was an Arab nobleman and physician, patron of translations from Greek into Arabic and ardent advocate of openness to truth, regardless of its source. Al-Rāzī was a Persian physician, participant in and critic of the Galenic tradition of medicine, iconoclastic cosmologist, and mildly ascetic Epicurean, who denied that any man had privileged access to intelligence, whether by nature or from God. Ibn Miskawayh was a Persian courtier, historian, and ethicist who naturalized Greek virtue ethics against the background of the command ethics of the Qur'ān.

Al-Fārābī was a logician and theorist of language and politics. Of Turkic origin, he championed the underlying harmony of Plato and

Aristotle and saw the Qur'ān as the poetic expression of truths known more directly through the insights of philosophers. He viewed all religions as imaginative projections, translating into norms and symbols the pure ideas that flow into the prepared intelligence of the inquirer from the supernal hypostasis known as the Active Intellect. Al-Ghazālī was an Eastern Persian theologian whose critical thinking brought him to a state of crisis that provoked him to flee the political instability and intellectual disorder brought about in his times by sectarianism and philosophy respectively. He found shelter and spiritual security in Sufism, rebuilding his faith through mystic praxis. Writing from the vantage point of his rebuilt faith, he exposed the inner tensions of the Islamic philosophical synthesis in his famous work, *The Incoherence of the Philosophers.*

Ibn Ṭufayl, a Spanish Arab, worked to rebuild that synthesis, through a philosophical fable, the tale of a child growing up in isolation on an equatorial island and discovering for himself the truths that underlie the symbols of the Qur'ān – truths that would reconcile the insights of al-Ghazālī with those of the Philosophers. Ibn Rushd (Averroes), a jurist and physician as well as a philosopher, was the scion of a long line of Arab *qāḍīs* at Cordova. Introduced to the Sultan by Ibn Ṭufayl, he was commissioned to write his extensive and faithful commentaries on the works of Aristotle. Struggling to defend the status and define the standing of philosophy in the Islamic milieu, he took up the challenge of al-Ghazālī, in his defense of the philosophic tradition, *The Incoherence of the Incoherence.*

Ibn Khaldūn was an Arab who spent most of his long and checkered political career as a minister and advisor on tribal affairs to the Princes of North Africa. He took advantage of one of his many political exiles to settle down in a small fortress under the protection of one of the tribes with whom he had good relations, and in a few months of intense activity, ideas pouring into his head "like cream into a churn," he wrote one of the most original works of social theory yet to be composed, the *Muqaddimah*, or introduction to his history of the world, laying out the dynamics of human social organization – the dialectic of civilization as it grows, declines, and succumbs to outside forces – and the motive force of that dynamic – group loyalty, a powerful but protean bond of loyalty, which religious ideas can sublimate into a universal rather than a merely particular motivation.

But the author, in the fullest sense, of the philosophic synthesis that al-Kindī and al-Rāzī never quite achieved, that al-Fārābī laid the foundations for, that al-Ghazālī criticized, that Ibn Ṭufayl and Ibn Rushd tried to defend or qualify or redefine to meet al-Ghazālī's attack, and that Ibn Khaldūn, like so many of his contemporaries who were lesser thinkers than he, quietly used but were often embarrassed to name, as the attitude of openness that al-Kindī had advocated waned in Islamic letters, was Avicenna, Abū Alī Ibn Sīnā, the Persian scholar, physician, and *wazīr* who is the subject of this book.

The great insight of Avicenna as a philosopher was recognition of the compatibility between the metaphysics of contingency, by which Islamic thinkers had tried to canonize the scriptural idea of creation, and the metaphysics of necessity, in which the followers of Aristotle had enshrined the idea that the goal of science is understanding as to why and how things must be as they are. The key to Avicenna's synthesis was his conceptualization of this world and everything in it as contingent in itself, but necessary with reference to its causes, leading back ultimately to the First Cause, the Necessary Being, whose timeless existence eternally authors the finite and determinate reality that we know.

While subsequent philosophers sharply criticized Avicenna's synthesis of necessity with contingency, none of his critics, Muslim, Jewish, or Christian, failed to profit from it. Even now, long after the cosmology that framed it has been shattered, leaving only a residue of words, the metaphysics of Avicenna remains an enduring source of insight into the logic of necessity and contingency and the enduring philosophic problems about freedom and futurity, temporality, and timelessness.

Avicenna's philosophy was not a bolt from the blue. It built methodically and thoughtfully upon the achievements of Plato, Aristotle, the Greek Neoplatonists and Peripatetics, and the Islamic thinkers, both philosophers like al-Fārābī, from whose work Avicenna gained his first understanding of the goal and point of metaphysics, and the creative and rambunctious *mutakallimūn*, the dialectical theologians of Islam. But although Ibn Sīnā's work was methodical and built upon the conceptions of his predecessors, it was no dry or scholastic construction of technicalities or pastiche of formalisms but a living and passionately engaged inquiry, in which the values motivating the inquiry are never wholly out of sight. Avicenna is a creative philosopher, and although he commented at length on the Aristotelian canon and responded at length to the work of his more immediate predecessors and successors, one can sense almost a relief in his reports of the loss of some of those works and an impatience bordering on exhaustion in his decision not to reconstruct or replace them and largely to abandon the polemical side of philosophy for the more constructive work of laying out original views and arguments that put to work the profits earned from probing study rather than simply plowing the outcomes of that study into yet more study, commentary, and ever deepening detail.

But perhaps I should not say more about Avicenna's philosophy here, since that is the story I want to unfold in the pages that follow: How Avicenna grew up at Bukhārā, saw the world that had nurtured him crash about him just as he was coming to manhood, fled from one toppling principality to the next and finally found refuge with a courageous and welcoming Persian prince; how his philosophical ideas emerged from his first youthful exposure to speculative thought and matured in the voluminous writings he composed during the intervals of tranquillity that his turbulent times afforded.

Besides exposition of the logic of his metaphysical stance, the distinction of essence from existence and its relation to the cosmological proof he devised, the argument for the existence of God from the contingency of the world, I want to explore Avicenna's ideas about knowledge and the soul, especially his distinctive defense of the individuality of the disembodied soul, and his famous Floating Man argument, a prototype of the Cartesian cogito, which Avicenna used to demonstrate the substantiality of the human soul. In my final chapter, I want to explore Avicenna's contributions to the history of logic – his insightful approach to the logic of the conditional, which, like much of the rest of his philosophy, has striking relevance for contemporary philosophical discussions; and his interesting ideas about rhetoric and poetics, areas in which he carried forward the Aristotelian approach but added to it the benefits of a new cultural setting and his own individual insights.

The study is intended as a philosophical appreciation of the work of Avicenna. I wrote it as a philosopher who is more than willing to apprentice himself to the great minds of the past. I have profited as a philosopher from that apprenticeship and commend it to others. But such an apprenticeship is not solely an end in itself. Comparative philosophy, the effort to inform our philosophical outlook by grappling with the thinkers of another age and culture, is not simply a descriptive discipline. Its goal is to make ourselves better at doing philosophy. I am convinced that Avicenna is not in a position to learn much from us. So while I will agree or disagree with him philosophically, it is not my object to correct or commend him but to discover the areas in which he has something useful and important for us to know.

The intended audience of this book is composed in good part of philosophers and students of philosophy who would like to know something, or something more, about the philosophical work of Avicenna. But I will not object too loudly if Arabists and Islamicists, and even straying Middle East specialists, read it too. I don't think one really can know much about Islamic culture or the Middle East unless one reckons with the intellectual achievements of its greatest minds. But I caution against the notion that one will learn from a book about Avicenna or any other philosopher who wrote in Arabic how "the Arab mind" works or what is typically Islamic about Islamic thought. Philosophers are individuals who work in a social, cultural, and indeed (lest we forget) natural context. The problematics of that context afford them the issues they confront. They do not present a set of ready-made solutions to those problems, as though answers could be plucked from the atmosphere and as though the work of the philosopher was no more than that of the ideologue or publicist, to articulate, expand, and uncritically expound what is already given, if implicit, in the attitudinal mother's milk of his upbringing.

On the contrary, for a philosopher the very act of seeking to articulate what may at first seem obvious or unquestionable raises questions that cannot be ignored and that cannot be answered without creative thought, analysis, and synthesis. Naturally such thought will draw upon the resources accessible to it, local or exotic, ancient and traditional, neglected, current, or devised *ad hoc*, literary, historical, scientific, or imaginative. The chief test of a philosopher is not faithfulness to the cultural givens. Still less is it typicality. Rather it is the adequacy with which values that seem, on critical analysis, to be in tension with one another can be reconciled or coordinated, to bring coherency out of pre-conceptual chaos. Such work, although it always originates within a tradition, is of cosmopolitan significance. For no human values should be so wholly alien to any one of us that we cannot see the usefulness of situating any of one them with respect to all the rest.

This volume was undertaken at the suggestion of Aziz al-Azmeh, and I want to acknowledge his warmth and friendship here. I should also acknowledge the patience of Richard Stoneman of Routledge, who waited patiently for the MS while I completed my book *On Justice* for Yale University Press. The manuscript of *Avicenna* was read in its entirety by Nicholas Heer, my Harvard mentor of nearly thirty years ago, now at the University of Washington in Seattle, who made many valuable comments and suggestions, and by Oliver Leaman of Liverpool, who responded warmly to the approach I took and again made valuable suggestions and voiced friendly differences. Parts of the book were read by other friends, whose good counsel it is my very pleasant duty to acknowledge here: my colleague George Simson, the Editor of *Biography*, who read the biographical chapter with a professional's eye; Clifford E. Bosworth of the University of Manchester, whose unrivalled historical expertise was invaluable in the same chapter; Herbert Davidson of UCLA, who read the metaphysics chapter and commented on it in detail and with his usual critical acuity; Thérèse Druart of the Catholic University in Washington, who read and commented on the chapter on Ideas and Immortality; my University of Hawaii colleagues Jim Tiles and Irving Copi, who commented copiously on the logic chapter and made valuable suggestions; and Jonathan Westphal of Idaho State University, who read good chunks of the MS and offered many helpful comments.

The book owes much to the growing body of scholarship on Avicenna's thought – the seminal work on his psychology by my friend the late Fazlur Rahman; the recent monograph of Dimitri Gutas, which explores the commitment of Avicenna to the Aristotelian tradition; William Gohlman's edition and translation of Avicenna's thumbnail autobiography and its biographical continuation by his disciple, al-Juzjānī; the monographs on Avicenna's logic, poetics, and rhetoric by Nabil Shehaby, Ismail Dahiyat, Deborah Black, and Selim Kemal, as well as the earlier work on Avicenna's metaphysics by A.-M. Goichon. There are many other tesserae in the scholarly mosaic – studies by Michael Marmura of Toronto, Kwame Gyekye of Ghana, Mohammed Achena and Henri Massé, and many other specialists. I have cited the literature wherever I have found it helpful, but I acknowledge the authors collectively here – from Emil Fackenheim and Gustave von Grunebaum to Miriam Galston, Nicholas Rescher, Nancy Siraisi, and Robert Hall – since it is only through the aggregate work of such committed scholars that we can recapture the enduring relevance of the philosophical traditions of other times and places. And without the broader perspectives to be gained from the study of philosophies other than the most familiar we can never acquire the critical range and cross cultural distance that are needed for triangulation and objectification in situating ourselves among the philosophically live options.

Once again, as in my earlier books, I thank the people of Hawaii, whose wealth of spirit sustains the possibility of comparative philosophy even on a large rock in the midst of the Pacific Ocean.

This book is dedicated to the memory of Fazlur Rahman, in the hope that his mild and progressive spirit, open minded commitment to tradition, and zest for inquiry will continue to spread through the influence of his writings among the adherents of the faith he loved so well.

Lenn E. Goodman
Manoa Valley, 1991

LIST OF ABBREVIATIONS

A.H.	Anno hegirae
AOS	American Oriental Society
ED	*Sefer ha-Nivḥar ba-Emunot ve-Deʿot*
EI, EI_1	*Encyclopedia of Islam, Encyclopedia of Islam,* original edition
IJMES	*International Journal of Middle East Studies*
IPQ	*International Philosophical Quarterly*
IQ	*Islamic Quarterly*
JAOS	*Journal of the American Oriental Society*
JHI	*Journal of the History of Ideas*
JHP	*Journal of the History of Philosophy*
JJS	*Journal of Jewish Studies*
JNES	*Journal of Near Eastern Studies*
JQR	*Jewish Quarterly Review*
JRAS	*Journal of the Royal Asiatic Society*
JSS	*Journal of Semitic Studies*
PAAJR	*Proceedings of the American Academy for Jewish Research*
PEW	*Philosophy East and West*
REI	*Revue des Études Islamiques*
REJ	*Revue des Études Juives*
SUNY	State University of New York
TF	*Tahāfut al-Falāsifa*
TT	*Tahāfut al-Tahāfut*
ZDMG	*Zeitschrift der deutschen morgenländischen Gesellschaft*

1

LIFE, TIMES, WRITINGS

1 SETTING THE SCENE

Shouldered between India and Arabia and pinched between the Caspian and the Persian Gulf, the great land mass of Iran that lies between the river systems of the Tigris and Euphrates to the west and the Indus and Helmand to the east, widens north of the Arabian sea, into the mountainous highlands of Khorasan, stretching north and eastward as it rounds the Caspian at Jurjān, to the cities of Nīshāpūr, Meshed, Ṭūs, Merw, Herāt and Balkh, the Pamir mountains and the Hindu Kush. North and east, beyond the Amū Daryā or Oxus river, which drains into the Aral Sea, lie Bukhārā and Samarqand, in the land the Muslim conquerors called Transoxiania, literally: *Mā warā' al-Nahar,* What-lies-beyond-the-River, bounded to the northeast in turn by the Jaxartes (Syr Darya) and the steppes, where Islamic military power and even Islamic faith never displaced the tribal way of life.

When the Arab Muslim armies came to Khorasan in the late seventh and early eighth centuries, they found a rich land, long the granary of Iran and its highway to the east. The rainfall in the highlands was light, less than ten inches annually, but the many fertile river valleys grew wheat, barley, and rice. Zones within the region were known for their oranges, apricots, peaches, pears, sugar cane, cotton, pistachios, pomegranates, rhubarb, melons, almonds, sesame, grapes, or currants, as well as plane tree bark, a remedy for toothaches. The earth yielded copper, lead, iron, mercury, vitriol, carnelian, silver, and gold. There was edible earth as well as turquoise in Nīshāpūr. In Badakhshān there were rubies, garnets, lapis lazuli, and asbestos. The craftsmen of Khorasan made steel, silk, iron, copper, and gold ware, textiles, carpets, incense, raisins, and soap. From 751, when Chinese prisoners of war brought the art to Samarqand, artisans made paper from linen, flax, or rags of hemp, gradually replacing papyrus as the writing medium. In the highlands there were horsebreeders and pastoralists who raised sheep and camels, producing butter, cheese, horns, fur, and hides.

The populace bore arms, but often little loyalty to the fallen empire of the Sassanian Shahs, or to the Zoroastrian priesthood, against which many had rebelled in the century before the rise of Islam. The village lords held their land and feudal privileges more tenaciously than their old Buddhist or Zoroastrian faith. So the Muslims pushed deep into Transoxiania, Farghānā, Kābul, Makrān on the Arabian Sea, spreading Islam to the Syr Darya, the west bank of the Indus, and the edges of the Panjāb and Kashmīr. But even by Ibn Sīnā's time the lands were not uniformly Muslim. Jews, Christians, Zoroastrians, and Buddhists had made up the population. By 750, only an estimated 8% of the people of an important Khorasanian city like Nīshāpūr were Muslim. The figure did not reach 50% until the early ninth century, but rose to 80% by the century's end. In rural areas and smaller towns conversion to Islam was much slower, with resistance to the building of mosques and persistence of Zoroastrian seminaries and fire temples into the tenth and eleventh centuries in such places as Musalla and Karkuy in Sistān, Bayhaq in Khorasan, and Varaksha west of Bukhārā. In Nīshāpūr itself, some 5,000 Zoroastrians, Christians, and Jews adopted Islam in 993. But there were active and activist Zoroastrians in Transoxiania until the late thirteenth century. Avicenna's hometown of Afshana outside Bukhārā acquired a mosque around 709 and a second by 741; but the citadel of Bukhārā got its mosque four years after Afshana, probably because the site had to be wrested away from the fire temple that still occupied the ground. As conversion continued, a new mosque was built in Bukhārā in 771, then a third, funded by a former Buddhist priest, in 793, and two more, built in the bazaars of the growing city, probably in the ninth century.[1]

Conversion to Islam was steady and perhaps inexorable, but it was not based largely on conviction. It was clearly a way of gaining or maintaining social status and economic position, or survival. For the *dihqāns*, or landholders, of Khorasan the differential taxes upon non-Muslims were a powerful incentive to conversion, along with the increasing social pressures of the emerging Islamic society. But such conversions could hardly be complete or sincere. Even when it was clear that Islam was in the region to stay, the numerous sectarian and schismatic movements and syncretistic trends reveal the spiritual restiveness of the newly and not fully converted. In Transoxiania acculturation to Islam was often violent, involving riots, first of the local populace, casting stones from the housetops at the Islamic call to prayer, but later, as the Muslims grew in numbers, centered on the Muslims' increasingly aggressive efforts to convert or displace the Zoroastrians, Manichaeans, Buddhists, and Nestorian Christians of such cities as Bukhārā. There were numerous conversions, dissimulations and reversions, removals, incentives (both positive and negative), forced confessions of faith, and apostasies. Within less than a century of the arrival of Islam, conversion was scornfully called "going Arab." And there were intercommunal riots between Muslims and Zoroastrians well into the tenth century.

Whether as Muslims or as Zoroastrians, the *dihqāns* valued being left alone in peace on their lands and were not overcritical about who received their taxes, so long as those in power could keep the peace. Indeed, the rival communities could unite in the face of an external threat, and did, even as late as the eleventh century. But the relative stability of Khorasan politically and of much of Transoxiania, precisely because of the value placed on civil security by the local populace, was not a fact of nature but an achievement. The *dihqāns* would pay their taxes with no more than the usual grumbling, provided the rulers could hold in check the tribal powers to the northeast. But their capacity to do so rested in turn on a paradox. For the chief source of military power in the eastern Islamic lands, and the most strategic export of the steppe land to the north was tribal manpower.

Islam had originated in Arabia but established an Arab kingdom in Syria soon after the death of the Prophet. The Muslim conquests of Iran and Khorasan shifted the center of gravity eastward and led to the 'Abbāsid Revolution of 750, whose rallying cry, in the name of Islam, was an end to the Arab hegemony imposed in the name of Islam. Baghdad, founded on the Tigris in 762 as the metropolis of the new Khalifate, gave substance to the eastward orientation of the Islamic state, but in less than a century of the revolution, the eighth 'Abbāsid Khalif, al-Mu'tasim, would withdraw to his newly built pleasure palace at Sāmarrā, sixty miles upriver, and surround himself with 4,000 Turkish retainers to protect him from the Baghdad mob and the turbulent Khorasanian soldiery that had been the backbone and the terror of the 'Abbāsid dynasty since its bloody rise to power. In the century that followed, the annual import of slave recruits from the northeast increasingly undermined the authority of Baghdad from within and visibly symbolized the threat from without.

By Avicenna's time, freebooters, mercenaries, and *ghulāms*, military slaves, seemed to pour out of central Asia inexhaustibly. The slaves were a byproduct of tribal warfare on the steppes. Islamized, trained, and promoted for intelligence, loyalty, and discipline,[2] they were easily destabilized in the rivalries of their immediate commanders and the more remote figureheads above them. The tribes themselves were another matter. Oguz Turks lived on both sides of the Aral Sea. Spreading down the Jaxartes valley, poised above Bukhārā and Samarqand from the watershed of Lake Balkhash, were the Qarluqs, restlessly ruled by Qarā-Khāns (or Ilig-Khāns). From them sprung the most aggressive of the many *ghulām* dynasts of the age, Maḥmūd of Ghazna. The Qarluqs had been pressing inward upon Muslim lands from the T'ien Shan Mountains of China since 840. East of them were the Uighurs. Still further east, like a great wave building force, that would not break on the Islamic lands until after Ibn Sīnā's death, were the Qarā-Khitāi, Cathay or China Mongols, whose khāns ruled China for two centuries (916–1125) before they were expelled. The incursions of other Mongols under Genghis Khān and Hūlāgū and of Turks such as Tīmūr in the fourteenth century would rain blows upon the Middle East from which it has never fully recovered.

In 945 the Khalif at Baghdad was made the virtual prisoner of his victorious Būyid (or Buwayhid) commander, chieftain of a clan of Shī'ite Daylamites from the highlands south of the Caspian, whose power rested in the ranks of their tribal soldiery, and whose quarreling family factions centered their authority not in Baghdad but in Shirāz. The following year the Khalif was blinded and a puppet ruler erected in his place. Until 1055, the Būyids ruled while the 'Abbasids reigned, often as prisoners in their own harems. Power was held by ministers and chamberlains and transferred through the intrigues of regents, queen mothers, palace eunuchs, or commanders of the guard. Rebels, raiders, sectarian armies, and disaffected governors beset the central authority. No power was too great or too petty to be defeated in battle or subverted from within by disaffected troops – mercenary, homeborn or slave – rival sons, tribal federations, or treacherous vassals and allies. As early as the 820s the 'Abbāsid Khalif al-Ma'mūn saw his general Ṭāhir set up an autonomous dynasty in Khorasan. The Khalif's power to respond was limited, since he was already facing a rebellion in Azerbaijān, and Ṭāhir's brother was his chief military commander.

Rivals to the Ṭāhirids, whose power was centered in Nīshapūr, the

Ṣaffārids arose in Sistān, south of Khorasān, initially from the popular defense efforts led by a coppersmith (*ṣaffār*) and his brother, against sectarian marauders. Up to the early ninth century the principal sectarian threat had been from the Khārijites, radical opponents of all existing Islamic states, for what they charged were hypocritical compromises of principle. The Khārijites held, heretically, that wicked deeds like allegiance to an illegitimate state are proof of misbelief; evildoers, and even associates of such sinners, must be hunted down and killed as unbelievers. Under the hammering of the Ṣaffārids and Tāhirids, the Khārijite forces, once swollen to armies of the disaffected, were reduced to mere bands of terroristic zealots and brigands. But in the tenth century a new threat emerged in the west, taking formidable shape with the conquest of Egypt by Ismā'īlī Shī'ites, radicals from the opposite end of the sectarian spectrum, and the establishment there of the Fāṭimid dynasty.

The Ismā'īlīs were the sect that became known as the Assassins. Their quest for authority in the name of the house of the Prophet was widely subversive of Sunnī claims, and their charismatic revolutionism often became the voice and vehicle of local ethnic or economic discontents. Yet their sense of frustrated legitimacy and clandestine action in behalf of a long persecuted cause also made the movement a seedbed of esoteric popular philosophy and spiritualism. The Ismā'īlīs were Sevener Shī'ites, holding that the last earthly Imām was Ismā'īl the son of the Imām Ja'far al-Ṣādiq, an eighth-century descendant of the Prophet through his daughter Fāṭimah and his nephew 'Alī, and seventh in the line of Muḥammad. Unlike the Twelver Shī'ites, who later came to prominence in Iran but now remained pensioners of the 'Abbāsid state, basking in the favor of the Būyids, and, unlike the Zaydī Fivers, who established themselves in the Yemen in 897 and maintained a moderate political stance, the Ismā'īlīs were militant revolutionaries. After the conquest of Egypt the Fātimid rulers founded Cairo in 973 on the site of an ancient Egyptian city and named it under the sign of Mars (al-Qāhirah), the planet of victory, establishing the great college of the Azhar as the seat of their learning and the base from which they sent missionary agents to propagate their faith throughout the east.

The Ṣaffārids broke the power of the Ṭāhirids, only to be thrust aside in turn by the dynasty Ibn Sīnā's father served, the Sāmānids, whose mandate rested on the powerful *dihqāns* of Khorasān. The Sāmānids came from Balkh, one of the four great cities of Khorasan, an ancient Buddhist and later Zoroastrian center, the capital of

Bactria in Greek times and called a metropolis (*umm al-bilād*) by tenth-century geographers, but today a mere village on the banks of a dried up riverbed in northern Afghanistan. The founder of the dynasty was the Sāmān-Khudāt, lord of the town of Sāmān, a Soghdian who embraced Islam early in the eighth century. Even as the Ṭāhirids were establishing themselves in Khorasān, the Baghdad Khalifate was finding a counterforce in the Sāmānids. For in 819 al-Ma'mūn rewarded four grandsons of the Sāmān-Khudāt for putting down a rebellion by making them the governors of Samarqand, Herāt, Farghānāh, and Shāsh (Tashkent). Nominally these princes were vassals of the Ṭāhirids, but as the Ṭāhirids grew more independent the Sāmānids were forging and testing their own strength, through internal struggles and battles with local warlords and rival groups. Aḥmad, one of the four, was able to set up his son Naṣr as an all but autonomous prince at Samarqand, rivaling the Ṣaffārids. Naṣr's brother, rival, and successor Ismā'īl defeated the Ṭāhirids in battle in 873 and established himself at Bukhārā. Two years later he was recognized by the Khalif al-Mu'tamid, although his succession of his brother was not recognized until Naṣr's death nineteen years later.

Strategically located on a large oasis on the banks of the Zarafshān River in what is today Uzbekistan, Bukhārā, like Balkh, Bayhaq and Shāsh, had grown from a cluster of oasis villages united by its market, its cathedral mosque, and its wall against nomadic marauders. Dry and sunny, but subject to temperature extremes, the city had roses as well as apples and apricots, cotton, vines, cherries, and melons. At the 39th parallel, its latitude places it in the same zone as modern Ankara, Athens, Lisbon, Washington DC, San Francisco, Tokyo, Seoul, or, in the southern hemisphere, Melbourne or Buenos Aires. Known for the political stability of its townsfolk, who had welcomed Ismā'īl as a champion of order, Bukhārā was raw in some respects and grew overcrowded and polluted. Yet in many ways it was the ideal capital. As one writer put it: "One who is seated there has Khorasan before him and Transoxiania behind him."

Hopes in Baghdad may have been that the Sāmānids and the Ṣaffārids would destroy each other,[3] but that was not to be. Responding to the Khalif's calls for help against the Ṣaffārids, Ismā'īl (r. 892–907) broke their power in a battle near Balkh in 900 and sent their leader to be executed at Baghdad in 902. He consolidated his power by subduing a number of vassal states in Central Asia; and his reforms of taxation, trade, and even land tenure, became the stuff of legend. His dynasty endured for just over a century. They were Sunnīs with an elaborate bureaucracy modeled on that of Baghdad, a class structure rooted in Sassanian Persia, and a dependency on Turkic troopers, fondly expected to counterbalance the *dihqāns.* As early as 914 the slave guard murdered Aḥmad b. Ismāʿīl, called "the martyred," in his tent near Bukhārā – some said for being too friendly with scholars and theologians. But the intellectual, theological, and artistic policy of the Sāmānids was no mere afterthought or ornament. It was emblematic of the order and stability the dynasts held forth as the foundation of their legitimacy, and expressive of the values of the landowners and administrators who anchored the civil authority of the dynasty and gave it its economic base. It was during the Sāmānid era that the poet Firdawsī (c. 939–1020) brought together the preliminary efforts and historical gleanings of several predecessors to create the Persian epic, *Shāh-Nāmeh,* the Book of Kings, celebrating the chivalric ideals of his independent-minded Persian sponsors, noblemen of Ṭūs, of the same class as that in which the Sāmānid princes found their core constituency. But equally emblematic of the age is Firdawsī's journey to the court of Maḥmūd of Ghazna, in about 1004, as Sāmānid power crumbled, to complete the enormous work at the age of seventy-one, and receive an indifferent to hostile response from the Turkish Sunnī monarch, who had no time to peruse the monumental epic that was the poet's life work, preferring short lyric panegyrics of himself to fantastic sagas of Persian lore, fairy tale, and romance, penned by a Shīʿite sectarian and rationalist heretic. The liberal *wazīr* who had drawn Firdawsī to the court had fallen from power, and the story circulated widely that Maḥmūd rewarded the poet not with the promised dinār for every verse of the great epic, but only a dirhem, twenty-thousand dimes, as it were, in place of twenty-thousand coins of gold.

The Sāmānids were loyalist toward Baghdad but seem never to have paid tax or tribute to the Khalif, beyond a symbolic gift. Yet the princes always called themselves *amīrs,* generals and governors, never khalifs. They sent formal reports of their doings to Baghdad and always included the Khalif's name on their coinage. When the Būyids seized control of Baghdad the Sāmānids remained loyal to the Khalifate and even sheltered the ʿAbbāsid pretender in 968 and attacked the Būyid power, only to be repulsed. They get a good press from historians because they were Sunnīs, well born (unlike the baseborn Ṣaffārids), and defenders of the local lords and law against brigands, Daylamte adventurers, and Ismāʿīlīs. They consulted the *ʿulamāʾ* or clerics, and exempted them from proskynesis (*taqbīl*), the Persian custom of prostration before the ruler, that had once so pleased Alexander the Great. Nūḥ b. Naṣr (r. 943–54) even made a learned Hanafī Imām his prime minister or *wazīr*. The geographer and traveler Ibn Ḥawqal wrote of the prosperity and plenty of the well-administered lands of Manṣūr b. Nūḥ (r. 961–76), the moderate taxes, the regular pay of the civil servants, the small reserves of the treasury and the security of the country.

After Ismā'īl's early conquests in Transoxiania, the Sāmānids' main security goal was to contain the tribes in Central Asia, in the interest of the caravan trade. In pursuing this goal they were relatively successful, commanding the respect of the tribesmen and gradually overseeing their conversion to Islam. The base of their success was the populace of their own realm. For as a complement to the power of the *dihqāns* of Khorasan the Sāmānids could call upon the freewheeling landowners of Transoxiania. These sturdy and independent frontiersmen were proud of their holdings and their hospitality. Istakhrī tells of a landowner in Soghd whose door had not been closed for a century and who fed and lodged one to two hundred travelers every night. The young and landless might join dissident bands of marauders or attach themselves to some rebel movement, but the more stable men of *Mā warā' al-Nahr* sustained the ideal of the *ghāzī*, or warrior of faith, and could always find a field of action in the direction of the tribal domains. When Sāmānid power broke, many followed Maḥmūd to India. But in their heyday the Sāmānids held the frontier, in part with the aid of volunteers organized in hundreds of *ribāṭs*, fortified abbeys, often funded by *awqāf* or eleemosynary trusts.

Secure for its day within its boundaries, the Sāmānid regime fostered the revival of ancient Persian culture in a new Islamic recension, based on sound administration, the produce of the land, trade with Russia to the north, and along the silk road to China. At Bukhārā, Naṣr b. Aḥmad (r. 914–43), who succeeded his martyred father at the age of eight, was called al-Sā'īd, the Fortunate. For his capable regent and *wazīr*, al-Jayhānī (in office 914–22, 938–41), a scholar and geographer, was able to put down several revolts by the youthful *amīr*'s fractious kinsmen and regain lost possessions in his behalf. The regime built a splendid capitol on the site of the ancient Bukhār-Khūdāh's palace, a royal residence with an adjacent office building for its nine diwans: *Wazīr*, Treasurer, Secretary of State, Chief of Police, Postmaster, Intelligence, Demesne Estates, *Muḥtasib* or Censor of Markets and Morals, and *Qāḍī* or Chief Justice. Many of the offices were held by professional, often familial bureaucrats. The finance ministry, under the *Wazīr*'s office, was particularly complex. There were twenty-six *daftars* or portfolios on financial and military affairs – the two being closely related. There was even a palace school for slave recruits, which became a model for later dynasties. Niẓām al-Mulk looks back on the procedure admiringly:

> This is the system that was still in force in the time of the Sāmānids: Pages were given gradual advancement in rank according to their length of service, their skill and their general merit. Thus after a page was bought, for one year he was commanded to serve on foot at the stirrup, wearing a Zandaniji cloak and boots. He was not allowed to ride a horse in public or in private, and if found to have ridden he was punished. After a year's service, the tent leader spoke to the chamberlain and gave him a report. Then they would give the page a small Turkish horse with a saddle covered in rawhide, a plain bridle and stirrup leathers. After serving for a year with a horse and whip, in his third year he was given a belt to gird on his waist. In the fourth year they gave him a quiver and bow-case, which he fastened on when he mounted. In his fifth year he got a better saddle and a bridle with stars on it, along with a handsome cloak and a mace to hang on his mace ring. In the sixth year he was made a cup-bearer and had a goblet to hang at his waist. In the seventh, he was a robe bearer. In the eighth they gave him a sixteen-peg tent with one peak and put three newly bought pages in his troop; they gave him the title of tent-leader and dressed him in a black felt hat decorated with silver wire and a cloak made at Ganja. Every year they raised his rank and responsibility, until he became a company-leader, and then a chamberlain. If he developed a reputation for being apt, able and brave, had performed some notable actions, and was known to be thoughtful of his peers and loyal to his master, then and only then, at 35 years of age, they would make him an *amīr* and give him command of a province.[4]

The Sāmānid court was elegant, but accessible to the *'ulamā'* and the notables, and every summer Naṣr took his army to Herāt, Samarqand or some such place on maneuvers.

Al-Tha'ālibī of Nīshapūr (961–1038) devoted a volume of his Arabic literary memoirs, *Yatīmatu 'l-Dahr*,[5] to anthologizing, celebrating, and appraising the Arabic poets supported by the Sāmānids.

He tells of his father's invitation to Naṣr's court at Bukhārā and the constellation of philosophers and writers he met there, whose like he knew he would never see again. Poets, historians, scientists, and theologians were welcomed at the court. The library that Ibn Sīnā would discover as a young man was established. The courtier Abū Dulaf was sent on an embassy to China, of which he wrote a full report. Among the luminaries drawn to Naṣr's court was the poet Rūdakī, who wrote *ghazals* (love poetry), panegyrics, and music for the lute. Rūdakī founded the Persian epic form, adapting the tales of Sindbad from the Pahlavi version of an Indian source and turning the Indian fables of Kalīla and Dimna into Persian verse. These had been translated into Middle Persian by Burzoe for Chosroes Anushirwan in the sixth century and into Arabic by Ibn al-Muqaffa' under the early 'Abbāsids. Their mildly satirical tone gave voice to the somewhat secular culture of the Islamic bureaucratic or "secretarial" class, and Rūdakī is best remembered for his straightforward and unaffected style that sharply contrasts with the mannerism of later Persian poets. But the fall of Naṣr's *wazīr*, Bal'amī, left the poet without a protector, and he died stripped of the wealth and honors his prince had lavished upon him.

The regent al-Jayhānī's years out of office came in part because he was suspected of secret Shī'ite leanings – some even said that his true faith was Manichaean dualism, as if Shī'ism was not bad enough. The *Amīr*'s downfall too resulted from the charge of Shī'ite sympathies. As the story was later told, Ismā'īlī agents from Khorasan infiltrated Naṣr's entourage, converted key courtiers, relations, and officers, and influenced the prince himself to support or tolerate the Ismā'īlī *da'wa*, mission or propaganda, in Khorasan. Naṣr's depositon by a cabal of sunnī officers was a direct result. His son Nūḥ was credited with snuffing out the plot. As the chronicles of the day report it, he saved his father's life, diverted the wrath of the conspirators, and retained the throne for himself, by pardoning and bribing all but the ringleaders of the abortive coup and turning the troops against the Ismā'īlīs and their sympathizers, whom he systematically suppressed in 942. The fragmentary remnants of the movement went underground.

Nūḥ (r. 942–54) sponsored the historian al-Narshakhī (899–959), who wrote the history of Bukhārā in Arabic in 943, praising the dynasty in general and his *Amīr* in particular, as the restorer of order. Under 'Abd al-Malik (r. 954–61) and his successor Manṣūr b. Nūḥ, a second Bal'amī, who served in the same office as his father, translated al-Ṭabarī's Arabic *Annals* into Persian, omitting the proliferation of variant versions and chains of authorities. Ṭabarī's voluminous *Qur'ān* commentary was translated soon after, and Persian works were commissioned: on drugs, by al-Muwaffaq in the time of Manṣūr b. Nūḥ; on astronomy, by Abū Naṣr al-Qummī; and on geography, by Abū 'l-Muayyad al-Balkhī, a bilingual author patronized by Nūḥ ibn Manṣūr (r. 976–97). This last, the eighth Sāmānid, was the prince whom Ibn Sīnā's father served. One of the officials at his court was the learned Muḥammad b. Yūsuf al-Khwarizmī (d. 997), not the great mathematician of the same surname, but an able and cosmopolitan scholar. His *Keys to the Sciences*, a classification of Arab and foreign knowledge, was written in 976 and dedicated to Nūḥ's *wazīr*. It reveals the excitement about the developing Islamic sciences and the Greek sciences made accessible to Muslims by the translation of Greek classics into Arabic especially under the 'Abbāsids.[6]

By the time Ibn Sīnā was born, the Sāmānids were losing their grip on their more peripheral lands, ceding them to hereditary vassals, losing control of the military governors appointed from the ranks of the slave troops. The costs of bringing loose vassals to heel or forgoing the full yield of their tax or tribute sapped Sāmānid revenues, alienated troops and retainers, and weakened the exercise of authority. As Ibn Sīnā grew to manhood in the last years of the first Christian millennium, Bukhārā itself was under threat, and as a young man he saw the state his father had served swept away by new and more rapacious powers.

2 IBN SĪNĀ'S YOUTH AND EDUCATION

Like the dynasty he served, Ibn Sīnā's father came from Balkh. He moved to the province of Bukhārā in the reign of Nūḥ b. Manṣūr and governed the demesne village of Kharmaythan, a town center, in behalf of the *Amīr*. Marrying a local woman, reportedly named Sitārah, he settled down in the nearby village of Afshana, where Ibn Sīnā was born in 980, followed five years later by his brother Maḥmūd. When the family moved to the capital, Ibn Sīnā was given a teacher of the *Qur'ān* and *'adab*, that is, literature, mastering (i.e., memorizing) the *Qur'ān* by the age of ten. That we know such details of the life of the philosopher, although far fewer than we might have wished, is due to the circumstance, unusual among Islamic men of letters, that Ibn Sīnā dictated a brief autobiography to his disciple al-Juzjānī, telling of his growth and education down to the time when the two met. Al-Juzjānī, devoted to the achievement of his master, continued the account down to Ibn Sīnā's death, including details about his manner of work and study much as the master himself had sought to reveal the origins of his interest in the problems his philosophy addressed and the basis of his method in attacking them.

The receptiveness of his father to the Ismā'īlī *da'wā* led to that official's being considered a follower of theirs. The suspicion was a grave one, for the aftershocks of Nūḥ's purge were still being felt. Niẓām al-Mulk, the great eleventh-century *wazīr* who founded Sunnī colleges in Khorasan, sponsored al-Ghazālī's polemic against the Ismā'īlīs, and ultimately lost his life to their tactic of assassination, writes that after the debacle of 942, when the "missionaries once more began preaching in Khorasan and Bukhārā, and again led the people astray, the majority of those converted were persons whose fathers and grandfathers had lost their lives because of this religion."[7] Despite his later claims that even as a boy he remained unconvinced by what he heard, Ibn Sīnā got his first exposure to speculations on the nature of the soul and the mind by overhearing his father's discussions of such notions, along with other topics of interest to the Ismā'īlī movement: philosophy, geometry, and what was called Indian arithmetic.[8]

He was sent to a greengrocer to learn that arithmetic, the system we call Arabic, with its distinctive use of the zero. This new system was displacing the ancient Persian dactylonomy or finger calculation; but Ibn Sīnā evidently remained adept at the latter as well, for in 1029 he invented a dactylonomy of his own to free accountants of dependence on counters, pen, or paper. The boy, marked for his swiftness as a learner, studied *fiqh*, Islamic law, with Ismā'īl al-Zāhid, a noted Ḥanafī jurist of the town. The Ḥanafī legal tradition, known as a moderate school and favored by the early 'Abbāsid Khalifs, was the mainstream school at Bukhārā, and the jurists, who were also clerics, would have a prominent role to play in the education of an important official's son. But law, studied in Arabic, was a typical secondary study in Islamic as in other scriptural societies of the day. The customary dialectic gave Ibn Sīnā his early exercise in practical logic; and these studies laid the basis of his later lawyerly employment.

Less typical was Ibn Sīnā's instruction by a philosophy teacher, al-Nātilī. Evidently the boy's skill in argument and his father's speculative bent justified the expense of a resident tutor in the subject. As a start, master and pupil read the Arabic translation of the *Isagoge* of Porphyry, which had served generations before them as an introduction to Aristotle's *Organon* and to philosophy itself. But Ibn Sīnā tackled the logic of genus and species in a way that was far more conceptual and less conventional than was familiar to his teacher. As he explains in his *Hints and Pointers* (*K. al-Ishārāt wa 'l-Tanbīhāt*), the usual procedure (then as now) was mechanical: It barely distinguished essential from accidental predications and rarely applied more general predications than conventional genera to the tasks of inference. Ibn Sīnā's own approach was much more in the spirit of Aristotle himself,[9] who urged that the syllogistic method is a framework of discovery and not merely a grammar of deduction, since its meat is the material content of predicates, not just the formal relations of propositions. Al-Nātilī was stunned by the originality of the youth's approach and urged the civil servant to save his son for philosophy. He himself could read logical works in a straightforward, linear way but was innocent of Aristotle's subtleties and left his pupil to study logic more deeply on his own.

Similarly with Euclid's *Elements*, Ibn Sīnā read only the first five or six theorems with his teacher and then forged ahead almost as independently as Pascal would later do. Moving on to Ptolemy's *Almagest*, the classic work of cosmology and astronomy in the middle ages, the teacher read the preliminary sections with his pupil but told him to work through the mathematical problems on his own, offering only to check them. So Ibn Sīnā studied the mathematical heart of astronomy essentially independently, nearly reversing roles with his master. Ibn Ṭufayl, a philosopher much influenced by Ibn Sīnā, portrays a similar reversal in his philosophical romance on the natural philosopher and mystic Ḥayy ibn Yaqẓān. In the Platonizing rationalism of Ibn Sīnā such autonomy is a mark of the truth: Teaching provides only a hint of the problems, which the real intelligence solves for itself. Symbols and conventions, on such an account, are hints at best and must not be allowed to distract direct conceptual insight. It was in such terms that Ibn Sīnā recalled the course of his education to his own disciple, al-Juzjānī: The heart of learning was a direct insight into the rational principles on which the world is constructed.

When al-Nātilī left Bukhārā for Gurgānj, the capital of the prosperous realm of Khwarizm to the northwest, Ibn Sīnā studied the texts and commentaries of Aristotle's *Physics* and *Metaphysics* on his own. But he made little headway with metaphysics and turned to medicine, which he found easy and accessible. It was the work of Galen, the second-century Greek physician of Marcus Aurelius and incisive writer of medical textbooks, that paved the way for Muslim physician philosophers like Ibn Sīnā and his predecessor the Arab al-

Kindī (c. 801–66), his Jewish successor Isaac Israeli (c. 855–956), and the Persian al-Rāzī (d. 925 or 932). Some 129 Galenic works had been translated by the Nestorian Christian Ḥunayn ibn Isḥāq and his disciples in the ninth century, and Galen's clarity allowed ready integration of Greek physiology and medical science into the larger world of the Greek philosophers – and clear discernment of the issues on which clinical experience or philosophical disagreement might require departure from Galen's views. Guided at first by Abū Manṣūr al-Ḥasan ibn Nūḥ al-Qumrī and the philosophically inclined Christian scholar Abū Sahl al-Masīḥī,[10] Ibn Sīnā soon began to practice medicine, finding methods of treatment that books alone could not convey. He was sixteen now and actively engaged in legal debates as well as medical seminars, in which other practitioners soon came to rely upon him to take the lead.

He now turned seriously to philosophy, spending a year and a half not sleeping through a single night but reading logical and philosophical works, organizing his knowledge in a file of syllogisms ordered according to their premises and recorded on papyrus cards. Writing on papyrus, unlike paper, could be readily scratched out and emended. When stumped by some question, Ibn Sīnā relied on prayer, wine, and even the thoughts that came to him in his dreams to clarify intractable obscurities by giving him the middle term that would bridge the gap between premises and conclusions. As a result of this intensive work, he says, he came to know as much as he would ever know in adulthood; and he understood all that he knew to the full extent of human capacity. Only First Philosophy eluded him. He had read Aristotle's *Metaphysics* forty times and could practically recite it by heart. But he could not see the point of it – a telling admission for the man who would soon revolutionize Aristotelian metaphysics to an extent that puts him in a class with only a handful of subsequent philosophers: Spinoza, Kant, Hegel, possibly Whitehead, Husserl, or Dewey – certainly not Augustine, Thomas, Maimonides, or Descartes, who are great thinkers in their spheres, but by no means radical as metaphysicians.

What must have troubled the still adolescent Ibn Sīnā about the aim or object of the *Metaphysics* was a question Aristotle himself had raised when he wondered whether metaphysics was a single science.[11] Specifically: What has the science of being *qua* being, as Aristotle describes First Philosophy, to do with Divine Science, the other challenging description Aristotle gives to the same study. A science of first principles, as Aristotle called metaphysics – a science of ultimates, as we might express it – may seem to deserve the name First Philosophy. But can there be a single science of whatever it is that proves to be ultimate? And what has that to do with the seemingly much more general yet much more specialized and rarefied science that we call ontology? Ibn Sīnā had despaired of an answer and come to the conclusion that metaphysics is unintelligible, when one afternoon in the booksellers market, a dealer approached him with al-Fārābī's little work *On the Objects of Metaphysics.*[12] Ibn Sīnā refused it at first, thinking that metaphysics must be worthless; but the owner had placed the book on consignment, trying to raise cash, and the bookseller pressed it on Ibn Sīnā for 3 dirhems. As he read, the objects of Aristotle's work that he had read so many times now suddenly came together in his mind, and he saw its point. In gratitude the next day he gave substantial alms to the poor.

What did Ibn Sīnā find in al-Fārābī's little book that set him on the right track? First, there was al-Fārābī's affirmation that the *Metaphysics,* often called Theology in Arabic, does not deal strictly with God, the mind and the soul, as unprepared readers might suppose. Its aim is not to be confounded with those of Islamic dialectical theology, *kalām,* which takes root in scriptural problematics and classically addresses the issues of divine unity and theodicy. Metaphysics is a far more general and independent inquiry. Other sciences deal with particular sorts of beings and notions – physics, with bodies in terms of motion and change; geometry, with magnitudes and their relations and the higher-order properties of those relations; arithmetic, with numbers; medicine, with the human body insofar as it is susceptible to diseases. But metaphysics is a universal science, dealing with whatever all beings have in common solely by virtue of their reality: existence and unity, for example. The point is to discover the kinds of being (that is, the categories, the ways in which things are, or can be said to be) and the most universal ways of characterizing beings – for example, as prior or posterior (ontologically and not merely temporally), actual or potential, perfect or deficient. Again, the object is to understand in the most general possible terms such relations as cause and effect, similar and different, essential and accidental, equivalent or analogous. There can be only one science that is truly universal in this sense; for if there were two, each would have its proper object, and neither would be universal. From the general principles learned in metaphysics will flow the appropriate methods and working assumptions of all the specialized sciences. But also, in discovering what all beings have in common, the student of metaphysics will discover what is properly conceived as divine. The branch of metaphysics that deals with what it means to say that God is the "principle of existence," its Ground, or Cause, Author, Goal, Source, or Benefactor, or whatever other interpretation we may give the idea of Primacy, is divine science, an inextricable constituent of the universal science, because God is the first principle of being in the broadest possible sense, and not of just the ground of one or a few specific sorts of being.

Metaphysics, al-Fārābī explains, takes its name from the fact that its themes and questions rise above the questions of physics about motion and change. Mathematics too deals with non-physical objects, but only by conceptual abstraction, whereas the objects of metaphysics may actually exist entirely beyond the physical realm, divorced from matter not just notionally but in actuality. The primary object of metaphysics is being and thus oneness (since unity or self-identity is the most general mark of being). But, correlatively, metaphysics must study non-being and otherness as well. Thus there are three sciences ultimately: physics, mathematics, and metaphysics. Physics deals with bodies; mathematics, with the abstract characteristics of bodies; and metaphysics, with being as such, its character, its kinds, its nature, and its basis. Armed with this schematic but trenchant account, Ibn Sīnā was ready not only to understand Aristotle's *Metaphysics* but in time to make his own profound and distinctive contribution to the enterprise it defined.

When Nūḥ ibn Manṣūr fell gravely ill, Ibn Sīnā was asked to consult with the court physicians; and, on the recovery of the *Amīr*, he was brought on to the Sāmānid staff as a physician. This gave him access to the royal library. He proudly recalled in later life the sight that greeted him: whole rooms of books for each subject, ancient or modern – Arabic language and poetry, philosophy, and the sciences – piled high in their special cases. Requesting works systematically from the catalogue, Ibn Sīnā "saw books whose very titles are unknown to many, and which I never saw before or since."[13] The learning he gleaned is evident in the rare works he sometimes cites in his writings. The experience, as he put it, enabled him to gauge the contributions of each ancient or modern scholar or commentator and confirmed him in a lifelong habit of scanning and sampling in the many derivative and repetitive works known in his day. His disciple al-Juzjānī reports: "One of the astonishing things about the Master was that in the twenty-five years I was in his company and service I never saw him when a new book came to hand simply work through it. He always went right to the hardest passages and the most baffling problems, examining what it had to say on these so that he could rate the author's learning and level of understanding."[14] In the age of manuscript literature, when a new copy was in effect a new edition, and a translation, paraphrase, or commentary could almost as easily become a new work, this method was a valuable asset to a thinker who did not wish to become bogged down in petty arguments and repetitious detail but hoped rather to place all that he had learned in a single coherent framework.

The period of study that culminated in his seeing the point of metaphysics completed Ibn Sīnā's education, at least the phase that was predominantly receptive and retentive rather than actively productive and synthetic. He was eighteen. His knowledge, he tells us, would mature, even as his memory grew less elastic in adulthood; but, he insists, he made no really new departure beyond this date. This sounds like a boast that he had nothing more to learn and may shock our sense of modesty or propriety, or seem hyperbolic in relation to our ideals of a lifetime of learning. But what Ibn Sīnā actually said (although consistently mistranslated), was simply this: "My memory for what I understood was keener then, but the understanding is riper now. Yet it is the same, not reconstructed or reborn (*yatajaddidu*) in the least."[15] What he meant was that the framework of his understanding was firm and his central beliefs would not alter radically as he matured. There is no dialectic of conflict and contradiction for the Hegelian intellectual biographer here, but the gradual unfolding of a set of central themes which deepen as Ibn Sīnā's knowledge extends into new areas, but which does not change its course.

We have evidence of this stability of outlook; for at seventeen Ibn Sīnā wrote what appears to be his first work, a short *Treatise on the Soul in the manner of a Summary*, still extant in Arabic and Latin in ten chapters, very humbly dedicated to Nūḥ ibn Manṣūr. The work is clearly a young scholar's essay, not a dissertation, as Gutas calls it, but more like a BA honors thesis, clearly dependent, as Gutas shows, on Ibn Sīnā's reading in Nūḥ's library.[16] The mature philosopher refers back to it at the close of his career as laying the basis in argument for his key demonstrations of the substantiality, incorporeality, and immortality of the rational soul. The work dealt also with the epistemic development which grounds the special ontic status of that soul. Ibn Sīnā did remain committed all his life to this cluster of problems and to the "unprecedented" approach he had taken to their resolution. Yet there was to be new growth in his development, for "Avicenna's unique theory of Intuition (*ḥads*), present in all his writings on the soul, had not yet developed" here.[17]

A scholar who lived in Ibn Sīnā's neighborhood, one Abū 'l-Ḥasan al-'Aruḍī, that is, the Prosodist, gave him the opportunity to write his first real book at the age of twenty-one, commissioning what Ibn Sīnā calls a "Summation" named in the sponsor's honor and treating "all the sciences except mathematics." Gutas calls it "the first medieval philosophical summa which can be said to have signaled the beginning of scholastic philosophy".[18] This claim is a bit excessive. The Jewish philosopher Saadiah Gaon's *Critically Selecting among Beliefs and Convictions*, deals systematically and thematically with the central issues of theology and morals. It was written in Arabic in 933, some sixty-seven years earlier.[19] Augustine's *City of God*, begun in 410, after the sack of Rome by Alaric and his Goths, was also a kind of summa, and there are similar works in the *kalām* and among its Christian prototypes, for example, the writings of John of Damascus. There is a problem in applying the term scholastic to Avicenna – not least because he never taught or studied in a school, doctrinal or otherwise. In many respects the Islamic *kalām* and its Christian predecessors have much closer affinities to the spirit of scholasticism than does the philosophy of Avicenna. But what Gutas is calling attention to is not scholasticism in the dogmatic or even the dialectical sense, but systematic comprehensiveness of plan, here seen at work in behalf of a secular (or at least, shall we say, non-sectarian) goal. This too, of course, is not unprecedented. For "scientific" works, philosophic works in Avicenna's sense, clearly the corpus of Aristotle is the model: The *'Arūḍī*, as Gutas explains, was the first of many attempts by Ibn Sīnā to treat within the confines of a single work all the sciences of the Alexandrian school tradition that elaborated on the Aristotelian canon.

The book appears to be extant, despite Ibn Sīnā's misgivings about the loss of his early writings. It survives in a unique if incomplete Uppsala manuscript (Number 364) copied from a scribe's copy of Ibn Sīnā's autograph and still preserving the record of changes made by the author's hand. The work includes Logic, although the surviving MS lacks the *Isagoge*, *De Interpretatione* in part, all of the *Prior Analytics*, and the beginning of the *Posterior Analytics*. It does include the *Rhetoric* and *Poetics*, which were grouped with logic in the school tradition, because they addressed specific modes of persuasion. The *'Arūdī* also included an Aristotelian *Physics* and *Meteorology*, a *De Anima*, and a *Metaphysics* with accounts of ontology, the hierarchy of being, potentiality, action, necessity, and possibility, the eternal and the temporal, universals, perfection, and imperfection, the four Aristotelian causes, priority and posteriority, the idea of essential creation, unity and plurality, and emanation from the necessary existent. The metaphysical themes are the very ones that al-Fārābī had called out as central, and Ibn Sīnā aligns them here into the distinctive plan of argument that would unify his own metaphysics. Whole pages and sections would be copied into his mature works.[20]

For another neighbor, Abū Bakr al-Baraqī, a Khwarizmian scholar of *fiqh* and *Qur'ān* who was also interested in philosophy, Ibn Sīnā wrote an appraisal of the philosophic sciences in some twenty volumes under the title *Sum and Substance* (*Kitāb al-Ḥāṣil wa 'l-Maḥṣūl* and another on morals entitled *Innocence and Guilt* (*K. al-Birr wa 'l-'Ithm*). These remained the private possessions of the scholar/official who commissioned them and were not lent out for copying. Yet both seem to have circulated among Ibn Sīnā's disciples and successors for a century or more, and some apparent fragments of the ethical work survive. In his mature summa, the *Shifā'*, Ibn Sīnā commends to his students the naturalistic theodicy defended in *Innocence and Guilt*: the triumph of good and truth over evil and falsehood, the fate of corrupt cities, and the truth underlying the popular belief in retribution and recompense, which operate in fact through nature, acts of human will, and the play of chance – all of which descend ultimately from God.[21] *Sum and Substance* aimed to be a commentary and distillation of the entire philosophical legacy. It seems to be cited by Ibn Sīnā in his famous correspondence with al-Bīrūnī (c. 1000), and Ibn Sīnā's Rayy disciple said that its comments on Alpha elatton of the *Metaphysics* were worth as much as the Christian scholar Abū 'l-Faraj ibn al-Ṭayyib's whole commentary. *Sum and Substance* evidently laid the foundation for the *Shifā'* and forms the precedent for the evaluative approach Ibn Sīnā later used in his *Impartial Appraisal* (*Kitāb al-Inṣāf*). Its loss lay at the heart of Ibn Sīnā's later unwillingness to revert to the commentary form.

3 *WANDERJAHRE*

On the death of his father, Ibn Sīnā acquired a government post. He was independent now, but "necessity compelled me to leave Bukhārā and move to Gurgānj." What necessity forced him to leave Bukhārā? The background is as follows:[22] To the southeast, in Afghanistan, territories Islamicized in the mid-seventh century and nominally dependent on the Sāmānids, the Oguz and Khalaj Turks held the high ground against the Hinduized population of the Indus valley. Two thousand Oguz slaves were in the annual tribute the rulers of Kābul had paid to Ṭāhir when he governed Khorasan. The Khalaj tribesmen fiercely resisted such civilizing, and Alptigin, a Turkmen commander of 'Abd al-Malik b. Nūḥ, dispatched his promising aide, Sebuktigin, to subdue them, which he did, recruiting many into his own forces, and thus building a power base. Alptigin and the *Wazīr* Bal'amī failed in a king-making coup attempt on the death of 'Abd al-Malik in 961. Undercut by the disaffection of his co-conspirator, Alptigin made for India, hoping to gain credit by warfare against the Hindu unbelievers. But en route his way was blocked by local warlords of the mountain fastness of Ghaznā in eastern Afghanistan. Forced to capture the place, he found it a formidable fortress and set up for himself there, carving out a little principality fed by the quarrels of his neighbors. He defeated the Sāmānid troops sent against him and acquired recognition from Manṣūr b. Nūḥ. After Alptigin's death in 963, the troops gained control of the place and held it against the freebooter's obsequious son and the Sāmānid soldiery he summoned to his aid. In the continuing fighting over the fortress, Sebuktigin, came to the fore. Originally a slave warrior purchased by Alptigin in Nīshapūr and inherited by the inauspicious son, this former *ghulām* had been rapidly promoted and even given a daughter by Alptigin. Now a warlord in his own right, he courted the troops and rationalized the feudal basis of their wealth. As a result, he held power and expanded his domains for twenty years, gradually elaborating and professionalizing his administration – in part with the aid of captured bureaucrats like the experienced Abū 'l-Fatḥ of Bust.

In 994 Sebuktigin scored a victory in behalf of Nūḥ b. Manṣūr and was rewarded with the rule of Balkh and other provinces, honors and dignities. His son Maḥmūd was given his father's old command in Khorasan. Sebuktigin saw himself as a loyal vassal of the Sāmānids, but, when he died in 997, Maḥmūd, the strongest or most ruthless of his sons, seized his father's authority, wresting away his brothers' portions. Drawn by the riches of Khorasan, he and his rivals the Qarā-Khānids set about carving up the domains of the Sāmānids and their vassals. His success bred in him an appetite for empire. The Sāmānids were rapidly falling into the kind of generational tailspin that Ibn Khaldūn, using historical experience to flesh out the dialectic of succession schematized in Plato's *Republic*, brilliantly captured in his model of the Islamic dynastic cycle. In 999 'Abd al-Malik ibn Nūḥ, placed on the Sāmānid throne by his officers and ministers after the blinding of his brother Manṣūr, was himself deposed. A secret treaty divided his realm among the Turks. Since the new *Amīr* was displeasing to the *dihqāns* the advancing forces of the Qarā-Khānid, Ilig Nasr, met little resistance from them. The town preachers of Bukhārā, salaried employees of the Sāmānid state, pleaded with the people to remember the good government they had enjoyed and rise up against Ilig Naṣr. But the masses and their traditional spokesmen, the independent *faqīhs*, unimpressed or alienated, decided that the invader was a good Muslim too and stood aside. 'Abd al-Malik's brother Abū Ibrāhim escaped and took the field, but he was defeated and executed in 1005.

Ibn Sīnā apparently remained in Bukhārā while this last Sāmānid struggled to revive the fortunes of his house, but the outcome became increasingly clear: In the long conflict that the epic poets projected into antiquity as an inveterate struggle between Irān and Turān, Persian power, in Bukhārā at least, was dead. In the words of Badī' al-Zamān al-Hamadhānī: "The house of Bahram is now subject to the Khaqan's son." Some two or three years before the final debacle, Ibn Sīnā left Bukhārā for Gurgānj.

Located in the fertile watershed of the Oxus in Khwarizm, an ancient center of Persian culture where Zoroastrianism was still practiced by a handful of adherents, Gurgānj, on the left bank of the Oxus south of the Aral Sea, lay at the gateway to the well-traveled caravan routes from the crossing of the Oxus to the Oguz steppes, the lands of the once Judaising Khazars of the Volga delta, the Caspian, southern Russia and Siberia. Long a bulwark and a base against the Turks, the country was Sunnī in orientation, but known as a center of Mu'tazilite sympathy. Gurgānj had grown rich on its trade with the Bulgars and Khazars, whose ties were to the Byzantine and Slavic west. Abū 'l-Husayn al-Suhaylī, a patron of scholars and admirer of the philosophical sciences, was minister there. Avicenna's medical teacher Abū Sahl wrote works for this *wazīr* and no doubt gave a good report of Ibn Sīnā at the court. The philosopher was introduced to the Khwarizm-Shāh, Alī b. Ma'mūn (r. 997–1009), leader of a local dynasty of former Sāmānid vassals that only a few years earlier had displaced the old Khwarizm-Shāhs of Kath across the river. The new Khwarizm-Shāhs were Arabs ethnically but heirs to many of the Persian ideals of the Sāmānids. Their court became a haven to al-Tha'ālibi and to Avicenna's older contemporary, al-Bīrūnī, himself a Khwarizmian Persian, as well as to Ibn Sīnā, who served "in lawyer's garb," with a *taylasan* "neckband tucked under my chin" and a salary "sufficient for a man of my station." He remained in Gurgānj until 1012, when again he cites necessity as requiring him to move on.

The name of the necessity in this case was Maḥmūd of Ghaznā. When the Sāmānid Manṣūr was blinded and deposed, Maḥmūd had already fielded an army to march against him, but the Sāmānid emeute allowed him to pose as the avenger of his intended victim, and he swept through Khorasan defeating 'Abd al-Malik and restoring the ritual homage in the mosques to the 'Abbāsid al-Qādir, whose usurpation the Sāmānids had refused to recognize. Only Maḥmūd's temporary withdrawal to fight his brothers for domination left the *coup de grâce* of the Sāmānids to the Qarā-Khānids. But once Maḥmūd's ascendancy was clear, he turned his attentions to clearing Khorasan of them as well, defeating Ilig Naṣr decisively in 1008. The new Khwarizm-Shāhs were not immune to the same pressure; by 1017 he had overthrown them and installed a *ghulām* of Sebuktigin's in their place. But by then Ibn Sīnā had been gone five years. Like intellectuals in other eras, he had the advantage of a kind of early warning, not through any special sensitivity to the target of Maḥmūd's next strike (for the warrior's most ambitious conquests were to be in India, against which Ghaznā was indeed the perfect aerie[23]), but because Ibn Sīnā himself was among the objects of the conqueror's covet, and his court would not have provided the ideal haven for a philosopher.

The Ghaznavids were militant opponents of the Shī'a and of the Mu'tazila, the rationalistic and voluntaristic school of *kalām* now reaching its full maturity in the work of 'Abd al-Jabbār in Rayy (d. 1025). The dynasts prized the role of defenders of orthodoxy, thus currying favor with the Khalif's party in Baghdad. But Sebuktigin and Maḥmūd also patronized the heretical Karrāmites and used them against the Ismā'īlī's. In 1015 Maḥmūd was accused of complicity in poisoning the famous traditionist Ibn Fūrak, whom he had investigated although the man was known to be quite orthodox, a Hanafite in law and Ash'arite in *kalām*, but an outspoken preacher against the Karrāmites of Nīshapūr. Even so, in Baghdad Maḥmūd was valued as a counterforce to the Khalif's Buyid Shī'ite "protectors." It was to recognize his power *de facto* and reward his loyalty *de jure* that he was given authority over Khorasan, as the Khalif's champion against the Qarā-Khānids and the Khwarizm-Shāh. Emboldened by Maḥmūd's support, in 1017 the Khalif would officially condemn Shī'ism and Mu'tazilism. Maḥmūd in *his* domains would set about to enforce the anathema. The significance for philosophy was dark. For the philosophers of Islam, if classified as *mutakallimūn*, would surely be pigeonholed with the Mu'tazilites. Ibn Sīnā sharply distinguished philosophy from *kalām*. But if philosophy was viewed as an ideology the analogy was a natural one, and the affinity of the Shī'ites to philosophy was well known. Ibn Sīnā usually avoids discussion of standard *kalām* issues, just as he denies any Shī'ite influence even on his youthful thinking. He also avoids all mention of a desire to stay out of reach of Maḥmūd. But when he finally gained a safe haven in his later life he would pulverize the radical atomists of the occasionalist *kalām* and make sport of Ash'arite orthodoxy.

It was clear in Gurgānj that the Khwarizm-Shāh was targeted by Maḥmūd, who would demand that the Khalif al-Qādir deal with the Qarā-Khānids and the Khwarizm-Shāh only through him. But Ibn Sīnā was targeted as well. Seeking to ornament his court, Maḥmūd diplomatically requested that Ma'mūn b. Ma'mūn (r. 1009–17), brother and successor to 'Alī, send him Ibn Sīnā, his Christian friends Abū Sahl and the physician Ibn al-Khammār, the mathematician Arrāq, and the polymath al-Bīrūnī (973–c. 1050). Ma'mūn, was in no position to refuse but reportedly gave his savants an opportunity to absent themselves.[24] Ultimately, Bīrūnī, Arrāq, and Khammār went to Ghaznā. Some later writers inferred that they were drawn by the reports of Maḥmūd's opulence. But in fact it seems that Bīrūnī, Khammār, and others did not leave Khwarizm until the year of its fall, when Ma'mūn was assassinated by his troops and Maḥmūd bore off the scholars and men of letters along with his prisoners. At the Ghaznavid court Ibn al-Khammār is said to have converted to Islam, reportedly at over a hundred years of age. Al-Bīrūnī went on to become one of the first great comparative scholars, adding the study of Indian culture and Sanskrit learning to his already voluminous erudition, and becoming, in effect, an intellectual Mahmūd. Sachau called him the greatest intellect of all time, and Frank Peters calls his work on India the "finest monument" of Islamic learning. He prospered intellectually in service to the conqueror, his son Mas'ūd, and grandson Mawdūd, as court astronomer – yet he did not follow Maḥmūd willingly to Ghaznā.

For Ibn Sīnā and Abū Sahl the choice was no less clear: Maḥmūd's frequent accusations of heresy against his subjects, the ruinous taxation and recruitment that fueled his campaigns, the cruel and dark side of his bright image as a *ghāzī* or champion of the faith, would bring death and suffering to thousands of his own people. If Ibn Sīnā did not fear complicity in this regime, he certainly did not need the inquisition and "straightening" of his ideas that would have dogged the steps of a Ghaznavid court philosopher. He was no poet, so the tenor of his ethnic loyalties remains implicit, rather than spun out in verses like the loyalties of a Firdawsī, but in his wanderings Ibn Sīnā consistently chose Iranian over Turkic patrons, and, while it is credible that he was no Shī'ite and certain that he was no Ismā'īlī, he seems to have seen a more welcoming refuge in Shī'ite than militantly Sunnite courts.[25]

Evading Maḥmūd's summons, Ibn Sīnā and Abū Sahl traveled south in 1012, as far as possible through the Khwarizm-Shāh's territory. Abū Sahl died in a dust storm, but Ibn Sīnā journeyed onward, and with great hardship made his way to Nasā, then a day's journey further, to Bāward, on to Tūs in Khorasan, in the domain of Maḥmūd, west to Samanqān and Jajārm, the western boundary of Khorasan. He was making for Jurjān, Abū Sahl's homeland on the southeast coast of the Caspian, where the Prince, Qābūs ibn Vushmagīr (r. 978–1012), was an ally of the Khwarizm-Shāh. A scion of the Ziyārids, who had originally brought fame to the Daylamite Iranians as warriors and had tried openly to restore Zoroastrianism less than a century before, Qābūs was a poet in Arabic and Persian and a sometime patron of Firdawsī. The Ziyārids had been allies of the Sāmānids, and Qābūs himself had spent long exiles at their court. His dynasty was to be swept away by about 1093, when the Ismā'īlīs overran Ṭabaristān. But, for the moment, although a reluctant tributary of Maḥmūd, he could offer refuge to Ibn Sīnā. The chroniclers report with delight how Qābūs maintained his hospitality to the philosopher (who had cured a kinsman), even when Maḥmūd sent men with Ibn Sīnā's portrait to inquire after him. But, before the year was out, Qābūs was imprisoned in a fortress, where he died in 1013. His son, who bore the Persian name Manuchir, was married to a daughter of Maḥmūd's, and it seemed prudent to Ibn Sīnā to move on.

Avicenna turned towards Dihistān near the border of Khwarizm, but fell deathly ill, and on recovering returned to Jurjān late in the year. There he was given a house by one Abū Muḥammad al-Shīrāzī, for whom he wrote a work entitled entitled *General Observations* (*Kitāb al-Arṣād al-Kulliyya*) and another called *Whither and Whence* (*Kitāb al-Mabda' wa 'l-Ma'ād*). The latter is extant in manuscript in the Ambrosian collection at Milan. Ibn Sīnā calls it the fruit of his studies of physics and metaphysics; and its subject, revealingly, is the origin and destiny of the human soul. Its three parts deal with God, emanation, and immortality. The general discussion that lays the groundwork in the first two parts is incorporated into the *Shifā'* and *Najāt*; but the metaphysics of the rational soul, the one part of the psyche that Aristotle had treated as capable of immortality, is expanded and reworked in a slightly later work, *The Situation of the Human Soul*, which is then incorporated into these mature compendia.[26]

The philosopher was thirty-two and living at Jurjān when he met his disciple, al-Juzjānī, who had forsaken his country to the west of Balkh to attach himself to Avicenna, after hearing of him and reading his works. He charmed Ibn Sīnā with verses about the philosopher's situation, one of which is preserved in the account of himself that Ibn Sīnā dictated to his pupil:

> I grew so big that no city could hold me
> But my price went so high every buyer has sold me.

The philosopher was, in effect, priced out of the market. Al-Juzjānī was devoted to his master and was to write commentaries on several of his works in different genres. Now he attended him daily to read the *Almagest* and take dictation in logic. Avicenna's *Middle Summary on Logic* and *Summary of the Almagest* were byproducts of this traditional method of instruction. Juzjānī was never to become a great scholar or thinker himself; but, as Porphyry had done for Plotinus, he made it part of his purpose to record the life of his teacher and to aid him by seeing that he devoted himself to writing and kept track of his works, not simply dispersing them without retaining copies. Thus in Jurjān in 1012 Ibn Sīnā wrote the beginnings of his great medical text, the *Qānūn* or *Canon on Medicine.*

The responsiveness of his patron and the disciples who gathered around him encouraged Ibn Sīnā to shift his focus away from summary appraisals of the "outcomes" of philosophical sciences and make good his transition to more original work, aimed at more universal intellectual purposes. The change is striking when we compare his achievement with that of even as insightful and synthetic a predecessor as al-Fārābī: The earlier philosopher regularly cloaks his own intentions in a descriptive and abstractive mode, writing about languages, cultures and religions, prophets, philosophers and theologians, statesmen and the credos necessary to diverse types of polity. But philosophy itself is often bracketed, even in the finest of his works, as the basis of a kind of ideology, the metaphysics of emanation becoming one core element in the system of "Principles behind the Beliefs of the People of the Outstanding State."[27] There are collections of discrete pronunciamentos, a reconciliation of Plato and Aristotle,[28] a brilliant treatment of the interactions of metaphysics, logic, and language,[29] trenchant commentaries, but no big synthetic work. Avicenna (who had nothing like al-Fārābī's eighty years) would produce, apart from his medical classic, at least three major conspectuses of his original philosophy and a number of related works: – one in a more direct, informal, almost tutorial format – the *Book of Hints and Pointers* – and several in more indirect, symbolic modes – his poem on the soul, and his philosophical allegories.[30] One result of the change in orientation was disappointing to Juzjānī, however: Ibn Sīnā was now unwilling to recreate his scattered longer works of evaluation and commentary.

As the quip about being priced out of the market shows, Ibn Sīnā did not see himself as settled in Jurjān. The shadow of Maḥmūd fell too close, and the role he thought best suited – and most likely to protect him from such a benefactor – required his presence in an independent prince's court. In search of such a berth, Avicenna and Juzjānī traveled to Rayy (near present day Tehran), bearing letters of reference and introduction to the Būyid court of Majd al-Dawla. The city was the richest in northern Persia, known for its manufactures and its central position on the road from Khorasan to Iraq. Ibn Sīnā entered the service of the court and treated the prince for melancholia, depression as we would call it. Medieval medicine associated melancholia with an excess of black bile, but carefully distinguished it from mere moodiness by its symptoms: anxiety, suspicion, unaccountable demands for isolation, obsessive appetites or constant washing, fantasies or loathings for particular objects or foods, fascination with dreams and predictions based on them. Physical symptoms like a black stool were confirmatory but secondary and inessential.[31] In Rayy Ibn Sīnā seems to have written *The Situation of the Human Soul*, in sixteen chapters, establishing his mature psychology. The work aims to show that our knowledge of universals betokens the immortality of the rational soul and its hegemony over (rather than dependence on) the body. Accordingly, the work argues for a Platonic doctrine of intellectual recompense – we gain immortality through the access intellect affords us to the eternal Forms. But it also argues against metempsychosis, which literal minded readers of Plato even today obtusely take to be Plato's literal thesis, rather than a part of his Orphic and Pythagorean symbolic apparatus.

Majd al-Dawla ruled with or was ruled by his mother, the Dowager Queen, known simply, but impressively, as the Lady. She had become regent when his father died and he was only four years old, but she refused to give up her power when the prince came of age, distracting him instead with wine and harem women. Despite his splendid title (Glory of the Regime), Majd al-Dawla was known as a weak ruler - weak enough, Maḥmūd said, to save him the trouble of keeping a garrison at Nīshapūr. Yet the riches of Rayy could not fail to attract Maḥmūd's appetite. In response to his threats, the Dowager is said to have written:

> As long as my husband was alive, I lived in fear that thoughts of conquering Rayy would come into your head, but since he died my heart is freed of that disquiet. For I said to myself, "Sultān Maḥmūd is a reasonable monarch; he knows that a ruler like himself ought not to make war against a woman like me." But, should you come, God knows I will not run. For there can be but two outcomes, since one army must be beaten: If it is mine that carries the day, I shall write to the entire world that I have broken Sultān Maḥmūd, who broke a hundred kings. . . . But if it is you who are the victor, what will you write? That you have broken the power of a woman?

When the Lady died in 1028, Majd al-Dawla was unable to control his troops and called in Maḥmūd for help - who obligingly deposed him and carried him off a prisoner. But once again, Ibn Sīnā had not waited for that denouement.

Still under pressure from Maḥmūd, he had moved on from Rayy, to Qazwīn and then to Hamadhān, where he acted as an agent of the Dowager and met Shams al-Dawla, a more aggressive brother of Majd al-Dawla, and successfully treated him for for the bowel disorder that the Arabic medical writers called colic. The Ghaznavids had gained control of Rayy, aided by the disgust of the local populace at the inability of Majd and his mother to control their turbulent Daylamite troops. But in the spring of 1015 Shams al-Dawla defeated and killed the Kurdish leader Hilāl ibn Badr ibn Hasanwayh (who had been released from imprisonment in Baghdad in order to curb Shams al-Dawla's power), routed the Baghdad armies sent against him, and retook Rayy from the Ghaznavids. Here Ibn Sīnā saw a promising protector. Shams al-Dawla had richly rewarded the philosopher for his medical treatment, but the two men hit it off personally as well, and in 1015 Ibn Sīnā joined the Būyid prince and became his close companion, accompanying him in the field when he took his armies westward to defend his claims in Kirmanshāh, and then serving as *wazīr* at Hamadhān when the troops fell back from the attack, probably in the winter of 1015/16. The troops at Hamadhān mutinied against this unwonted *wazīr*, besieged his house, hauled him off to prison, and looted his belongings. When Shams al-Dawla returned from the field, they demanded Ibn Sīnā's life, but the prince mollified them by merely banishing the philosopher, who went into hiding for forty days in a friend's house, until Shams al-Dawla, stricken with colic once again, recalled and reinstated him, amid profuse apologies.

All the while, Ibn Sīnā was struggling to keep on with his writing. He had begun the *Qānūn* in Jurjān in 1012, continued it in Rayy in 1014, and now completed it in Hamadhān over the years 1015–23. Juzjānī saw the administrative responsibilities thrust upon his teacher and then wrested from him, as "a waste of our time." He was eager to see more writing by the master, especially since it was clear that the lost early works were not likely to be recovered. Ibn Sīnā had not the heart or the inclination to undertake another exhaustive commentary or verbal analysis of the Aristotelian classics, but he agreed (probably around 1020) to write an original comprehensive work in the order that seemed best to him and without detailed responses to the prior tradition. He committed himself to writing two pages each morning before his official duties began. This was the origin of the *Shifā'*. Each night, after his ministerial work had been completed, he would gather with his students for a double session, Juzjānī reading from the newly finished pages of the *Shifā'* and another student reading from the first book of the *Qānūn*. When the session ended, all sorts of singers would appear, and a drinking party would begin.

This schedule was not ideal for sustained new writing, but the immediate response of the hearers spurred on the philosopher, and the period was productive in its way. But it lasted only briefly. Shams al-Dawla died in 1021, retreating from a campaign aborted by his old complaint. His heir, Samā' al-Dawla, and the young prince's *wazīr* Tāj al-Mulk, sought to confirm Ibn Sīnā in office. For the philosopher was by now quite an experienced politician; the list of his books in fact includes a work on *The Management and Provisioning of Soldiers, Slave Troops, and Armies and the Taxation of Kingdoms.*[32] But the philosopher, not confident of the staying power of his new would-be patron, entered into secret correspondence with a rival monarch, 'Alā' al-Dawla of Isfahān (r. 1008–42), called Ibn Kākūya, by reference to his kinship with the Lady; for in Daylamī *kākū* meant maternal uncle, and that was his relation to the unfortunate Majd al-Dawla. Awaiting an invitation to join this prince's entourage, Ibn Sīnā again went into hiding, lodging with a druggist friend.

The need to stay out of sight proved an opportunity for sustained work on the *Shifā'*. Ibn Sīnā asked for paper and ink and in two days wrote out his main rubrics in some twenty octavo quires. Then in a few weeks of spirited labor, reportedly writing some fifty pages a day, without a library (but clearly with access to his own *De Anima* and Metaphysics materials), he completed the Metaphysics and Physics (except for the Zoology and Botany) of the *Shifā'* and began the Logic and his general introduction. But now Samā' al-Dawla and his *wazīr*, infuriated by the discovery of the secret correspondence and informed by Ibn Sīnā's enemies of his whereabouts, arrested and imprisoned him in a castle known as Fardajān in the Jarrā district about fifty-five miles outside Hamadhān. As he wrote at the time:

> That I go in you see, so that's without doubt.
> What's uncertain is whether I ever come out.

For four months Ibn Sīnā remained in the castle, and there he wrote his *Hidāyah* or Book of Guidance, his allegory of the human intellect, *Ḥayy Ibn Yaqẓān*,[33] and his medical treatise, *Colic*. But, as Hamadhānī might have explained, had he overheard Juzjānī's complaints of the blows of fate, fate has tricks as well as blows to deal out. The city of Hamadhān fell to 'Alā' al-Dawla in 1023, and the routed prince and *wazīr* took refuge in Fardajān, along with Ibn Sīnā. When the Kākūyid withdrew, Ibn Sīnā returned with the ruler to Hamadhān, where he was put up by an 'Alid friend, in whose honor he rapidly wrote a work on *Cardiac Therapies*,[34] while hearing out the blandishments of the young prince, who now more than ever desired his service.

But Ibn Sīnā had not survived the collapse of so many regimes to make so obvious a mistake. In company with his brother, his faithful disciple, and two slaves, all disguised as Sufis, he set out to the southeast for Isfahān, where the Kākūyid ruler held a glittering court and used his revenues to support Turkmen forces that would hold off Maḥmūd. After an arduous journey, Ibn Sīnā's little company were met by 'Alā' al-Dawla's men not far from Isfahān with fresh clothing and fine mounts, and the philosopher was given furnished lodgings in the city and the warmest of welcomes by the ruler.

4 THE YEARS AT ISFAHĀN

With Aristotle's writings at hand, offering points of agreement and disagreement, Ibn Sīnā worked toward completion of the *Shifā'*, finishing the Logic and incorporating his early summaries of Ptolemy's *Almagest* and Euclid's *Elements*. The work was intended as a compendium of knowledge, and its title, literally, *The Cure*, is indicative of Ibn Sīnā's hope that it would "help to clear away the veils of fancy." As Gutas writes, "It is tempting to see in Paul [the Persian's sixth-century] description of Aristotle's oeuvre as a 'course of treatment' (*shifā'*) that cures 'the diseases of ignorance' the source of Avicenna's title."[35] But the work was clearly no mere summary. Even in its mathematical sections, as Juzjānī stresses, Ibn Sīnā was always original, adding ten figures to the Almagest to illustrate the effects of parallax, and developing Euclid's geometry, the traditional mathematical treatment of music, and the obligatory discussions of arithmetic in ways that the ancients had not anticipated. Only the Botany and Zoology remained to be done.

At 'Alā' al-Dawla's court scholarly assemblies were held on Friday nights, and Ibn Sīnā took part with delight, often contributing to literary and linguistic discussions and not confining himself to the sciences in which he had won fame. One Abū Manṣūr, whose adopted surname, al-Jabbān, boasts of his learning the niceties of Arabic usage from the desert Bedouins, criticized Ibn Sīnā for his apparent hubris: Knowledge of philosophy and medical science does not make one a philologist. Piqued, Ibn Sīnā studied Arabic philology for three years, sending off to Khorasan for one key textbook – for the scholars who made a science of Arabic grammar and diction were often Persians, in this case a native of Herāt who had lived two years as a prisoner in a Bedouin tribe. Then, as a hoax, the philosopher composed three odes filled with rare words and obscurities of the sort that delighted the literary dandies of the day. To complement the poems, he wrote three short works, each in the style of a different essayist noted for his brilliant prose. He had all this bound into a single volume, whose leather was suitably aged and antiqued, and then prevailed on the *Amīr* to present it to al-Jabbān as a curious tome found while hunting in the desert. The man of letters soon caught on to the joke, when Ibn Sīnā began citing chapter and verse to explain the rambunctious Arabic usages that the philologist could not tie down, and he apologized for underestimating his fellow scholar. The philosopher capped his *jeu d'esprit* by writing a learned work called *The Arabs' Tongue*. His disciple attests that it was peerless, but it was still in draft form at his death, "and no one could see quite how to put it together."

A favorite at the court, Ibn Sīnā was made *Wazīr*, and served as such until his death. He regularly accompanied the *Amīr* in the field, and it was on the way to Shābūr Khwāst that he completed the *Shifā'*, perhaps during 'Alā' al-Dawla's campaign against the Kurds, whom he routed at Nihāwend in 1027. In all, the *Shifā'* contained nine books on logic, eight on the natural sciences, four on the quadrivium of arithmetic, geometry, astronomy, and music, and of course the metaphysics.[36] Juzjānī was proud to be the godfather of the work, as he makes evident in his introduction, but his conception of it is rather different from Avicenna's. He emphasizes the feats of memory and the difficult circumstances of composition, as though pleading extenuating circumstances for the failure of the *Shifā'* to measure up to the Aristotelian original.[37] But the author stresses its originality and completeness, urging that it omits nothing of value to be found in the ancients. Ibn Sīnā does not see himself as an Aristotle manqué, but as a conscious reformer and synthesizer of the Aristotelian disciplines.

The main divisions of the *Shifā'*, Logic, Physics, Mathematics, and Metaphysics, show that it is not intended to be an encyclopedia in our sense. It made no attempt to include medicine and does not at all celebrate the vastness of human inquiry that is so much a theme of Diderot or Bayle. Indeed, if we are seeking an encyclopedic mind in Ibn Sīnā's time, al-Bīrūnī would be the man, combining as he did, chronology and astronomy with the medical and mathematical sciences, history, geography, language studies, and what we would call anthropology. It was Bīrūnī, not Avicenna, who found a way for a single man, at a single moment, to measure the earth's circumference, by trigonometric calculations based on angles measured from a mountaintop and the plain beneath it – thus improving on Eratosthenes' method of sighting the sun simultaneously from two different sites, applied in the ninth century by astronomers of the Khalif al-Ma'mūn. Rather, Ibn Sīnā's work was a summa in the proper sense, a compendium (*jumla*), as he called it, pulling together not vast learning and erudite detail but related themes and ideas into a coherent pattern. It was with this notion of comprehensiveness in mind that he called it the *Shifā'* or Healing, a cure for the ignorance of the Soul. For it was only through understanding, and the remedying of its deficiency in this respect, that the human soul could regain its true home. Thus the Latins were not wrong to render Ibn Sīnā's title for the work, *Sufficientia*. In the mid-fourteenth century Muḥammad

Tughluq, the Sultan of Delhi paid 200,000 mithqals of gold for a fine calligraphic copy of the work.

On completing the *Shifā'*, Ibn Sīnā immediately began work on the *Najāt*, apparently beginning the task en route to Shābūr Khwāst around 1026 and finishing it by the following year. His friends had asked for a practical, even minimal treatment of philosophy: basic logic, physics, geometry and astronomy, the arithmetic needed for calendars and astronomical tables, basic musical theory, metaphysics enough to grasp the destiny of the soul, and practical ethics as needed for salvation from the sea of errors. The title *Najāt* means Salvation. Here again, and even more than in the *Shifā'*, the emphasis was on unity and coherence, overcoming rather than reveling in the proliferation of knowledge, marshaling and ordering the solid outcomes of those sciences whose use of rigorous argument entitled them to the designation "philosophical," i.e., scientific. The *Najāt* was not a new work – nor, as it is often represented, a summary of the *Shifā'* – but a patchwork quilt, incorporating the short summary of logic that Ibn Sīnā wrote in Jurjān around 1013 or 1014, the physics of the *'Arūḍī* that he wrote at twenty-one in Bukhārā, the *De Anima* from *The Situation of the Human Soul*, and the metaphysics from *Whither and Whence.* Juzjānī completed the work by tacking on chapters on geometry, astronomy, and music from his copies of Ibn Sīnā's early works, his own abridgement of a work of Ibn Sīnā's on arithmetic, and a foreword on the provenance of these parts. Avicenna had stopped writing about mathematics in his mature works after the *Shifā'*, finding no philosophical disagreements on this subject.

Carrying on his medical work – clinical research as well as writing – Ibn Sīnā found a way of curing himself of headaches with ice compresses, and of curing a tubercular woman with large quantities of a sugar-rose preserve, whose virtue was perhaps in the vitamins it contained. He hoped to record his medical discoveries in the *Qānūn*, but most of his clinical notebooks were lost. As a result, al-Rāzī, a philosophical iconoclast who was proud of his hospital experience with many classes of patients, became known as the better clinician. Still, the completed *Canon*, because of its clarity, concision and order, became the most widely used comprehensive work on medicine in the Middle Ages. Translated into Latin by Gerard of Cremona between 1150 and 1187 and printed in Arabic at Rome in 1593, along with samples of Avicenna's philosophy (this version of his name being itself an artifact of the translation), the *Canon* became the authoritative compendium of Greco-Roman scientific medicine for Europe as well as for the Islamic lands. As Da Monte put it in his Commentary (1554): The ancient Hippocratic corpus was enigmatic, Galen prolix, Rāzī confusing. Avicenna wrote the *Canon* "because he saw that neither the Greeks nor the Arabs had any book that would teach the art of medicine as an integrated and connected subject."[38] In the last thirty years of the fifteenth century the work went through fifteen editions in Latin and one in Hebrew. The Renaissance was in part the throwing off of the authority of this *Canon*, with many thinkers from Leonardo to Harvey fighting its influence. But in the medieval practice of medicine, it was the trunk to which lesser vines could cling. Even the pre-Harvey discovery of the lesser or pulmonary circulation of the blood through the heart and lungs was recorded by Ibn al-Nafīs (1256–1345) in a commentary on Avicenna's *Canon*, and some physicians in the Middle East continued to find valuable clinical advice in it down to our own age. Goichon mentions a Dr Abdallah Ahmadieh in Tehran, who achieved good results in treating rheumatism with therapeutics derived from his study of Ibn Sīnā.

The work is of five parts. The first is on the the nature of the human body, anatomy, physiology, the definition of health, illness, and medical treatment, the causes and symptoms of disease. Diseases are ascribed to an imbalance of the temperaments, a bodily malformation, or a dissolution of bodily order – for example, in obstructions. Urine and pulse are valuable monitors of the inner complexion. Diseases may result from diet, air, motion and rest, sleep, or the passions of the soul. Special regimens are needed for children, adults, travelers, and the elderly. Therapies include emetics, cathartics, enemas, sedatives, and other drugs, bleeding, blistering, and cauterization.

Part Two of the *Canon* deals with medical simples and the conditions they treat. But it also contains Ibn Sīnā's important early prescription of a scientific method, formulating the canons of agreement, difference, and concomitant variation, and laying down seven rules for the isolation of causes, analysis of temporal and quantitative effects, and constancy of recurrence. Goichon sagely connects this discussion with the Stoic hypothetical logic and theory of signs.[39] The key to that connection is Ibn Sīnā's general, Aristotelian principle of never reducing the terms of reasoning to empty abstractions or mere formalisms. Aristotelian science, without the hypothetical method of the Stoics, was far too essentialist to allow genuine experimentation. As I have written elsewhere, Aristotle's failure to share Plato's enthusiasm for mathematics enlarges into a general bias against the significance of measurement and overemphasis of qualitative over quantitative variations. His normative preference for the natural regards artificially contrived situations as "accidental" and so intrinsically uninteresting. His tendency to view cosmogony as mere myth deflates the importance of efficient causes, relative to the formal, final, and even material cause. In principle at least Ibn Sīnā's openness to the hypothetical logic of the Stoics (which he learns from Galen), overcomes some of these structural deficiencies in the Aristotelian method and gives him a more historical and experimental view of science and discovery.

The method Ibn Sīnā develops clearly expresses his emanative understanding of causality, which is both Neoplatonic and in a way Mu'tazilite. For the Mu'tazilites understood the imparting of sound limbs and capacities (including the capacity for moral choice) to be among the principal expressions of God's grace, much as the Stoics understood divine providence (*pronoia*) to operate through an immanent rather than a merely external causality. For a Neoplatonist like Ibn Sīnā, this immanent causality would act through the emanation of forms from the Active Intellect. But the empirical study of the working (or materially grounded dysfunction) of those forms in the body would be a matter of reasoning about the signs that mark the presence (or absence) of the pertinent forms. This could be done by using the special hypothetical syllogisms by which the Logic of the *Shifā'* brought Stoic conditional logic within the framework of the Aristotelian predicate calculus.

The pathology of each organ or system, twenty-one in all from head to toe, is surveyed in the third Part of the *Qānūn*, with an accompanying review of anatomical and physiological data and the assignment of appropriate treatments for each ill. There follows in Part Four a discussion of diseases not associated with a particular locus, because they affect the body as a whole or might lodge in various parts. Part Four opens with a celebrated treatise on fevers and develops the important concept of crisis, discussing medical signs, symptoms, diagnostics, and prognostics. It also teaches minor surgery, the treatment of tumors and pustules, wounds, bruises, sprains and ulcers, dislocations, fractures, poisons (mineral, vegetable, and animal, including bites and stings), and skin conditions. In the west, Paracelsus (1493–1541) fought against the traditional division of medicine from surgery; but he was pilloried for it by his fellow physicians. Ibn Sīnā is completely uninhibited about combining the two.

The fifth and final Part of the *Qānūn* is the pharmacopoeia, a manual for the preparation of compound medicines. Here too, where we separate pharmacy as an independent art, Ibn Sīnā made it an integral part of medical studies. Paracelsus, who publicly burned the *Canon* of Avicenna as a display of his hatred for ancient authority as against empirical study, followed Avicenna (and earned the ire of the apothecaries) by pursuing the study and practice of pharmacy for himself.

Of the general plan of the *Qānūn* Siraisi writes:

> If one wishes to use the *Canon* as a reference tool, the arrangement . . . works well for some subjects, but a good deal less well for others. . . . One can, for example, relatively easily find an answer to any of the following questions: When and in what conditions is bleeding an appropriate treatment? What are the medicinal powers of cinnamon? What treatments are recommended for deafness? For various kinds of fevers? How is theriac compounded? . . . Least satisfactory, in some respects, is the arrangement of the physiological and anatomical material. Principles of physiology and the anatomy of bones, muscles, nerves, veins, and arteries . . . are scattered . . .[40]

Despite its pioneering formulation of empirical methods, the *Qānūn* remains a compendium largely of traditional material, much of it Galenic, ordered and accepted on the authority of what is taken, erroneously, to be a rather mature and well-established science.[41] Thus the practical tenor of the work: A canon, in Arabic as in English, is a rule, yardstick, or standard. Ibn Sīnā's intent, all too successful, was to give practitioners ready guidelines for immediate application, without too much worry over theory, and with a minimum of skeptical doubt or radical experimentation. The practitioner, he argued, should investigate the material, formal, and final causes of the body's health and sickness for himself, by means of the senses, and must know anatomy, regimen, symptoms, and medications, but should take the fundamentals of physical science such as the theory of the four elements from natural philosophy. The role of a physician does not call upon one to investigate such philosophical matters independently.[42] This workmanlike approach has its benefits: The physics and chemistry of the age were not adequate to physiological application, and it was generally true as a matter of practice that the less a medic became embroiled in them, the better off his patients would be. The ancient Skeptics, Methodics, and medical Empiricists made much the same point within the framework of their own epistemologies.

Few medical practitioners even today perform original research in physics or chemistry. Most take their "first principles" from authority, i.e., from textbooks. This said, we must recognize that Avicenna's great medical compendium was egregiously outdated even when he wrote it. Galen was eight centuries old and was himself a synthesizer, not the most advanced Greek medical scientist of his day. Ibn Sīnā's reliance on tradition was a great boon in that it did lay down a canon of practice that was scientific rather than merely traditional or haphazard. But in many ways even such a canon was as much a disservice to patients as a convenience to physicians. Ibn Sīnā's avoidance and discouragement of radical probing of the suppositious foundations of medieval physiology held back medical progress. Even his experimental modes, with their emphasis on careful observation and detail, were the rules of what we would call "normal science" – as though the medicine of his day had any title to authority based on the very limited successes it achieved in treatment. And there was little in the milieu that would put those methods to work as a genuine experimental method.

But all this is said only with the benefit of hindsight. The *Qānūn* was not a modern work; and its author, like such predecessors as al-Rāzī, while appreciating the need for progress and recognizing the shortcomings in the ancient texts, could not see how radical a break with tradition real progress in medicine (or astronomy) would require. He was not a Francis Bacon, not having the Renaissance *animus* against the past. Indeed, although he influenced them both, he was not a Roger Bacon or a Robert Grosseteste, lacking Roger Bacon's discontent with the authority of an all too integrated tradition, and lacking Grosseteste's idiosyncratic drive to a self-generated rather than communally shared system of thought and investigation.[43] Yet the *Canon* did distinguish between pleurisy and infections of the mediastinum, rightly attributed ancylostomiasis to an intestinal worm (the nematode we call hookworm), observed that phthisis can be contagious and that diseases are spread by water and soil, not only by "bad air." Its *materia medica* knows some 760 drugs. And we, for our part, should not be too superior about our modernity. To begin with, modernity as we know it is not ours alone but is itself part of a tradition. Besides, the breach of continuity that was the ticket to modernity for most thinkers of the Renaissance and Enlightenment makes exceedingly difficult for many of us renewed access to the metaphysical and moral insights of the ancient and medieval tradition. Rediscovery of that tradition can aid us in addressing perennial problems of philosophy that modernity has often failed adequately to address.

At 'Alā' al-Dawla's request, Ibn Sīnā made original astronomical observations, not for astrological purposes (indeed he wrote a work against astrology[44]), but to clear up obscurities in the established tables of observation that piqued the curiosity of the Prince. Juzjānī was charged with engaging skilled artisans to manufacture the necessary instruments, including some of Ibn Sīnā's invention, on which the philosopher wrote a treatise. Also at the Prince's request, Ibn Sīnā wrote a conspectus of philosophy in Persian, like the *Shifā'* covering Logic, Physics, Astronomy, Music, and Metaphysics – but in a discursive and explanatory tone genuinely inviting to the lay reader. Entitled *Danesh Nameh Alā'ī*, or *The Book of Sciences for 'Alā' al-Dawla*, this was Ibn Sīnā's only major work of philosophy written in his native Persian, an Indo-European rather than Semitic language, whose survival against the onslaught of Arabic the epic of Firdawsī in great measure assured. Arabic, the language of international scholarship in Muslim lands, would not have been too comfortable a medium for the Prince to read so seemingly remote a subject, already so studded with the distinctive abstract vocabulary that Arabic translators and the polyglot philosophers who wrote in Arabic introduced in their encounter with Greek thought. The French translators of the *Danesh Nameh* note Avicenna's clear, natural, and lucid Persian equivalents for Arabic terms and describe his Persian style as the fairest and finest that Persian has to offer: short, solidly constructed sentences, without any hint of Arabism, and a direct and serious tone, leavened by irony and good humor. This natural style was ideally suited to philosophic writing and far removed from any supercilious mannerism – or even from the conventional '*Know that . . .*' and '*One might say that . . .*' of the *Book of Hints and Pointers*.[45] It is a grave challenge to the notions of linguistic determinists, that Avicenna readily transposed from Arabic into Persian the original philosophical insights that he had built upon the earlier work in Arabic of the Soghdian speaking Turk al-Fārābī, which were founded in turn upon the ideas of philosophers who wrote in Greek and of inspired poets and prophets whose message was conveyed in Hebrew, Aramaic, and Arabic.

Ibn Sīnā's Persian work, dedicated humbly to the Prince at whose court he had at last found "safety, dignity, honor, respect, and cultivation of the sciences," and modestly confessing the author's sense of his own inadequacy to the task,[46] was modeled on the same practical, minimal scheme as the *Najāt*. The Persian work formed the basis of al-Ghazālī's celebrated critique of the Philosophers of Islam, and al-Ghazālī followed it verbatim in *The Objects of the Philosophers* (*Maqāṣid al-Falāsifa*), which formed the groundwork of his celebrated refutation, *The Incoherence of the Philosophers.* It has long been known that Ibn Sīnā was the chief target of al-Ghazālī's attack on the Islamic tradition of philosophy. Indeed Averroes (Ibn Rushd), in responding to that attack in *The Incoherence of the Incoherence*, and in readjusting his own philosophical posture after confronting al-Ghazālī's polemic, often thought it sufficient simply to distance himself from the philosophic stance of Ibn Sīnā. But we can say more than that: "Contrary to what one might suppose from the introduction to the *Maqāṣid*, this book was not the original work of al-Ghazālī. It was a literal translation into Arabic of the Persian philosophic treatise of Avicenna, the *Danesh Nameh*," although Ghazālī nowhere in it mentions Ibn Sīnā by name.[47] Moreover, despite his failure to cite his source, al-Ghazālī was clearly much impressed with the argumentation of Ibn Sīnā, and not only as a philosophical stalking horse: He adopted the idea of emanation, although rejecting the accompanying thesis of the world's eternity, and, as I have shown in my studies of al-Ghazālī,[48] adopted the core of Ibn Sīnā's emanative idea of causality (rejecting only aspects of its necessitarianism). He plainly accepted Ibn Sīnā's extensive argumentation in this work against the radical atomism of dimensionless substances associated with the occasionalist schools of *kalām*, and he even used elements of the ethics of Ibn Sīnā in modifying the humanistic ethics of the Persian writer Miskawayh to his more pietist and ascetic presentation.[49] Later partisans of Averroism sometimes saw al-Ghazālī as a secret follower of Ibn Sīnā – the *Maqāṣid* expressing his true views; and the polemic against philosophy, a mere symptom of the political ills of his time.[50] That is an obvious overstatement. But al-Ghazālī's express position is that *Falsafa*, meaning most emphatically the views of Ibn Sīnā as represented in the *Danesh Nameh*, was to be rejected only on the twenty crucial theses rebutted in the *Incoherence.* All the rest was true.

When a group of Shirāz scholars wrote to Ibn Sīnā with objections to the short work on logic that he incorporated into the *Najāt*, he stayed up most of the night with candles and wine, until midnight accompanied by his brother and Juzjānī, filling five quires of "Pharaonic" style paper with his replies, saying that he did not wish to keep the messenger waiting too long for his reply. The monumental *Kitāb al-Inṣāf*, or *Impartial Judgment*, was written as a pastime in a similarly combative spirit in the first six months of 1029. It adressed nearly

28,000 questions of text, interpretation, and philosophy drawn from the Aristotelian corpus and its commentaries. Included in the discussion were those excerpts from Plotinus' Sixth to Ninth *Enneads* that circulated in Arabic, ill disguised, as the *Theology of Aristotle*, which Avicenna himself labeled suspect. A fair copy of the *Kitāb al-Inṣāf* would have filled twenty volumes. It took up some 6,000 folios in cursive and would, we are told, have occupied 10,000 in a square hand. It was a controversial work in which Ibn Sīnā sought to judge dispassionately, as the title suggests, between what he called eastern and western philosophers. Much ink has been spilt needlessly in efforts to identify the adherents of these two tendencies, some taking the Westerners to be Christians or Peripatetics, the Easterners to be mystics or theosophists. But Ibn Sīnā's target, as he tells us himself, was the Baghdad school of *falsafa*, the school we associate with al-Kindī and his followers, including the second generation disciple, Avicenna's older contemporary at Bukhārā, al-Āmirī,[51] who read Aristotle's *Metaphysics* theologically and seemed to Ibn Sīnā to miss the differences between natural theology and religion – or the nexus between ontology and theology, which al-Fārābī had taught so clearly and which Ibn Sīnā had consummately understood. The Easterners are the thinkers of Khorasan.[52]

In the prologue to the *Shifā'* Ibn Sīnā refers to a work of his that can be dated to this period, the *Eastern Philosophy*. He says that it contains the unvarnished truth, without reference to existing opinions and without his usual concern to avoid provoking controversy. Most of the work, he says, was packed up in quires and lost, along with passages from another work called the *Throne Philosophy*. The *Eastern Philosophy*, he says, would not be difficult to recreate. It was a work of one volume and included a discussion of "the invariable element in animals," that is, the life principle, and an "Eastern proof" of the incorporeality of the rational soul. Thus it voiced the same Platonizing rational mysticism that sounds throughout Ibn Sīnā's oeuvre. But some modern scholars, playing on the vocalization of the word 'Easterners' (*mashriqiyyūn*) have sought to father upon Ibn Sīnā a later tradition of mystical theosophy that is more pantheist, immanentist, and gnostic in orientation than the traditions of "sober" Sufism or Neoplatonic Aristotelianism in Islam would normally countenance: the tradition of the "illuminists" (*mushriqiyyūn*). Even Ibn Ṭufayl suggests a strong dichotomy between Ibn Sīnā's view of the truth and his Peripateticism. But the mysticism Ibn Ṭufayl adapts from his reading of Avicenna, al-Ghazālī, and Ibn Bājjah does not depart from the ambit of Neoplatonic and indeed neo-Aristotelian thinking and outspokenly relies on that tradition in the arguments by which it rejects the pantheistic tendencies that admirers of illuminist theosophy were to prize most highly.[53] Clearly the Persian illuminist tradition takes its point of departure in the metaphysics of Avicenna. But Suhrawardī, the true founder of the illuminist school, testifies decisively against the idea that the Prince of the Philosophers had any hand in founding the distinctive traditions of theosophy that go beyond what is stated in any of Avicenna's familiar philosophical writings: He saw the work on eastern philosophy (even if only the parts now extant), and found that it differed only in slight verbal respects from Peripatetic *falsafa*.[54] A hint of what is meant by such differences remains visible to us: Ibn Sīnā remarked in a surviving passage from the introduction to the work that Easterners may have their own name for logic. We know that some scholars, uncomfortable with philosophy, held that philosophical logic applies only to the Greek language and that the name for logic (*manṭiq*, from the root *n-ṭ-q*, meaning speech, on the analogy of the Greek *logike/logos*) implies the dependence of its rules on the conventions of a particular language.[55] Avicenna scotches such debate when he argues that logic would be the same regardless of the name it is given. Eastern Philosophy to Ibn Sīnā meant original but rigorous speculation in the Neoplatonic and Aristotelian tradition, a tradition that did not exclude mystical fulfillment of the quest of reason, but also, as we shall see, a tradition that did not sharply distinguish rational from mystical intuitions, and one that saw the power to forestall pantheistic excesses as one of the greatest strengths of philosophy.

The luxury of sustained speculation, even intellectual play and experimentation, were not to endure. In 1029 Maḥmūd captured Rayy north of Isfahān, destroying the Būyid palace library, and burning its learned tomes "at the feet of the corpses of the Ismā'īlīs, Rāfiḍīs, philosophers, and other unbelievers that hung from the trees."[56] Not satisfied with tribute, his son Mas'ūd dispatched a governor to Isfahān; but 'Alā' al-Dawla bravely turned him away, and Mas'ūd marched against the city. The fighting did not go well, and 'Alā' al-Dawla was forced to evacuate. In January, 1030, as Ibn Sīnā and others were streaming out of the city with the Prince, the philosopher's baggage was plundered near the gates. The manuscript of the *Kitāb al-Inṣāf* was lost. Evidently it was not destroyed, for a bibliophile claimed to have bought a complete copy in Isfahān in 1150, but only fragments of the work survive.

Isfahān fell to Ghaznavids repeatedly. On one occasion, five thousand Isfahānīs were killed for rebeling against the garrison left there by the Ghaznavids. But the Kākūyid did not give up his resistance. Although his son became a vassal to the Seljuqs, 'Alā' al-Dawla never succumbed to the Ghaznavids, and the tribute they exacted from him in defeat, 20,000 dinārs and 10,000 bolts of fabric annually, besides several annual festival gifts, was regularly in arrears. In 1034 Mas'ūd's Kurdish cavalry commander, al-Ḥamdūnī, systematically pillaged 'Alā' al-Dawla's treasury and library, including the works of Ibn Sīnā. As a result Mas'ūd possessed what must have seemed the very best of Ibn Sīnā, works the plunderer would never read, but to which the philosopher himself now had no access. Years later the *Eastern Philosophy* and *Throne Philosophy* were still to be found in Mas'ūd's library at Ghaznā, down to the time of its burning in 1151 by Gurid troops under the command of Jahān-sūz, the "World-burner." But all that lay in the future.

In 1030 'Alā' al-Dawla retreated south toward Khuzistān and was seeking aid from a Būyid ally there when the news arrived of the death of Maḥmūd. Mas'ūd, as the Isfahānīs anticipated, rushed back to Ghaznā to do battle with his brother, just three months after conquering the region. 'Alā' al-Dawla recaptured Rayy, Qum, and Kashān, and at Rayy a disciple urged Ibn Sīnā to recreate the lost *Inṣāf.* He promised to try, but found even the thought disheartening. Yet he seems to have made a start and to have abandoned the task, not because of its immensity but because of its limited value: He sought to buy the works of Abū 'l-Faraj ibn al-Ṭayyib (d. 1043), his old Khwarizm colleague Ibn al-Khammār (b. 942), and Abū 'Alī ibn al-Samḥ (d. 1030), evidently egged on by students who thought that such writings would goad him into rewriting the *Inṣāf.* Abū 'l-Faraj, the only one of the three still alive, set an exorbitant price, but Ibn Sīnā met it with the aid of a wealthy backer. Rumors flew about the motives of both men, but in the end Ibn Sīnā got the books, found them muddled, and told his students that he had felt all along the Baghdad school was not worth the trouble of a refutation. The books were sent back and Abū 'l-Faraj allowed to keep the money. Beyond the *beau geste,* which a Hamadhānī would have appreciated, Ibn Sīnā was again choosing original work over philosophical pedantry. Rather than attempt to recreate the *Kitāb al-Inṣāf,* Avicenna devoted the early 1030s to his *Book of Hints and Pointers* (*Al-Ishārāt wa 'l-Tanbīhāt*), a mature expression of his own philosophical views, insights, and cautionary advice directed to the intellectual work of his disciples as philosophers in their own right and not as mere interpreters of Aristotle, of Islamic Neoplatonism, or even of his own thought. All through his life his patrons and disciples were begging him to be a scholastic, to be Averroes, and write the great extended commentary on Aristotle and all things Aristotelian. But in philosophy Ibn Sīnā was never to be a scholastic, and what Mas'ūd's troops could capture of him was never the living philosopher. By about 1031 he had stopped referring to Eastern Philosophy and does not mention it in the *Ishārāt* or *On the Rational Soul.* The contentious spirit that had led him to react so voluminously to the "Western" authors, cooled as he recognized that in philosophy there are no rivals but only clearer and more comprehensive, and obscurer and more negligible thinkers. In the final, valedictory piece of advice in his *Hints and Pointers* Ibn Sīnā writes:

> Dear Brother, I've churned my best cream for you and fed you my finest dishes, words whipped from the froth of wisdom. Keep it safe from boors and touts, and any whose wit is not lit up with insight, whose character is unschooled by practice, who leans to listen to the crowd, renegade philosophers and the gnats that buzz around them. But if you find someone you're sure is of good faith and upright living, who can stand up to the sallies of temptation and keep his gaze fixed on the truth cheerfully and sincerely, supply him what he asks from this, gradually, bit by bit, and piecemeal, watching his reactions and responses, and make him swear to God by oaths that brook no backing out that he will follow calmly where you lead him. But if you spread around this knowledge and squander it, God judge between us. For God is the surest guarantor.[57]

Ibn Sīnā's Rayy disciple reports that writing the *Inṣāf* greatly cheered Ibn Sīnā as he got what he had to say off his chest.[58] But once that was done, there was no need to rake over stale disputes and sort out the muddles of the Baghdad school or any other derivative thinkers.

Life was too short. Mas'ūd by now was ready to turn back to Isfahān, for it was critical to his power to make a brutal example of the rebellious 'Alā' al-Dawla, who had refused to send him his son as a hostage and proof of allegiance. Mas'ūd sent his general, Tash Farash, against Rayy, his army committing numerous atrocities once the city was taken, the *Schrecklichkeit* of Turkic military policy, designed to inspire terror and obedience. In the battles that followed, 'Alā' al-Dawla was defeated repeatedly but never conquered. Achena and

Massé wonder justifiably if Ibn Sīnā did not have his Prince in mind when he wrote:

> The prevalent notion among the commonfolk is that the most powerful and overmastering pleasures are the sensory ones, and that pleasures that go beyond these are weak, imaginary, even illusory. We can awaken those who have discernment by saying: . . . you know that one who has a chance of winning, even in some low pastime like chess or backgammon, will scorn food or sex in favor of this purely notional joy of winning. . . . And in the same way, the great souled holds hunger and thirst paltry next to honor. He disdains the fear of death and sudden destruction when battling in the fray. He may plunge in of a sudden, mounting on danger's back, with no greater pleasure awaiting him than praise, and that when he is dead . . .[59]

As Achena and Massé remark, of all the monarchs Ibn Sīnā knew, 'Alā' al-Dawla was the only one to whom he offered praise, and the only one at whose side he remained, through victory and defeat. As for the Prince, his face shone with happiness, according to the historian al-Bayhaqī, when the philosopher presented himself at court and took his place at the *Amīr*'s side, beautifully dressed in brocaded robes, leather boots, and linen turban.

Readers both Muslim and non-Muslim are sometimes surprised to learn of Ibn Sīnā's resort to wine. But we must remember that the philosopher never set himself up as a paradigm or paragon of Islamic piety. Al-Sijistānī tells us that Ibn Sīnā justified his drinking on the ground that he was a Ḥanafite – as though Ḥanafite latitudinarianism extended to the permission of intoxicants. But even in explaining the material requirements of logical rigor, Ibn Sīnā stuck to his rejection of moral rigorism, pointedly choosing as an illustration of loose reasoning the proposition "Wine intoxicates," and arguing: "One should take into account whether potentially or actually, and whether a little or a large amount."[60]

The philosopher's fate did not allow him the luxury his father had enjoyed, of marrying, settling down, raising a family, and educating his children. We know of no wife or offspring, and it is clearly impossible for any such impedimenta to have accompanied him on his desperate odyssey in search of refuge and a home. Yet female slaves were as plentiful as male ones in this Islamicate society, and Juzjānī writes candidly that "the master was vigorous in all his powers, the sexual being the most powerful and predominant of his concupiscent faculties, and he indulged it often" – ultimately to the detriment of his health. During the campaign of 1034, when 'Alā' al-Dawla and Ibn Sīnā were in retreat before Mas'ūd's troops, and the treasures of Isfahān were being looted, Ibn Sīnā fell ill of a colic, which he treated too strenuously, taking eight enemas in a single day, trying to rush his recovery, lest his illness prevent him from keeping up with the retreating army and he fall into the hands of the invaders. The result was an ulcer and a visible suppuration, which the hasty retreat of the army toward Khuzistān did not allow to heal. Seizures followed, a familiar sequel to colic. Ibn Sīnā continued trying to treat himself with enemas. Hoping to "break the wind of the colic," the philosopher ordered a small amount of celery seed added to his enema, but his physician overdosed him, either intentionally or by accident, aggravating his ulcer. A slave similarly overdosed him with mithridate, an electuary of opium that he was taking for his seizures. According to Juzjānī, this was done because the slave was stealing from the master's coffers and hoped to avoid detection. By the time the party reached Isfahān, Ibn Sīnā was unable to stand, but he continued to treat himself until he could walk again and present himself at court. Relying on the memory of his youthful vigor more than on his best medical judgment, he took no special precautions now and continued in his habit of frequent sexual intercourse. As a result of this self-neglect, he suffered repeated relapses, the final one, in June of 1037, en route to join his prince at Hamadhān. There his resistance ebbed, and he said: "The governor that used to rule my body is too weak to rule any longer, so treatment would be of no further avail." After lingering a few days, he died and was buried in Hamadhān, where his grave can still be seen. He was fifty-eight years old by the Muslim lunar reckoning, but by the solar calendar he had not yet completed his fifty-seventh year.

NOTES

1 See *Kitāb aḥvāl-i Nishāpūr*, in R. Frye, ed., *The Histories of Nishapur*, Harvard Oriental Series 45 (1965) 40a; Richard Bulliet, *Conversion to Islam in the Medieval Period: An Essay in Quantitative History* (Cambridge: Harvard University Press, 1979) 18–63; Jamsheed Choksy, "Conflict, Coexistence, and Cooperation: Muslims and Zoroastrians in Eastern Iran during the Medieval Period," *The Muslim World* 80 (1990) 213–33.

2 See Roy Mottahedeh, *Loyalty and Leadership in an Early Islamic Society* (Princeton: Princeton University Press, 1980); Daniel Pipes, *Slave Soldiers and Islam: The*

Genesis of a Military System (New Haven: Yale University Press, 1981).

3 See R. Frye, ed., *The Cambridge History of Iran* 4 (1968) 137.

4 *The Book of Government or Rules for Kings*, Hubert Darke, tr. (London: Routledge and Kegan Paul, 1960) 106.

5 The title may be translated *The Unique Pearl of Time*, or even, as by R.A. Nicholson (followed by Sir Hamilton Gibb), *The Solitaire of Time*. The term *yatīma* refers to an orphan child, and thus poetically to a rare jewel or pearl. In al-Tha'ālibī, it is a flowery allusion to the unrivalled cultural riches of the era, time's one and only, never to be repeated.

6 See G. van Vloten, ed., Al-Kwarizmī, *Mafātīḥ al-'Ulūm* (Leiden, 1895; repr. 1968) and C.E. Bosworth, "A Pioneer Arabic Encyclopedia of the Sciences: Al-Kwarizmī's *Keys of the Sciences*," *Isis* 54 (1963) 97–111.

7 Nizām al-Mulk, "Siyāsat-nāma," *The Book of Government*, tr. Hubert Darke, 227. Arberry remarks that "Avicenna seems almost certainly to have belonged to a Shī'ite family," noting that all the names in the philosopher's immediate family were of the sort favored by Shī'ites; see A.J. Arberry, *Avicenna On Theology* (London: Murray, 1951) 5.

8 For the "Indian" arithmetic of Ibn Sīnā's youth, at the time of its entry into Islamic culture, see Abū 'l-Ḥasan al-Uqlīdisī, *The Arithmetic* (written in 952/3), tr. A.S. Saidan (Dordrecht: Reidel, 1978).

9 See *Prior Analytics* I 31; cf. Dimitri Gutas, *Avicenna and the Aristotelian Tradition* (Leiden: Brill, 1988) 70, no. 6, and 222–5.

10 See Manfred Ulmann, *Die Medizin im Islam* (Leiden/Köln, 1970) 147, 151.

11 Aristotle, *Metaphysics* Beta 2; cf. Giovanni Reale, *The Concept of First Philosophy and the Unity of the Metaphysics of Aristotle*, tr. John R. Catan (Albany: SUNY Press, 1980; 3rd Italian edn., 1967).

12 *Maqāla fī aghrād mā ba'da al-Ṭabī'ah* (Hyderabad: Dā'irah al-Ma'ārif, 1349 A.H.); tr. in Thérèse-Anne Druart, "Le Traité d'al-Fārābī sur les Buts de la *Métaphysique d'Aristote*," *Bulletin de Philosophie Médiéval* 24 (1982) 40–3. Some eight pages in the Arabic edition, the essay fills only three and a half pages in French, including the colophon and editorial notes.

13 *Autobiography*, in William Gohlman, ed., *The Life of Avicenna: A Critical Edition and Annotated Translation* (Albany: SUNY Press, 1974) 36. Arberry reasons that the Sāmānid library, whose loss Ibn Sīnā so regrets, would have reflected Nūh's Shī'ite sympathies and was doubtless destroyed by "those Sunnī zealots who did not scruple to whisper that the torch which fired the treasury of learning was lit by the philosopher himself, jealous to keep to himself knowledge he had there imbibed." See *Avicenna on Theology*, 5.

14 Al-Juzjānī, in Gohlman, 68; the translation here is my own.

15 Arberry renders: "My memory for learning was at that period of my life better than it is now, but to-day I am more mature; apart from this my knowledge is exactly the same, nothing having been added to my store since then." (p. 13); Gohlman: "nothing new has come to me since." (p. 39); Gutas, as in Gohlman. See Régis Blachère, Moustafa Chouémi, and Claude Denizeau, *Dictionnaire Arabe-Français-Anglais* 2 (Paris: Maisonneuve et Larose, 1963) 1356, for the sense of the verb as 'reconstructed' or 'reborn.'

16 *Maqāla fī 'l-Nafs 'alā sunnati 'l-Ikhtisār*, German translation by S. Landauer as "Die Psychologie des Ibn Sīnā," in *ZDMG* 29 (1875) 335–418; translated by Edward van Dyck, as *Avicenna's Offering to the Prince: A Compendium on the Soul*

(Verona, 1906). See Dimitri Gutas, *Avicenna and the Aristotelian Tradition* (Leiden: Brill, 1988) 82–7.

17 See Gutas, 83.

18 See Gutas, 87.

19 This is the first systematic work of Jewish philosophy, the famous *Kitāb al-Mukhtār fī 'l-āmānāt wa 'l-I'tiqadāt*, best known by the title of its Hebrew translation, *Sefer ha-Nivḥar ba-Emunot ve-De'ot*. It is misleading to render this, "The Book of Beliefs and Opinions," as Samuel Rosenblatt does (New Haven: Yale, 1948), missing the nuance of 'convictions,' omitting the participle, and ignoring the preposition. Saadiah's title emphasizes the role of argument in the determination of our views. For the date, see H. Malter, *Saadiah Gaon: His Life and Works* (New York: Hermon, 1969; 1920). Malter shows how Saadiah constructed the work using essays or treatises (*rasā'il, maqālāt*) on specific problems as the building blocks. The *Isagoge* genre, discussed by F.E. Peters in *Aristotle and the Arabs* (New York: New York University Press, 1968) 79–87, was vital to Saadiah in establishing thematic organization, as his exegetical writings make clear.

20 The Meteorology and key portions of the Metaphysics were copied into the *Najāt*. But in the psychology of the *Najāt*, Ibn Sīnā took only the first page from the *'Arūḍī* and the rest from a later work called *The Situation of the Human Soul*, in Arabic, *Ḥāl al-Nafs al-Insāniyya*; see Gutas, 89–90.

21 See Gutas, 95.

22 See W. Barthold, *Turkestan Down to the Mongol Invasion* (London: Luzac, 1968) 249–93; C.E. Bosworth, *The Ghaznavids* (Beirut: Librairie du Liban, 1973).

23 Maḥmūd made seventeen expeditions against India, fulfilling a vow of *jihād* to render thanks to God for the Khalif's recognition of his authority in Khorasan. His army of 30,000, as the poetry in his praise reveals, were moved as much by visions of booty from Hindu temples as by visions of the paradise awaiting martyrs. See Achena and Massé, *Le Livre de Science* 1 (Paris: Les Belles Lettres, 1986) 262 n. 30.

24 See F.E. Peters, *Allah's Commonwealth*, (New York: Simon and Schuster, 1973) 589; E.G. Browne, *A Literary History of Persia* 2 (Cambridge: Cambridge University Press, 1964; 1902) 96.

25 Cf. Louis Gardet, "L'Humanisme Gréco-Arabe: Avicenne," *Journal of World History* 2 (1954) 812–34. Describing three dynasties whom Avicenna served, Joel Kraemer writes,

> The Buyids and their rivals … to the east, the Sāmānids, sovereigns of Khurāsān and Transoxiania, created what Vladimir Minorsky has felicitously termed 'the Iranian intermezzo' in Islamic history – i.e., between the rule of the Arabs, which lasted until the tenth century, and the domination of the Turks, which began in the eleventh. The Ziyārids, erstwhile patrons of the Buyids, had also attempted to revive Iranian traditions. The Iranian orientation of the Buyids was evident mainly in the political sphere . . . whereas the Sāmānids stimulated Persian letters and were responsible for an Iranian cultural renaissance.

26 See note 20 above.

27 That is the *K. Mabādi' ārā' ahli 'l-madīnati 'l-fāḍila*. The title does not mean "Principles [i.e., essential features] of the Views of the Citizens of the Best State," as

Walzer supposed, as though the work made no distinction between beliefs and knowledge. Rather, *ārā'* are beliefs, and *mabādi'* are the conceptual ideas that underlie them. See R. Walzer, ed. and tr., *Al-Fārābī on the Perfect State* (Oxford: Clarendon Press, 1985) 1.

28 Translated by M. Mahdi as *Alfarabi's Philosophy of Plato and Aristotle* (New York: Macmillan, 1962).

29 This is the *Kitāb al-Ḥurūf* or Book of Letters, M. Mahdi, ed. (Beirut: Dar al-Machreq, 1969); cf. my review, *Philosophy East and West* 21 (1971) 220–2, and my chapter "Jewish and Islamic Philosophy of Language," in Kuno Lorenz *et al.*, eds, *Handbuch Sprachphilosophie* (Berlin: De Gruyter, forthcoming).

30 See H. Corbin, tr., in *Avicenna and the Visionary Recital* (London: Routledge, 1960), translated from the French by Willard Trask.

31 See al-Rāzī's excerpts from Rufus of Ephesus in F. Rosenthal, *The Classical Heritage in Islam* (London: Routledge, 1975) 198–200.

32 Gohlman, 107, item 62.

33 The title, which is the name of the protagonist, is allegorical and can be rendered "The Living the Son of the Wakeful"; it alludes to the enlightening role of the Active Intellect.

34 See M.S. Khan, "Ibn Sīnā's Treatise on Drugs for the Treatment of Cardiac Diseases," *Islamic Quarterly* 27 (1983) 49–56. As Khan explains, the heart is not just a physiological organ for Ibn Sīnā but the seat of the emotions and regulator of the animal heat, by which "spirit" mediates between the mental and the physical. Such thinking remains central in Ibn Ṭufayl and even in Descartes, who resisted Harvey's discoveries out of unwillingness to give up so seemingly effective a model of the mind-body relationship. Ibn Sīnā, like his younger Jewish contemporary Ibn Gabirol, is very interested in the physiology of the emotions but does not adopt a strict physiological determinism: A weak hearted person need not be melancholic, nor a strong hearted person sanguine. Among the heart conditions Ibn Sīnā treats are angina, palpitations, and loss of consciousness; some sixty-five simple and seventeen compound drugs are recommended. The simples include exotics like silk cocoon, saffron, ruby, pearls, Egyptian clover, wild ginger, silver, gold, musk, and ambergris, and domestic remedies like egg yolks and meat soup.

35 Gutas, 205.

36 M. Horten, tr., *Die Metaphysik Avicennas* (Halle, 1907).

37 See Gutas, 111.

38 Quoted in Nancy G. Siraisi, *Avicenna in Renaissance Italy: The* Canon *and Medical Teaching in Italian Universities after 1500* (Princeton: Princeton University Press, 1987) 20.

39 *Livre des Directives et Remarques*, tr. A.-M. Goichon (Paris: Vrin, 1951) 56–9.

40 Siraisi, 22–3.

41 Ibn Sīnā *defined* medicine as a science, having both a theoretical and a practical part: "Implicit in the definition is the repudiation of any notion that medicine is merely a practical art, technology or craft," as Hugh of St. Victor and many others took it to be; Siraisi, 24.

42 See Siraisi, 24.

43 See R.W. Southern, *Robert Grosseteste* (Oxford: Clarendon Press, 1986).

44 Gohlman, 109, item 83, "Treatise on the Refutation of Astrology."

45 See Achena and Massé, 1, 41–2.

46 Achena and Massé, 1, 63–4.
47 Achena and Massé, 1, 44.
48 L.E. Goodman, "Did al-Ghazālī Deny Causality?" *Studia Islamica* 47 (1978) 83–120; "Ordinary and Extraordinary Language in Medieval Jewish and Islamic Philosophy," *Manuscrito* 11 (1988) 57–83, esp. pp. 74–5, nn. 30–1.
49 See L.E. Goodman, "Islamic Ethics and Social Philosophy," in the *Encyclopedia of Asian Philosophy* (London: Routledge, 1992).
50 See Moshe Narboni, *Commentary on the Guide to the Perplexed*, ed. M. Hayoun (Tübingen: Mohr, 1986) and my review in *JQR* 81 (1990) 161–5.
51 See Everett Rowson, *A Muslim Philosopher on the Soul and its Fate: Al-'Āmirī's* Kitāb al-Amad 'alā 'l-abad (New Haven: American Oriental Society, 1988).
52 See Gutas, 127 n. 26, 130 n. 28, 134–9.
53 See Ibn Ṭufayl, *Hayy Ibn Yaqẓān* (New York: Twayne, 1972; repr., Los Angeles: Gee Tee Bee, 1983) 95–102; 150–2. For the uses later theosophy made of Avicenna's metaphysics, see S.H. Nasr, "Post-Avicennan Islamic Philosophy and the Study of Being," *International Philosophical Quarterly* 17 (1977) 265–71. Nasr writes: "While in the West gradually the possibility of the experience of Being nearly disappeared and the vision of Being gave way to the discussion of the concept of being and finally to the decomposition of this very concept in certain schools, in the Islamic world philosophy drew ever closer to the ocean of Being itself until finally it became the complement of gnosis . . ." 265.
54 Gutas, 118.
55 D.S. Margoliouth, ed. and tr., "The Discussion between Abū Bishr Mattā and Abū Sa'īd al-Sīrāfī on the Merits of Logic and Grammar," *JRAS* (1905) 79–129.
56 Quoted in Achena and Massé, 1, 26.
57 *Ishārāt wa 'l-Tanbīhāt*, ed. Dunya, 903–6, citing *Qur'ān* 4:83, 131, 169.
58 Gutas, 132.
59 *Ishārāt* 8.1, ed. Dunya, 749–51, tr. Goichon, 467–8; the translation here is my own.
60 *Ishārāt*, tr. Goichon, 132.

2

METAPHYSICS

1 CONTINGENCY AND NECESSITY

Al-Ghazālī's teacher Abū 'l-Ma'ālī al-Juwaynī (1028–85) was called Imām al-Ḥaramayn for his four years of teaching at Mecca and Medina while self-exiled because of the early Seljuq leader Tughrul Beg's suspicions of even Ash'arite theological reasoning. He was favored for his orthodoxy by Niẓām al-Mulk and preferred to a theological post in the Niẓāmiyya of Nīshāpūr, where al-Ghazālī later taught. He opens his *Kitāb al-Irshād* or *Book of Right Guidance*, with a statement meant to couch in the language of orthodoxy a duty to pursue natural theology: "The first religious obligation of every intelligent boy who comes of age, as marked by years or by the dreams of puberty, is to form the intention of reasoning as soundly as he can to an awareness that the world is originated".[1] From here the lad can make his way to terra firma. For the originatedness (*ḥudūth*) of the world, the fact that it is not eternal, implies its creation and thus the existence of God – wise, powerful and purposive Determiner of what need not have been in the design of creation. Recognition of the Creator leads naturally to the recognition of God's sovereignty and acceptance of our role in His plan.[2]

The roots of Juwaynī's reasoning are Platonic. Plato argues in the *Timaeus* (27–30) that if we distinguish what is fully real from the temporal realm, where nothing is real absolutely but everything is continually becoming other than it is, we will find that the world is not eternal but generated and so requires a cause. That cause must be good, since the world is good and reflects the goodness of its cause, whose very pattern for the world must be everlasting and intellectual, shedding on the world all the goodness and wisdom we discern when we understand things scientifically or when, as we should, we acknowledge the grace and bounty of nature.

The argument as Plato presents it is highly problematic, assuming that what 'becomes' in the sense of changing must also be originated and thus dependent on a cause for its origination. How does Plato move from 'becoming' as changing to the sense that means originated? Later thinkers like Philoponus argue that what is temporal is subject to destruction and decline, and that what is destructible must be created.[3] The tenability of such an argument rests upon Plato's bifurcation of reality into the realms of being and becoming: Only the timeless transcends change, destruction, and creation; if a thing is changeable it is both destructible and possessed of an origin. If anything originated, it did not originate itself but stood in need of a cause, and ultimately, of a Creator. With the structuring aid of the dichotomy between being and becoming, a rugged chunk of Platonic reasoning becomes, not an article of faith but the goal of a proof which is itself a matter of religious obligation for every Muslim male capable of abstract reasoning.

In the Arabic translation that preserves Galen's Compendium of the *Timaeus* the preliminary byplay of Plato's dialogue is cut away, and the stunning and enigmatic argument from becoming is thrust to the fore, on the first pages of the Aya Sofia manuscript. Here Galen relates how Plato uses "the *mutakallim* Timaeus" as his spokesman, abandoning "his customary mode of question and answer" and

> assigning the whole discourse to Timaeus alone . . . who asks: 'What is it that exists eternally and has no coming to be, and what is it that is constantly coming to be and never *is* at any moment whatever?' To one schooled in the other books of Plato, the answer is obvious. For Plato divides substances that are understood by the mind and are not bodies from those that are sensory, which he customarily calls 'becoming,' rather than substances at all . . . . Having laid down as a premise that there are two sorts of things, one eternal and the other constantly coming to be, Timaeus says that whatever comes to be must necessarily come from some cause. He affirms this without proof, since it is one of those truths that are plain to reason. For if anything at all remains as it is, neither coming to be nor passing away, then it has no generative cause. But anything that has come to be had a cause that made it; and anything that is in a state of becoming has a cause at present that makes it what it is. With regard to the world, Timaeus judges categorically that

it is in a state of becoming, since Socrates had made this clear to him elsewhere in his teachings. And as to the world's being eternal or having an origin, he specifies further on that its becoming did have a beginning, saying that the character of its creator is difficult to find out, and that one who had found the truth about him would be unable to reveal it to all mankind.[4]

The *Compendium* allows for the apparent looseness of Plato's argument, paralleling Plato's bracketing the argument in the dialectic of a living discussion, by painting Timaeus as a faithful disciple of Socrates and casting the intended reader as a diligent student of the dialogues, including the *Republic*, which is cited for the doctrine of Forms: Timaeus was simply taking for granted Plato's distinction of being from becoming, as a *mutakallim* would take a scriptural doctrine for granted; and Galen himself is simply filling in an ellipsis in Plato's argument, as a *kalām* commentator would resolve an ambiguity in the *Qur'ān* with the aid of the appropriate dialectic and sound theological principles, buttressed by passages drawn from other contexts in the authoritative text. Timaeus was not merely presuming that whatever is temporal is generated but tacitly inferring (*a*) that all becoming has a cause, and (*b*) that the world is caused because it is originated. The basis of *a* is a pre-Cartesian, pre-Galilean, conception of inertia, reflecting the assumption that inactivity requires no cause but that any action requires an energizing principle. The key to *b* is the creation idea of Genesis, explicated in the thought that the world need not have existed: Whatever *is* as it need not have been requires a cause of its being as it is. This was a standard *kalām* argument, applied to the existence of anything in particular, and to the world at large, which required a cause to determine its existence over non-existence.[5] The argument depends, of course, on a metaphysical construction of the causal principle, treated here as an a priori truth.

Philosophers on the fringes of *kalām* were very open to such arguments. For example, the early Jewish philosophical *mutakallim* David al-Muqammiṣ (d. c. 862+), who was educated in Christian circles, argues at length that the substances in the world are never free of accidents that arise in time and are therefore themselves originated and dependent on a Creator.[6] Ibn Sīnā's elder contemporary al-'Āmirī, an exponent of the "Western" thought that Ibn Sīnā hoped to surpass, characteristically ascribes to "Empedocles" the view that God's existence "is not like that of any of the beings in the world, since worldly beings realize a contingent (*imkānī*) existence, dependent on their creation, whereas His Identity is necessarily existent . . ."[7] The Arabic Galen naturally ranked Timaeus as a *mutakallim* rather than an astronomer when he saw the apparent dependence of his thinking on the idea of the world's contingency.

Plato's actual argument, that all things temporal have a beginning, is faithfully repeated by al-Ghazālī, who has learned to be suspicious of the argument from contingency. But he too reverts to the *kalām* idea of a determinant, what Leibniz will call a Sufficient Reason, to link the extreme terms of the inference, the engine to the differential, urging that all temporal becoming is bounded and so requires a Determiner of its temporal bounds.[8] The assumption that all temporal becoming is temporally bounded is question begging with respect to the thesis that the world had an origin: Aristotle, who denies that time had a beginning quite consistently affirms that all events, and thus all temporal *segments* have both a beginning and an end. When Ghazālī tries to argue that "what depends for its existence on events in time must itself have come to be in time," his argument declines into circularity or comes to rest on an equivocation between becoming as changing and becoming as having an origin. Ultimately, if anything was to be made of Plato's argument, temporal boundedness would have to drop out of the premises and contingency would be the critical issue: Was the world such as it need not have been? Was it an event in *that* sense – that its existence was not necessary and so required a cause? Only so, it seemed, could Plato's reasoning be made unanswerable. What is changeless, as the *Compendium* argues, does not require a cause, but what is changeable is contingent and therefore does require a cause. The core insight of the *kalām* was that all determinate being is contingent. Only God stands outside the system, unbounded and undetermined, determining all things.

As philosophers like al-Fārābī always suspected, the *kalām* idea of contingency is a kind of theological descant on the Scriptural idea of creation.[9] The poetry of Genesis uses silence about the character, physiognomy, motives, and intentions of God to set itself apart from the cosmogonies and theomachies of Babylonian myth and to set the transcendent God vividly apart from the things of His creation, placing God above time, change, passions, embodiment, dependence, or manipulation. The *Qur'ān* echoes this conception when it speaks repeatedly of God as the Creator of heaven and earth, and of all things – men, animals, angels, *jinn*, formed from a smokeless fire. And the Qur'anic God continues to create, in Galenic terms causing not only the world's origination, but its continual becoming, making fire from the heart of a green tree, men and women from a drop of liquid, formed in the womb into a clot of blood and a living embryo.[10]

Plato does argue in the *Republic* (VI 509) that the Highest Reality provides for the growth and generation of all things, gives them both essence and existence, and imparts all their beauty, truth, and understanding. Was this not essentially what the *Qur'ān* was saying when it linked God's eternity, ultimate reality, and providential bounty in the celebrated Throne verse (2:255): "Allāh, there is no god but Him, the Living and Everlasting. Neither sleep nor slumber overtakes Him . . . His throne spreadeth vast over heaven and earth, and He is unwearied in preserving them." Even today Muslim exegetes gloss *al-Qayyūm*, which we render "Everlasting," as "The Self-subsisting Supporter of all."[11]

It was the linkage of contingency with creation that made contingency vital to the metaphysics of the *kalām*: Being is what God made and is as God makes it. For the atomist occasionalists this means that nothing can be presumed as to any being beyond the initial posit of existence: A "substance" does not endure beyond an instant, and for its instant possesses only the characters God gives it. All traits then, are accidents; to single out any as essential might suggest that they would appear regardless of God's act. No "substance" extends beyond a point, for the givenness of one point of being does not imply that of another; and no accident entails the presence of another, lest we limit God's omnipotence and the fundamental datum of contingency.

To the radicals of the *kalām* this meant that God might create intelligence in an atom, or in no substrate at all, without the prerequisite, say, of life. There were arguments over the fate of atoms that God does not please to replace with new created ones, once their instant of existence has expired. Do they simply fail to reappear, or does God create an atom with the accident of non-existence, or create non-existence in no substrate, to assure each disappearance? The whole debate, among a wide diversity of schools, went on for generations without the aid of Aristotelian formal logic, using disjunctive and hypothetical inferences, arguments from analogy, and reductions to absurdity. Public disputations were the ideal, and the typical volume of *kalām* was an armory of responses and objections, rational or scriptural, designed to silence an adversary.

The *kalām* doctrine of contingency was dedicated, of course, to the establishment of divine creation. As Maimonides explains, in their anxiety to demonstrate the reality of creation, *mutakallimūn* typically tried to show that creation was necessary. In the process they proved too much, making creation in effect a necessary truth and the act of continuously recreating the world a continuously recurrent responsibility of God.[12] At the same time, their emphasis on the urgent and immediate dependence of the world on God undermined the continuity of nature and in a way overstated, indeed misrepresented the immediacy of God's involvement, in effect rendering the very act of creation a sham: The being God was said to have imparted did not seem capable of standing on its own legs and *acting* or causing anything. For such reasons Maimonides was dissatisfied with the *kalām* and warns his reader not to overrate the achievement of the *mutakallimūn*: They sacrificed nature, denatured heaven and earth, in the vain attempt to make the world's createdness a matter of demonstration.[13]

Not all *mutakallimūn* were radical occasionalists, but the prejudice against any delegation of divine authority was preserved in the more moderate schools like that of the Ash'arites, even when they did not press the radical atomism and resultant phenomenalism of the extremists. Any assignment of power to act or judge, any notion of enduring dispositions or even objective human value judgments seemed to threaten the absoluteness of God's rule. So, even where radical atomism was rejected, a tendency toward radical analysis persisted: God need not follow His familiar course in nature or in norms; there is no moral necessity, as the Stoics and their Mu'tazilite successors had urged, for God to reveal His will to humanity, or for God to do what we suppose is right. There is no natural necessity for the world to follow its accustomed course, since one fact does not imply another. The only necessities are vertical: our duty to obey God's commands, the world's necessity of being, at each instant, as God makes it.

What Ash'arite metaphysics preserved from the radical occasionalism of the earlier *kalām* was the sharp, ultimately Biblical contrast between God and creation, temporality and eternity, self-sufficiency and contingency. The resultant scheme could not be more antithetical to the voluntarism and objectivism of the Mu'tazilites or to the rationalism, naturalism, and humanism of Aristotle. By Aristotle's account, being *is* determinacy. Whatever is a this or a such – above all, whatever holds together and functions in a unified, coherent pattern – has the definiteness expected of a substance. It is not that Aristotle simply presumes nature to abide by laws; rather it is those things that do preserve a pattern, always or for the most part, that are identified as substances – those among them, that is, that are not in or of something else, as suggested by the common usages of language. For we say "the color of the horse," not "the horse of the color."

Aristotle found substance by searching for constancy and stability – persistence through change and definiteness of identity and character. He would not accept the mere posit of "this now" that seemed to satisfy the *kalām*; for Plato, following the arguments of Cratylus and Heraclitus, had shown that there is no "this now." The immediate phenomenal particular is always contextual and always changing. Aristotle was looking for that being of which the Parmenidean dicta were true: what does not change, come to be or pass away, but is one and self-same, in some sense acceptable to a logic tolerant of phenomena. So it is not surprising that species, essence, Aristotelian form, as the locus of determinacy in nature, should take the palm as the most promising claimant to the title of substance: Form/species is the object of scientific knowledge and the subject of universal and necessary, changeless predication.[14] Nor is it surprising that the runners up, that meet at least some of the criteria of substantiality, should be the concrete particular (as the unchanging substrate of all changes short of coming-to-be and passing away, substrate of the accidents, referent of all other categories, and unit of arithmetic identity in the realm of multiplicity and change) and matter (as the ultimate notional substrate of change and predication, ground of arithmetic unity, and basis of potentiality).

Invariance was the grail sought by Greek philosophers from the time of Parmenides, and Aristotle departed most strikingly from Plato not in denying reality to Plato's Forms but in finding their invariance within the world of change, in the species of things, but also in time, which never varies, and in matter, which is indestructible and constant even through transformation. Science, for Aristotle, far from being a recognition of contingency, is the discovery of why things must be as they are.[15] The foundations of necessity, then, are both intellectual, in the formal essences that are the very being of things, and material, in the binding of each thing to the rest in the spatial plenum, and of each event to its antecedents and consequences in the temporal continuum.

Like the presocratics, Aristotle expected the ultimate principle of being to be divine. He found divinity most effective as a principle of explanation when it acted immanently, *through* rather than upon things like a *deus ex machina* in a bad play, whose doings are not organic to the action and the characters. But this called for God somehow to be given access to the rational principle of all things while at the same time standing apart and moving the world. Teleology was the key to explaining how this happens. For all processes pursue perfection, even if only by constantly reclosing the circle of a natural cycle like that of rain and evaporation, or that of the generations.[16] Yet Aristotle does not say exactly how the perfect actuality of the pure Intelligence that is his God becomes a goal for beings below the heavens. Nor does he convincingly explain how God's knowledge can be perfect if its sole object is Itself. Later philosophers found ample means for answering these questions.

The Neoplatonists, who mediate the teachings of Plato and Aristotle to Avicenna and al-Fārābī, saw it as their task to answer Aristotle's objections to Plato – in particular, how could Plato's Forms be real when they lack the discreteness of sensory particulars, each one of which is "a this"; and how could they be causes of events in nature, when Forms themselves do not change? To answer Aristotle's objections to the self-subsistence of the Forms, the Neoplatonists placed them within Nous, the Aristotelian principle of intelligence, pure actuality, now identified with Platonic Being, and hence with the eternal Forms. Since the Ideas are now identical with the mind that knows them, they are no longer isolated but alive, in and *as* divine Intelligence. The same expedient makes clear how that Intelligence, in knowing itself, can know and govern the world. For the forms are the patterns of the world, the ideals all things pursue through their actions.

In modeling the causal relation of the Forms to the world, the Neoplatonists drew upon Stoic cosmology. The Stoics were materialists but also pantheists. They assigned spiritual, creative, and intellectual powers to the physical energy of the divine pneuma, which resonates through the Stoic plenum much as a modern field of force pervades the void.[17] The Neoplatonists, abandoning Stoic materialism, transformed this idea of radiant spiritual energy into a powerful metaphor: Being, goodness, truth, and beauty, are diffused through nature as light is diffracted through the heavens and spread upon the earth. The Forms, which are the very being of things, shed their influence as a fountain spreads its lifegiving waters, but inexhaustibly and without diminution of the Source, since what is imparted is intellectual and formal and is never really lost. In the words of Plotinus, God is a circle whose center is everywhere. Being is imparted by the pure Form of the Good, the One or God, which is above the definiteness and so the finitude of Nous. What is imparted is in fact a specification and thus a differentiation of the absolute goodness of the One, a proliferation of its simplicity, through Nous to the temporality of Soul – the World Soul – and down ultimately to the relative unity and specialized goodness of individual subjects and objects in the realm of becoming.

The schematism of emanation vividly revealed that the bond between the Forms and nature is no mere logical relation of class membership but a dynamic nexus. It gave a concrete and energizing content to the Aristotelian idea of God as the first mover, since the attraction of all beings for perfection is their very essence, derived ultimately from the emanative goodness of the One. So the purposiveness Aristotle discovered in God's moving all things as subjects drawn to an end is now clearly linked to the yearning of the Intelligences that guide the spheres. The heavens express an intellectual contemplation of God's perfection, bodying it forth in their cosmic choric dance. But every being seeks realization of the divine perfection within it, and each becomes in its own way a prime mover, exemplifying the forms shed upon it from the source of forms above, as dancers in a darkened room catch the light of whirling mirrors on their parti-colored garments and join in the dance that is first figured in the revolving orbs above their heads.

But the scheme demands a measure of compactness of nature with its cause. Overcoming the alienation and isolation of nature from the divine, an estrangement that Plotinus combatted in the pessimism of the Gnostics, seemed to risk a smothering dependence of nature upon God and a host of related problems: Is there really any freedom, contingency, or change if everything is linked so intimately with the Divine? How is ignorance possible, if each of us lives in unbroken contact with absolute and eternal truth? What is evil, and are such epiphenomena of otherness as matter, privation, difference, variation, individuality, mere illusions? For even if it is said that these are obstacles to be overcome, it remains to be explained how and why the overflowing abundance of divine grace and truth leaves room for any obstacles at all – or any of the individuality that Neoplatonists sought to affirm and to protect with the rhetoric of imparted powers and (relative) self-sufficiency.

Emblematic of the many problems of compactness is the doctrine of the world's eternity, a thesis of Aristotle's adopted by Neoplatonists on the authority of his strenuous arguments against creation, his prejudice against the ancient cosmogonies that seemed to substitute a story of origins for an explanatory account, a religious respect for the rational continuities of nature as discovered by science, and a rationalistic insistence on preserving God from becoming the mere precipitating cause of nature, compromised by the act of creation into a sullying temporality. Aristotle rejected what he saw as the creationism of the *Timaeus*; and later Platonists, except for Plutarch and Herod Atticus, took Plato's argument from temporality as portending emanation rather than creation. They read Plato's affirmation of the creation of the world as a mythic expression to be refined into the subtler stuff of a timeless ontic dependence of the temporal upon the eternal. The Neoplatonists, like the Arabic Galen, saw Timaeus in the dialogue as a kind of theologian. As Plotinus put it, emanation is not a process but a procession.[18]

Species in the Neoplatonic cosmos, as in Aristotle, never change, let alone come to be or pass away. Their eternity is earnest of the constancy of intellectual emanation, which belies the surface inconstancy of nature and signals the reality known under its universal forms through science, which never studies mere particulars as such. The heavens too never change, and the world is uncreated. Its "principal parts," the limbs and organs of the great macrocosmic organism, have always maintained the same relations and moved in invariant patterns, expressive of the perfection they embody. There is no generation or decay above the sphere of the moon, where matter itself is deemed simple and without an opposite to threaten its stability. Here change gives way to a kind of constancy that points to complete transcendence of the physical. Not only are divine forms present in nature, but at the celestial level even matter partakes of the constancy of the intellectual, indestructible, and uncreated. Ibn Sīnā was very much a disciple of this tradition. It was what he had in mind when he spoke of God's primacy as ontic rather than temporal, and of creation as involving causal ultimacy rather than any mere temporal event.

But in the scriptural tradition stemming from the Torah and enshrined for Muslims in the *Qur'ān* the constancy that Aristotle found in all natural kinds and in a way even in composite particulars was reserved to God, one and transcendent, regnant, as Qur'anic language put it, over all. Only God is eternal and everlasting. Nature's light is commanded into being by God's creative word, and man's life is not his own but breathed into him by God. In the words of the *Qur'ān* (28:88; cf. 55:27), "All things perish, except His face." To the commentators, this meant, "All things but God are contingent; only He is a Necessary Being."[19] The species of things are not eternal, nor are the succession of day and night, the elevation of the heavens, or the separation of land from water. All is the work of God. Heaven and earth were created by God, and nothing in nature needed to be determined as it was. What God imparts to being is not eternal and inalienable wisdom, implicit in the very natures of things, like Aristotle's intrinsic wisdom of means and ends, but an unsought bounty providing extrinsically for all beings beyond what they unaided could afford. The radical imparting of being, *creatio ex nihilo*, is the ultimate content of God's grace. If the account of creation is mythic poetry, then what it portends is not captured in the idea of the eternal emanation of self-sufficient creatures from a timeless Source.

When the attempt was made to barter new lamps for old, the metaphor of emanation proffered, for example by al-Fārābī, as the philosophical truth behind the scriptural myth of creation, what seemed to creationists most palpably left out in the intended exchange was the ultimate sense of creatureliness, the radical Scriptural idea of contingency. This was the value most clearly bespoken by the Biblical idea of creation, the idea that the world need not have been, elevated to a central axiom of metaphysics in the *kalām*, but tacitly ignored in Aristotelian metaphysics and explicitly rejected when Aristotle and his followers argued against the origination of the world. To be sure al-Fārābī and all the followers of Plotinus sought to preserve and thought they *had* preserved the world's dependence upon God when they argued that an effect could be coeternal with its cause. But where, if the world was eternal, was its lack of necessity? What kept nature as a whole from being itself immortal and divine, as the ancient pagan philosophers had imagined it to be, a partner or "associate" of God of the sort that the language of the *Qur'ān* so emphatically denied?

The creationist metaphysic of grace is one of contingency, based on abstraction of the empiric characters of things: God need not have made this being so, need not have provided this. Generalized, this abstraction becomes the contingency of being, the non-necessity of creation. As for the intellectualist metaphysic of wisdom, which leads Aristotle to say, in his immanentist language, that nature does nothing in vain, it leads to the necessity of all true beings – the eternity of matter, form, species, minds, and the celestial bodies that form what are later called the "principal parts" of the cosmos. Being is necessary by its nature, and the task of science is to discover in specific and in general terms the grounds of that necessity. In so doing the philosopher discovers and makes his own the wisdom of nature, which is divine.

The value celebrated in Aristotelian metaphysics is self-sufficiency, and the object of Neoplatonism is to integrate the relative self-sufficiency of particulars into the larger self-sufficiency of species, the cosmos, the Forms, Nous, and the One. If there was no ontological argument for the existence of God in Aristotle or in his Neoplatonic successors, it is because they succeeded so well in their work of integration: God was not unique as a necessary being but shared necessity and a kind of absoluteness with all things.[20] Species were necessary, eternally reflecting the eternity of their ultimate Source, and the cosmos as a whole was necessary and divine, all its laws expressive of an implicit and changeless wisdom that was not the hallmark of an external craftsman's plan, but the sign of an inwardly working intelligence.

The ancient idea of immanence, first adopted for philosophy by Thales, allowed Greeks to integrate being and the cosmos in a single scheme, under a single rule. Indeed, on Aristotelian premises, integration did not seem possible without the idea of immanence and the ultimate divinity of the cosmos and of all things. So natural theologians in the Aristotelian and Neoplatonic tradition held as fast to immanence as Biblically inspired thinkers held to divine transcendence, creation, and exclusivity, without which they too were certain that the scheme and law of nature would unravel into an anarchy of warring principalities and projective passions.[21]

The rival schemes of the neo-Aristotelians and the scriptural creationists had much in common. Both were theistic. Both deferred to a higher Unity as the source of goodness and grace. Abstracting from the formulaic, both schemes were pursuing the same goal, saying the same thing in different ways, even sharing some of the same ambiguities and ambivalences. But in conceptualizing the linkage between this world and the divine the two pursued competing values. Creationism was most struck by the contrast between divine absoluteness and creaturely dependence; Neoplatonism, by the flood of divine light shining through in nature. Creationists see natural objects by their opacity. For Neoplatonists seeing, ultimately, can only be of light, and true being is always transparent to the flood of light from above. Yet it was the emanationists who seemed to make of matter a thing apart, eternal, preexistent, uncreate, and who seemed to make matter a scapegoat in dealing with the problem of evil, treating our embodiment almost as a curse instead of as a gift of God. And it was the creationists who continually praised God for the goodness of His acts, rejecting the Gnostic idea that creation itself was a dreadful error and celebrating life and finitude, not for the privations that are among its conditions, but for the grace and wisdom that are its content, and even for the uniqueness and particularity of each created thing.

When eternalist Aristotelians and Neoplatonists criticize creationists, it is for exempting the first moments of time from the universal sway of causal law, disrupting the flow of divine wisdom; or for drawing down God into the temporal maelstrom, failing to preserve the very transcendence that the image of creation was intended to express. When creationists criticize the eternalist philosophers of the Neoplatonic tradition, it is for treating matter as unassimilable to God's wisdom or intractable to His will; or for locking the world and man in a determinism so strict as to deny human freedom or even change itself. Both critiques, then, appeal to common standards, charging that the rival scheme underrepresents the integration of nature under God and at the same time fails to respect the distinctness of God from man and nature. That the inner conflicts of either approach were more visible to its adversaries than to its advocates and the family resemblance between the sister philosophies so little emphasized in the heat of the polemic is an expression not only of the familiar limitations of human charity but also of the enormity of the task that medieval thinkers set for themselves. For it was a tacit goal of all medieval metaphysics to see the world as God sees it.

2 IBN SĪNĀ'S SYNTHESIS

Part of the achievement of Ibn Sīnā is his creation of a synthesis between the two opposed accounts – the metaphysics of being as an eternal given, bearing within itself its logic and its law, and the creationist metaphysics of radically contingent being. Both positions by his time had grown extreme, hardened by centuries of polemic, resting on rival premises, and canonizing in each case a cosmology that seeks to recognize the fundamental moral and metaphysical truths about the world but finds them in opposing crystallizations. Where Aristotle finds divinity and wisdom in the necessity each kind bears within itself, the *kalām* points to a transcendent Deity, found not by uncovering the seeds of eternity in finite things but by recognizing the radical contingency of all that is and acknowledging the absolute emptiness of the world without God's creative act. The polarity left a middle ground, large and identifiable, but not well tenanted and fortified, or even well defined.

It was clear to the more scripturally inclined monotheists that the followers of Aristotle and Neoplatonism intended to be theists, although they did not rely on arguments from creation. It was clear too that they were advocates of the design of nature, which the sciences that loomed so large among their writings celebrated brilliantly. Jewish, Christian, and Muslim thinkers had no difficulty in transforming the pagan gods of Neoplatonic cosmology into angels and assimilating them, as the Greek philosophers had done, to the intelligences of the spheres. For the Greek philosophers were not pagan in the sense of tolerating ungoverned or unintegrated deities to wander through the cosmos wreaking random havoc. It was clear that monotheists had much to learn from the Greeks. Miskawayh, for example, appropriated Aristotle's virtue ethics and used it to reinterpret the command ethics of scripture and scriptural law. Not just al-Fārābī and Ibn Sīnā but al-Ghazālī and Maimonides followed him in this, sketching an ideal of humanity from the virtues that the scriptural commandments seemed to intend. Al-Fārābī not only incorporated the emanationist scheme, but applied Platonic politics and Aristotelian poetics to take the measure and plumb the intentions of prophetic rhetoric and legislation.

In the theory of action and the metaphysic of morals, it seemed clear to Muslim and Jewish philosophers, regardless of what theological authority might seem to teach, that men act and judge between right and wrong by divinely imparted powers. The Mu'tazilites had treated these on the analogy of a healthy or diseased limb; but the Aristotelian psychology of faculties and dispositions brought to the discussion a coherence that overwhelmed the Ash'arite theory that we "appropriate" our actions without ever exercising determinative or deliberative control over our choices. Looking back on that debate, Maimonides could dismiss the Ash'arite theory of "acquisition" as mere doubletalk. He argues, following Aristotle, that the same imparting of a nature that makes rocks fall makes men capable of choice, and he thanks God that no one of his confession has ever called freedom of the will into question.[22]

But the way to handle the core of metaphysics was less clear. The earliest Muslim and Jewish philosophic thinkers to encounter the fruits of Greek philosophy in Arabic translation adopted an accommodationist policy. Al-Kindī and al-'Āmirī, among the Muslims, Isaac Israeli and Saadiah Gaon among the Jews, developed schemes in which creation was made to coexist with emanation.[23] But as the full apparatus of the Philosophers was unlimbered and the full extent of its rigor and extensiveness of its crosslinkages, indeed, of its rigidity, became visible, mere accommodation seemed increasingly unworkable. Through the hostile reports of an adversary, we can still glimpse al-Rāzī, Ibn Sīnā's medical predecessor, fighting a losing battle for a kind of Epicurean/Platonic *formatio mundi* in the early tenth century: Only if we acknowledge matter, time, space, and the world Soul as eternal along with God, Rāzī insists, can we vindicate creation and overcome the arguments of the eternalists.[24] To philosophers like al-Fārābī such compromises seemed clearly a lost cause.[25] The Aristotelian sciences depended on causality; and causal necessity as well as the natures of time, space, matter, and potentiality, and the logical structure implicit in the essences of things, all seemed to demand the eternity and essential unchangeability of the world. The rigor of this position would be shaken when al-Ghazālī and Maimonides acquired the philosophical tools to penetrate its underlying assumptions and discover a measure of arbitrariness in them.[26] But even their response would have been impossible without the work of Ibn Sīnā, which showed them how one could reject rigid necessitarianism without wholly abandoning the naturalism that was the glory of the Philosophers.

Avicenna himself was convinced by arguments like those of al-Fārābī that creationism was untenable, and he adopted and elaborated al-Fārābī's eternalist emanative scheme. He saw what we would call the argument from design as nothing better than a sophism, based ultimately not upon the weak analogy between the cosmos and, say, a house, but on the suppositious premise that whatever has form must have an origin.[27] In the polarized rhetoric of the polemics of his day, he was an eternalist. But in his philosophic argumentation Ibn Sīnā fused the Aristotelian metaphysics of self-sufficiency with the monotheistic metaphysics of contingency. It was this remarkable synthesis of seeming opposites that enabled him candidly to identify emanation as the real meaning of creation and to drop the descriptivist mode of exposition so often favored by Fārābī, warmly advocating his own new metaphysics that celebrates and shares in the poetry of creation while respecting the scientific and theistic values enshrined in its seemingly irreconcilable alternative.

The core of the new metaphysics is Avicenna's argument for the existence of God, a cosmological argument that combines the *kalām* appeal to contingency with the Aristotelian search for a first cause – not of motion now, but of existence. The central theme, then, is the Biblical quest for an absolute Creator.[28] The starting point is Plato's dichotomy of the temporal from the timeless, modified, in Islamic fashion, to a dichotomy between the necessary and the contingent. Ibn Sīnā had used his papyrus card file well. The argument runs as follows:[29]

1 Existence is always either necessary or contingent.
2 What exists necessarily requires no cause; its existence cannot be denied without a contradiction.
3 What is contingent might or might not exist without any internal contradiction, so if it exists it requires a cause that makes it necessary, not in itself, but relative to that cause.
4 But something exists: This exists.
5 And this is either necessary or contingent (by 1).
6 If it is necessary, there exists a necessary, i.e., uncaused being (*QED*).
7 If it is contingent, it has a cause to determine or give precedence to its existence over its non-existence (since nothing in its own nature requires it to exist and there is no contradiction involved in its never having existed.)
8 Turning to that cause we ask whether it is necessary or contingent.
9 And so we follow the series until we reach a necessary being.
10 For there can be no infinite series of causes that reach an end in an actual effect; but the effect is here before us, by hypothesis (4 and 7). Nor can a complex system of causes sustain itself and overcome the contingency inherent in all complexity, since that would make effects ultimately their own causes, transforming what is contingent in itself into something necessary in itself.[30]

So there is a necessary being, *QED*.

The nub of the argument is the axiom or truism that the contingent can never be self-sufficient. Even a complex system where each part contributes to sustaining the whole, as in Strato's cosmos or Hume's Hindu image of the world as a spider that simply spins itself out according to its own nature, will not attain self-sufficiency through the complexity of its inner interdependencies. Rather, these will only compound its contingency. The only alternative to Avicenna's reasoning, then, is to reject the notion that the contingent depends upon the Necessary and give up the project of rendering the world intelligible by reference to its causes. As I argued in *Monotheism*, this is to adopt the positivist expedient of saying that the world just is and cannot be made sense of by causal explanations. One cannot stop half way and apply causal explanations to particular phenomena but not to the world as a system. For in a complex and interactive system of interdependencies all explanations will lead back to some common basis (the spheres in an Aristotelian cosmos, the subatomic particles in our own) and these will be either explained or left as surds. But in the latter case, the whole fabric of explanation crumbles, since everything was explained in terms of something that now proves inexplicable. Ibn Sīnā's strategy is to press on with the rationalist quest even to the point where the categories of natural explanation are exhausted and to find a general explanation for the being of the world at large, as a system, and for the character of all its inner interdependencies globally. His thesis is that what affords such an explanation will be the Necessary counterpart of all the contingencies we discover in particulars, the Necessary Being whose act resolves those contingencies into the relative or causal necessity that the sciences discover.

Our present concern is not with Avicenna's theology but with his metaphysics. Having established the existence of a necessary being, he is well positioned to argue for the uniqueness, simplicity, and causal primacy of that being, that is, to show that it is God. He goes on to develop his philosophical versions of the traditional attributes of omniscience, will, wisdom, and bounty.[31] But what concerns us here is how the existence of God is reached. For, in any cosmological argument, the manner in which the existence of God is proved orients not only the conception of the divine but also the conception of the world, as the springboard to the divine.

Ibn Sīnā's dichotomy between necessary and contingent existence, his assumption that the contingent requires a cause since there is no logical contradiction in its non-existence, and his reliance on the *kalām* idea of a determinant of existence over non-existence, all bespeak his rationalism as clearly as his reliance on the assumption 'This exists' bespeaks his realism. Rationalism here means the assumption that the universe can be made intelligible by way of explanations. Even the Aristotelian denial of an infinite causal regress is of a piece with Ibn Sīnā's rationalism. It requires simply that the demand for causal explanations of any given phenomenon not be infinitely put off or deferred with unsecured promissory notes, anchored in moorings that themselves have no anchor. Popkin notes that the causality implicit in the disjunction of necessary and contingent beings makes it equivalent to *ex nihilo nihil fit*.[32]

By Avicenna's standards, causal explanations are, in the truly Aristotelian manner, reductions of phenomena to necessity. If a thing is not necessary in itself, it is necessary through another. Something made it as it is, or it would not have been so. But here 'as it is' means existent rather than non-existent. Aristotle would apply such reasoning to particulars, but not to the cosmos as a whole.[33] Ibn Sīnā feels no such inhibition. For, he argues, even if a thing is eternal or infinite it may owe its existence to something else, being necessary not in itself but through another. In true monotheist fashion, Ibn Sīnā sees no grounds for stopping the chain of causes at the celestial beings, for example. They too are contingent and not necessary. They are not gods. There is no self-contradiction in denying the existence of the entire world, affirming that it need not exist, even though it always has existed. Thus its existence is dependent on God. The truest cause is not the merely transient efficient cause that officiates at the origin of a thing but the enduring cause that sustains and perpetuates the existence of its effect giving it a reality of its own, as God sustains and perpetuates the world. A preoccupation with efficient causes is the mark of materialism, but metaphysics seeks the ultimate ground or basis of the existence of all things.[34]

Causes in general and God in particular necessitate their effects. The relation, ultimately, is an intellectual one: A necessary being is intelligible in itself, without reference to any external thing. A contingent being's existence is not intelligible in itself. It is for that reason that there is no contradiction in denying its existence. But, given the existence of its cause, taking that assumption into consideration, there is a contradiction in denying the existence of a contingent being that actually exists. Note the departure from Aristotle. In Aristotle necessity itself is delegated to nature. Here all beings but God are contingent; the specificities of their determinations, their being so rather than otherwise, crucially, the "precedence" of existence over non-existence, are not accounted for by their own natures, need to be accounted for externally, and *are* accounted for with the assumption of their causes. Thus again, Ibn Sīnā's departure from the radical contingency doctrine of the *kalām*: The causes of a thing do make it necessary, although it is never necessary in itself.

The key to Ibn Sīnā's synthesis of the metaphysics of contingency with the metaphysics of necessity lies in a single phrase: *considered in itself.* Considered in itself, each effect is radically contingent. It does not contain the conditions of its own existence; and, considered in itself, it need not exist. Its causes give it being. It is by abstracting from its causes that we can regard even the world as a whole as radically contingent. But considered in relation to its causes, not as something that in the abstract might never have existed, but as something concretely given before us, with a determinate character, the same conditionedness that required us to admit its contingency requires us to admit its necessity: Considered in relation to its causes, this object must exist, in the very Aristotelian sense that it does exist, and must have the nature that it has in that its causes gave it that nature. A thing might *have been* other than as it is, it might yet be other than it is, but it cannot now be other than as it is. This is not an argument that even the most radical occasionalist of the *kalām* can afford to dismiss. For although *kalām* occasionalism is founded on the eclipse of horizontal causality in favor of the vertical causality of God's creative act, no *mutakallim* will categorically deny causality, since the central theme of the *kalām* is the nexus between particulars and the absolute act of God, who establishes all determinacy in things, down to the determination of existence over non-existence.[35] And, of course, no causal determinist can deny contingency either, since the very meaning of imputed causality rests on the counterfactual conditional, "Had the cause not occurred the effect would not have taken place."[36] Statements of causal determination are impossible if it is impossible to abstract from the givenness of the relevant causes and fictively presume their non-occurrence.

Following a distinction Aristotle makes between the question what a thing is and the question whether such a thing exists, Ibn Sīnā, then, can draw up his famous distinction between essence and existence, which will enable him to find a truth in both the metaphysics of Aristotle and the rival metaphysics of creation. This will not be simply a matter of calling creation a mythic symbol of emanation, but of assigning to each of the rival views its due measure of truth. Since all complex beings are contingent, inasmuch as we can abstract from whatever assumptions we make when we assume their existence, existence is a separate notion, over and above the essence of the thing. It is not, as Aristotle strove to establish, identical with the very essence of each thing, so that for a thing to be is for it to be the kind of thing it is. On the contrary, Aristotle's own distinction of *what* from *whether* shows that this cannot be so, and Ibn Sīnā has only to expand that distinction from the realm of particulars, where Aristotle introduces it, across the realm of species (which Aristotle would not allow it to traverse[37]) and to the cosmos at large, which is, despite Aristotle's views as to its necessity and divinity, a finite and composite thing by his own account, and therefore, as Ibn Sīnā reasons, itself contingent.

Historians of philosophy can be rather opaque in describing what is at stake in Avicenna's distinction of essence from existence, sometimes because they presume upon an interest in later discussions – Thomistic disquisitions on the analogy of being, or even existentialist debates about the priority of existence to essence, as a way of voicing the claims of human freedom. But I think if we are to understand Ibn Sīnā's contribution to philosophy and his impact on subsequent discussions we must read him first in the framework of his own thinking and against the backdrop of the metaphysical discussions that formed its problematic. The most profound of these was Aristotle's, and the most fruitful for Ibn Sīnā's synthesis of Aristotle with the scriptural metaphysics crystallized in the *kalām* was in the technical work of Plotinus in the last of his six *Enneads*.

Aristotle analyzed existence in terms of essence[38] – not because he was unaware of a distinction between the two, as is suggested in all the talk of Avicenna's "discovering" the distinction. Aristotle clearly formulated the intuitive distinction between what a thing is and whether such a thing exists, and it was he who defined the idea of essence that all subsequent philosophers would use as their point of departure, bringing the Platonic Ideas down out of the clouds, as undergraduates invariably are taught. But it was a central thesis of Aristotle's that when we come to the end of our inquiry about being, we shall find that the being of a thing is what makes it what it is, its essence. Just as there is for Aristotle no distinctively moral sense of "good," but the term is applied in different ways in each of the categories, so there is no distinctively existential sense of the verb to be, but "being" is applied in as many and as diverse senses as there are categories, and what it means for a thing to be is for it to have unity (Platonic self-sameness, or identity) and a definite character (suchness), to belong to its own kind and exemplify its nature, whatever that nature may be. In other words, for a thing to be is for it to have the essence that it has. That is why the verb *to be* is "systematically ambiguous." There is a structural resemblance among its different senses, but no univocal, material semantic content, because what it is for a thing to be depends on what the thing is. What it is for a man to be a man and what it is for a number to be a number or a color to be a color are not the same, as though existence were some character that, say, numbers, persons, and colors had in common. This is what Aristotelians understand by *pros hen* equivocity. "Being" does not signify the same notion in all these cases. Yet it signifies in the same way: What it is for a man to be a man is *for a man* the same as what it is for a number to be a number is for this number, and the same for a given color as what it is for any color to be a color. That is, to have a definite character, belong to the class it does belong to, to preserve a certain continuity and discreteness, self-sameness over time, and distinctness from all other things. Kantians express the same idea when they say that "exists" is not a proper predicate: It adds nothing to the characterization of what we say exists beyond what is already posited as pertaining to the nature of that thing, whatever it may be and whatever category it may be found in.[39]

The Aristotelian answer to the question about the nature of existence may seem disappointingly flat, even tautologous. It seems to say no more than that the nature of being is to be, that things are what they are. But that was part of the appeal of this approach for Aristotle. It seemed to complete Parmenides' project of founding the account of being upon the logic of the idea of being, but in an eminently more commonsensical way, resting the idea of being on the logic of identity, as Plato had proposed, but taking a bit less seriously than Plato had the challenge of the Cratylean idea of change: Change does not really violate the constancy Plato sought as the basis of identity, so long as we remember the Heraclitean truth that there is always constancy in the *pattern* of change. Beings then, or substances, are whatever preserves continuity and uniformity through change. That is why matter is called substance, and so are particulars. But the outstanding exemplars of constancy through change in nature are species. And it is in Aristotle's doctrines about species that we see the material, indeed prescriptive requirements of his seemingly innocuous near tautology about being: in the fact, for example, that there is no evolution or extinction of species, no generation or destruction among the heavenly bodies, no change of essences at all. Parmenides was wrong, in Aristotle's view, to have interpreted the law of identity and the law against contradiction as debarring change and multiplicity altogether. But he was right not only in the question he asked about the nature of being *per se*, and in seeking his answer in the logic of the term "being," but also right, profoundly, as Plato had understood, in supposing that being in the ultimate sense does not change.

> He who knows what man or any other nature is [Aristotle argues] must know also that it exists. For no one knows the nature of what does not exist . . . . But "being" is not the essence of anything, since "what is" is not a genus. So the existence of anything requires proof, and that is what the sciences do in fact.[40]

Thus existence is constitutive to the essences of all natural species, and it is only because "being" is too general and polymorphic a notion to define a specific essence, that we can make no deductions from it about the actual properties of the things that are but must examine them as given in nature. Yet their existence is of necessity, or they would have no constant natures to be studied.

The power of the Aristotelian analysis of being lay in the doctrine of the categories, and it was here that the Stoics, who were penetrating and radical logicians, placed their mines and mortars: If a category was, as Aristotle claimed, a way in which things are or are said to be, then the broadest categories would not be those of being, as Aristotle supposed, but a higher category that includes being and non-being. For even things that do not exist, and nothingness itself, are said to be. To engulf this larger grouping, the Stoics devised their own category of "the something," *to ti*, entities, as we might say, including all the things that are or are not but might be spoken of, including nothingness. What profit was there in this, since the Stoics themselves, with their Megarian, ultimately Eleatic heritage, would be the last to claim reality for the unreal considered as such? But again, as with Aristotle, an innocent sounding logical exercise has a profound material impact on metaphysics. If "the something" is the broadest class of categories, then "being" is a real predicate, distinguishing the real from the unreal, and it is possible to speak of being as imparted or acquired rather than intrinsic in the characters of things. What makes this observation relevant for all the subsequent tradition, at least down to Spinoza's conception of diverse powers of being,[41] is the fact that "the something" includes virtual as well as actual beings.

Despite his strident polemic against Stoic materialism, Plotinus was not slow to grasp the usefulness of the Stoic approach in constructing a Platonic response to Aristotle's categories. Thus, where Aristotle held (somewhat inconsistently) that the category of substance does not allow for variation in degree – one may be more or less pale or sunburned, but one either is or is not human – Plato's reasoning and even Aristotle's own notions of the realization of potential and the life that most fully realizes our humanity, make humanness something to be lived up to rather than merely something we either do or do not exemplify. That means that even in the category of substance, where "being" is said of us in the primary sense, a distinction must be made between essence and existence. Or, as Ibn Sīnā would put it, existence is a notion superadded to that of essence. To be sure, Aristotle was right that there is no common trait that all beings share in sheerly by the fact that they are beings. But, as Plotinus saw, the very fact of differentiation from absolute unity, the attempt at self-affirmation and at turning back toward the unity of the One, are in a way something that all beings have in common, not in *how* they interpret the possibilities of existence, but in the fact that each being and kind *does* in its own way interpret those possibilities.[42]

The Stoic approach, as adapted by Plotinus, allowed for the imparting of being by the One and for the completion of Aristotle's thought about the causal role of Nous, allowing Nous to share out to all beings whatever actuality they may have as members of their kinds. For the history of any being's activities is the story of its efforts to attain or achieve the potential represented by the form it receives, to become what it most truly is. Clearly this implies that things are not simply what they are in the passive or static, pigeonholed sense of the logician. A conative character is resident in every being, as Spinoza later would insist. Such a character formed the very basis of the human project for Plotinus as well, the project of self-discovery and self-creation. Socrates had hinted as much in his revisionist reading of the Delphic oracle as calling on us to discover the god within ourselves. And Plato had voiced the same thought, projected in an imperative mood, in saying that the task of man is to become as like to God as humanly possible, that in this way, by realizing our kinship with the divine, we perfect humanity in ourselves, become fully or truly human. This is the common theme that each being interprets in its own way. Aristotle himself spoke of it in terms of the pursuit by all beings of their own ends; he found the perfection of nature, transcending the limitation and even conflict of natural ends, in the self-containedness and complementarity of the system of those ends.

Summing up the contribution of Plotinus, Jean Trouillard writes,

> No matter how narrowly specialized a thought may be, it never ceases to be total (IV 9.5; VI 7.9). Every finite point is an integral participation in the integrality of the intelligible. . . . What meaning would such a movement of thought give to the distinction between essence and existence? On the one hand existence would express the inadequation of the essential determination in relation to its act. . . . Act, on the other hand, is frequently looked on as something external, superimposed on a determination indifferent in itself and burdening it with a complexus of extrinsic relations. In that case, existence would be more than an accident; it would be the source of every accident.[43]

This is the turning taken by Ibn Sīnā.

Linking the work of Plotinus and of Plato in the *Symposium* with what would later be said by many Sufis, Kabbalists, Christian mystics, and Renaissance Neoplatonists, Ibn Sīnā conjoins earthly with the celestial love, the sacred with the profane:

> Every essence under God's plan, striving by its nature towards its own perfection, which is the very goodness imparted to it as an essence from the Essence of Pure Good, shuns the lack specific to it, which is its evil – materiality and nonbeing. For all ills stem from attachments to matter and nonbeing. So clearly every being subject to God's design has a natural yearning and innate love. The love in such a being is necessarily a cause of its existence. For everything that is called real may be classed under one of these three rubrics: Either (*a*) it stands at the summit of its perfection, or (*b*) it is afflicted with utter lack, or (*c*) it seesaws between these two states. Now at the lowest rung of privation is pure nonbeing, wholly lacking in all attachments and rightly called utter nothingness and judged nonexistent. It may be counted as a "being" notionally or in some scheme of classification, but its "existence" is never considered real, and the term "existent" is never applied to it appropriately in any but a figurative and wholly accidental sense.
>
> Real beings are either those that are predisposed for utter perfection or those that are described as swinging back and forth between an inadequacy arising from some quarter and the perfection inherent in their nature. So no being is ever devoid of some converse with perfection of some kind and a resultant love and natural attraction for whatever will realize its union with that perfection and strengthen its converse with it.
>
> The same point becomes evident teleologically. For every essence directed by God's design has its own specific perfection and does not suffice in itself to realize that perfection, since the beings under God's governance receive their perfections from the outflowing emanation of Him who is Perfect of Himself. And it is unacceptable to suppose that this Source and Origin of all perfections singles out each individual recipient of bounty, as the Philosophers have made clear. So it is necessary in His wisdom and benevolent governance that He implant a general love in each of them, enabling it to preserve the portion of perfection it has received by emanation and to strive to realize

or enhance it where it is lacking. He does this in the interest of the governance of the cosmos, which is thereby wisely ordered.[44]

Avicenna took full advantage of the work of Plotinus (and of Aristotle himself) when he argued that the concept of existence is not included or entailed in any of the Aristotelian categories, nor is unity entailed in the notions conveyed by any of those categories. These are "accidents" relative to the concepts conveyed under the ten categories, for there is no contradiction in denying the existence of any color, body, shape; and no contradiction again in proposing the multiplicity of such entities. The argument is eminently sensible, but it cuts deeply into the metaphysical structure of Aristotelian thinking, exposing a tendentiousness that Aristotle's own profoundly commonsensical exposition conceals. Of course Aristotle does not imagine that the existence of some hypothetical dog or cat is necessary. But he does think that a world without dogs or cats is inconceivable, that the non-existence of the cosmos at large is absurd, and that it is absurd to deny the existence of what we see before us.

Ibn Sīnā uses the *kalām* scalpel of analysis to expose the suppositiousness of Aristotle's position, the simple but razor-sharp device of assuming the contrary of what we take to be the case, to see if reason can exclude it. If there is no contradiction in assuming the non-existence of species, or even of the cosmos, these are contingent and not necessary beings – even if they are eternal. Being is necessary, intrinsic, not an accident, provided one confines one's attention, as Aristotle did, to actual beings, or beings whose actuality is presumed. But then, in effect, one begs the question as to whether the actual beings are all that there might be. Aristotle himself, when expressing his impatience with Megarian determinism, similarly inclined to view possible beings and events as possible.[45] But when we consider virtual beings as virtual, or, as Ibn Sīnā did, contingent beings as contingent, "existence" does become a predicate and makes all the difference in the world between what Avicenna likes to call one essence and another. For, as Parviz Morewedge rightly frames the distinction in our own vocabulary,[46] one is instantiated and the other is not. Ibn Sīnā puts it succinctly: A thing considered in itself is something altogether different from a thing considered in relation to the actuality of its causes.[47] But that there is no contradiction in conceiving the non-existence of the entirety of nature is demonstrated by Scripture, for all readers of Scripture do conceive the non-existence of the world of particulars.

It was at this juncture between the Aristotelian givenness and the Scriptural gift of being that Ibn Sīnā created a third major option in metaphysics, subsuming the creationist contingency of the *kalām*[48] and the essentialist eternalism of Aristotle. Ibn Sīnā's cosmos, by contrast with Aristotle's, was contingent. But, by contrast with the cosmos of the *kalām*, its contingency did not negate natural necessity, or the efficacy of natural causes and potentialities, including human actions and dispositions. Ibn Sīnā's scheme did not impugn the authority of science or the reliability of human moral judgment, even as applied to life and the act of creation itself. Finite things were contingent in themselves but necessary with reference to their causes and ultimately to God, who is the Cause of causes. Thus the natural order retains its integrity and the continuity of its categories – time, space, causality, the wholeness of human intelligence, and moral sense. God's wisdom guarantees that integrity and continuity, while the integrity and continuity discoverable within the world bespeak God's superintendent wisdom and outpouring benevolence. Like Aristotle, Ibn Sīnā relies on proximate causes between the ultimate Principle and the final effect, but unlike Aristotle he made God not only the cause of the world's orderly movement but also the cause of its existence.

Proclus (410–85), the great systematizer of Neoplatonism, criticized Aristotle for making God the cause of motion in the world and not, as in Plato, the cause of the its existence. Ammonius, a student of Proclus and leader of the philosophic school at Alexandria, urged that the Final Cause of Aristotle is in fact the artificer or demiurge of Plato. Simplicius (sixth century), a student of Ammonius, rationalizes this identification, arguing that the Prime Mover is in effect the sustaining cause of the existence of the cosmos. But this Platonizing reading strains Aristotle's text and the fabric of his thought.[49] The discussion was known to al-Fārābī. And Abū Bishr Mattā (d. 940), the Christian translator and commentator who defended logic against linguistic relativism at the court of the *Wazīr* in Baghdad, and who taught one of al-Fārābī's teachers, took up this line, arguing that the cause of motion in the world is the cause of its existence as well. Avicenna rejected the claim along with the idea that physics is the proper place to prove the existence of God.[50] Among the ten practical guidelines that he offered in logic for avoiding the pitfalls that fallacies present, he included advice against the Prime Mover argument, which was the mainstay of Aristotelian theology: "Avoid ambiguous or problematic premises like the proposition, 'All that moves must have a mover, since nothing can be self-moving.'"[51] His Rayy disciple reports hearing Avicenna explain his discontent with the Prime Mover argument and his assignment of a strictly metaphysical (sc., teleological) interpretation to the argument of the *Metaphysics*:

> We also heard him say: "It pains me that belief in the eternity of the First Principle and its eternal unity should be reached by way of motion and the oneness of the world that is set in motion – as if the *Metaphysics* can yield up its riches concerning the Almighty only in this way. But this distressing reading is found not only in the Moderns but even in their masters, all of them alike." He went on: "Had they comprehended the inner meaning of the *Metaphysics*, they would have been ashamed to put forward such a view and would never have felt the need to hold that the course to be taken involves both a physical and a theological approach – a course that is totally unwarranted, since the text specifies the theological line of argument exclusively.[52]

Physics, Ibn Sīnā insisted, gives only the faintest inkling of God – a sound observation, if we consider how far removed the Prime Mover of *Physics* VIII is from the ontic absoluteness that metaphysics expects, and if we recall that Aristotle's *Physics* lacks the teleological nexus by which an unmoved mover can impart goal-directed change (let alone existence) to all things in nature.[53]

What Avicenna seeks, as contrasted with the traditional appeals to the movements of the spheres, is a properly metaphysical argument, based on the concept of being itself, and it is for this reason in part that he insists that God is not the subject of metaphysics. For a Peripatetic science postulates its subject, as physics assumes but does not prove the reality of matter and motion. But metaphysics will prove the existence of God using elemental, undefined notions of existence, possibility, and necessity, which it does not (circularly) concoct from derivative notions but which it intuits directly. It is for this reason that the syllogisms leading to the recognition of God's existence are not demonstrative, as though God were the product of causes represented in their middle term, but are evidentiary, arguing, by what Peirce will call abduction, from effect to cause.[54]

Echoing a Sufi turn of phrase, Ibn Sīnā says that a metaphysical argument will call existence itself to testify to the reality of God. In a way this anticipates Anselm's (1033–1109) desire to mirror the self-sufficiency of God in the self-containedness of his argument.[55] But I must stress, in all deference to my old friend Parviz Morewedge,[56] that

Avicenna's contingency argument is not an ontological argument in any strict sense at all, and it is misleading to call it one. The argument does use the idea of a necessary being and does conclude by ascribing necessary existence to God. In this it has much in common with the approach employed by Norman Malcolm in recent years and, I have argued, by Descartes and many others before him, seeking to show that the kind of existence God has, after God's existence is already established, is that of a Self-sufficient being.[57] But Ibn Sīnā does not, like Anselm, seek to prove the existence of God a priori. For he does employ at least one a posteriori premise when he assumes the existence of something here before us.[58]

We can argue further, supported by Ibn Sīnā's own classification of his argument as evidentiary rather than apodeictic, that even in its analysis of being, although the concept of being is said by Avicenna to derive from pure rational intuition, his proof works from experience. For the claim that this item before us, and indeed the world, are not the necessary being we seek but are contingent and that this is known by our power to conceive the non-existence of any single item and to suppose without contradiction the failure to come together of any composite of matter and form or essence and existence, shows that the argument rests on experience. Ultimately, it rests on the same Cratylean experience of change that Plato appealed to, regardless of how high into the empyrean we may project that experience. Thus Davidson rightly classifies the argument as a special case of the cosmological proof. It is the very argument, in fact, that Kant said was too well known to require detailed statement.[59] What is metaphysical in the argument, as Davidson explains, is that it could have taken its starting point from any existent whatever. Where it brushes against the ontological argument, we can add, is where it reflects on the conception of a necessary being. But that, of course, is inevitable in any argument that addresses itself to the idea of an ontic absolute.

Necessary being is an a priori concept regardless of the route that reaches it. It was recognition of this fact that led Kant to discover the terms of the ontological argument in the Leibnizian restatement of Avicenna's cosmological proof. Kant was sensitized by Leibniz' born again Platonism, which resonates deeply with the underlying Platonism of Avicenna. But to think of God in Platonizing terms is not to commit oneself to demonstrate the existence of God from the idea of God, as the ontological argument seeks to do. In fact, it is no more than to recognize that a God who is perfect must transcend sensory experience and is to be apprehended only through the pure concepts of reason. It is this recognition that Anselm and Avicenna hold most clearly in common – along with most of the major philosophical theologians of the west.

As Fazlur Rahman stressed,[60] Avicenna's doctrine of the contingency of being is easily misunderstood. One of its most prominent slogans, the thesis that existence is an accident "superadded to essence" is too readily taken to suggest that existence is a thing, a factor or principle, mixed like an ingredient in the natures of particulars. But the only two "factors" in natural particulars for Ibn Sīnā are form and matter, and these, as in Aristotle, cannot exist without one another. In fact, for Ibn Sīnā matter and form individuate each other; their combination is the basis of all individuality. This combining of matter and form, by which the virtuality of existence is made fact, is bestowed by antecedent causes leading back to God. It is in part because matter cannot exist without form that Ibn Sīnā rejects *formatio mundi* and insists on the eternity of the world – or, as he prefers to understand it, the absolute (but timeless) creation of the world.

Both Islamic and European thinkers sought to impose more familiar conceptions on Ibn Sīnā's idea of existence. In the Islamic East Suhrawardī (d. 1191), the true framer of the Illuminist theosophy, and Naṣīr al-Dīn al-Ṭūṣī (1201–74) fostered an idealistic reading, treating essence as the reality and existence as a mere notional addition. Both men argue that, if existence is an accident, essence must come first to receive the accident. But when Ibn Sīnā calls existence an accident he means simply that existence is not implied in the essence of any composite thing. As he argues in the *Ishārāt*, no effect can be caused by its own essence; for when a thing does not yet exist, it does not yet have an essence to cause it.

In the Islamic West, Ibn Rushd, who exercised a profound impact on the Latin scholastics and Jewish philosophers who wrote in Arabic and Hebrew, accused Ibn Sīnā of violating Aristotle's definition of substance as that which exists in itself. But this is just an attempt to revive Aristotle's metaphysics through the authority of a definition. It may be true that substances do not depend on the secondary categories in the way that, say, qualities, quantities, or relations depend on substances. But that does not show that Aristotelian particulars are self-sufficient in the sense of not depending for their existence on any other thing. (Surely all of them depend on their causes.) Nor does it obviate Ibn Sīnā's argument that the nonexistence of any finite beings – including species, the heavens, or the world itself – is conceivable and contains no self-contradiction.

For Ibn Sīnā, as Rahman emphasizes, existence is not posterior to the essence of a thing, an accident *of* it in that sense, but is prior logically and ontologically to the full determination of any essence. God's bestowal of existence, through the imparting of form to matter by the Active Intellect, is the basis of the instantiation of any essence. As Ibn Sīnā explains:

> While it is possible for the essence of a thing to cause certain others of its qualities or attributes – for example, that its general differentia cause its more specific properties – it is not possible that the attribute called "existence" be caused in a thing by its essence, which is quite distinct from its existence or any other attribute. For the cause precedes the effect ontologically, but nothing is prior to existence.[61]

That is, before a thing exists, it does not have a nature to determine it.

Creation for Ibn Sīnā does not mean the imparting of existence to what previously lacked it, for the temporality invoked by such a notion presupposes a physical order as its clock and thus precludes the absoluteness of God's creative act. Indeed, to speak of God's bestowing existence on what previously lacked it is to talk as though what is given existence already existed before receiving that gift. On the contrary, creation for Ibn Sīnā means the ontic priority of God to all things: Without God's imparting of existence nothing in nature would have been, since all natural substances are compounded of matter and form, neither of which can exist of itself. This non-temporal reading of creation, in Avicenna's view, is what is understood, or rather, what is best understood, by the absolute imparting of existence to the world. In Avicenna's view this is, in fact, the only logically coherent reading of the scriptural story of creation. Any merely temporal or pictorial reading would imaginatively presuppose some or all of the categories that were to be created. In trying to imagine absolute creation such temporal stories and images undermine themselves, undercutting the very absoluteness they seek to signify and celebrate.[62]

Avicenna's critics, clinging to their myth, accuse him of denying creation by virtue of his affirmation of the Aristotelian dogma of the eternity of the world. The tradition is to assimilate his views to those of Aristotle and ascribe his eternalism to a naturalism that borders on atheism. That traditional, antipathetical reading of Ibn Sīnā survives as a mainstay of later scholarship. But, in fact, Aristotle's eternalism was as religious as it was naturalistic or rationalistic. These values are not discriminated in the fully unfurled philosophy of Aristotle. And Ibn Sīnā's eternalism, quite unlike Aristotle's, is as motivated by allegiance to absolute creation as it is by naturalism. To Avicenna's early critics his affirmation of creation easily appeared to be a subterfuge, a passport, or a semantic quibble. But Avicenna was quite serious about the point: What the myth of creation represents is the reality of ontic dependence. That dependence, in Avicenna's view, cannot be absolute if it is temporal. Not only is God compromised into temporality, as the pagan Neoplatonists had feared, but time, potentiality, matter itself seem (at least imaginatively, if not in fact) to be presupposed as the preconditions of God's act. Surely no creationist worthy of the name would take Rāzī's Five Eternals as an adequate expression of the world's absolute dependence on the unique and absolute act of God. Thus Ibn Sīnā reasons that only the idea of contingency can capture what is at stake in the scriptural idea of creation.

As Rahman sums up the position,

> all beings other than God are inherently infected with contingency ... temporal beings, which are already composites of form and matter ... the heavenly bodies which are composites of an eternal form and an eternal matter ... the transcendental Intelligences, which are free from matter and are not subject to any change, yet are composites of essence and existence ... a contingent can never shed its contingency at any stage of its career and become self-necessary like God. ... This is the true meaning of the famous metaphysical dictum "Existence is accidental to essence." It means that the contingent is never rid of its contingency. ... This, of course, does not mean that the contingent world is accidental in the entire scheme of things, since it is necessarily involved in God's self-knowledge ... in the context of its cause the contingent does attain necessity; it does not become self-necessary but "necessary-by-the-other," as Ibn Sīnā invariably puts it.[63]

Ibn Sīnā echoes the Qur'anic Throne verse (2:255) by calling God *Qayyūm*, ever-enduring or self-subsistent.[64] The expression confirms for him the scriptural legitimacy of linking the world's contingency with God's Self-sufficiency. Maimonides similarly appropriates the name *Shaddai*, interpreting it as containing in small the idea of God's Self-sufficiency, which he takes to be the sense of the Tetragrammaton, a miniature ontological argument, spelled out in the revelation of God's most explicit name, I AM THAT I AM, as Maimonides glosses the passages where that name is revealed to Moses. The Throne verse is particularly well suited to Ibn Sīnā's purpose, since it links God's creation and providential care with His everlastingness: "He is the Living and Everlasting. . . . Neither sleep nor slumber overtake Him . . . His throne spreadeth vast over heaven and earth. His are all things in heaven and earth . . . and He is unwearied in preserving them." A modern Muslim commentary writes of this verse, "Who can translate its glorious meaning, or reproduce the rhythm of its well-chosen and comprehensive words. Even in the original Arabic the meaning seems to be greater than can be expressed in words. . . . The attribute of *Qaiyūm* includes not only the idea of 'Self-subsisting' but also the idea of 'Keeping up and maintaining all life.'"[65] But the richness of meaning here results in part from the accretion of layers of interpretation deposited by the *kalām* and even by the philosophy of Ibn Sīnā, which the glossator silently uses. Indeed, the Qur'anic language itself *is* a translation here, the Arabic *al-Ḥayy, al-Qayyūm* echoing the Hebrew *Ḥayy ve-Qayyom* (Berakhot 32a) and the *lā ta'khudhuhu sinatun wa lā nawmun* rendering the *lo yanūm ve-lo yishan* of Psalms 121: 4, even to the extent of using the corresponding words.[66] Rahman rightly reappropriates the sense that Ibn Sīnā adopted and enriched.

For many later thinkers what was most striking in Ibn Sīnā's metaphysics was the concession of temporal creation to the arguments of the Aristotelians. The continuities of time and causality were allowed to overspill the finite cosmos into eternity. But even those who blamed Ibn Sīnā and al-Fārābī for conceding the eternity of the world and making the seeming automatism of emanation the ultimate meaning of creation adopted both the emanative scheme of the Neoplatonists and the distinctive Avicennan solution to the question of the world's relationship to God.[67] Both al-Ghazālī and Maimonides, for example, reinstate creation but within an emanative universe; both allow – and Maimonides insists upon – the integrity of causal bonds and independent valuative judgments within the natural realm of finite being. And both make the necessities, values, and categories of nature relative to nature's ordained scheme rather than absolute requirements of disembodied logic, as their predecessors in philosophy had been inclined to do.[68] Although Ibn Sīnā does not make quite the same journey, it is his creative synthesis in metaphysics that makes their achievement possible. For it is he who reinstates the Platonic recognition that all necessities in nature, in the realm of becoming, are relative, not absolute.

It is al-Fārābī, clearly, who paves the way for Ibn Sīnā's synthesis, when he vindicates Aristotle's account of future contingency[69] by distinguishing between intrinsic and relational necessity: the necessary implication of an event by the corresponding fact or truth or knowledge, even if it is God's knowledge, does not in any way render the event necessitated in itself. What necessitates events can only be the complex of their causes. In abstraction from these, the event is not necessary but contingent. In the same way, one can reason, even the implication of an effect by the givenness of its causes in no way entails the intrinsic necessity of the effect. Students of Ibn Sīnā who imagine that his doctrine of the world's eternal implication by the act of God somehow entails its necessity (and so its self-sufficiency), or entails the necessity of all events, have simply fallen prey to the dialectics of an anti-eternalist polemic. They fail to observe that the same specious reasoning would make a necessitarian of anyone who affirms any causal judgment and neglects the relevant distinction between absolute or intrinsic necessity and a necessity of implication between effect and cause when a causal relation is presumed or posited. Such necessities are a matter of logic. But that very fact is sufficient to reveal that they obtain only in a context where the proper relations have been stipulated.[70]

In a textbook exposition of Ibn Sīnā's thought what would follow now might be a rapid slide down the surfaces of the spheres that in medieval cosmologies rotate about the earth as viceregents of Providence, bearing the stars, planets, sun, and moon, guided or driven by starsouls and celestial intelligences that mediate the influences of the Divine toward nature. Since God is absolutely simple, and since only what is simple can arise from what is simple, Ibn Sīnā, like al-Fārābī rationalizes the emergence of the world's multiplicity from God's unity via the Neoplatonic expedient, still important to Spinoza, of discovering a moment of differentiation in the purity of divine thought, distinguishing the subjective from the objective and thereby allowing the primal diversity from which all subsequent multiplicity will arise. Ibn Sīnā exploits his own idea of relative necessity to account for the emergence of bodies: The celestial intelligences in his system precipitate the spheres by reflecting on their own contingency. Stated in more modern terms, bodies are the very image of the object, the *in itself* as distinguished sharply from the subjective *for itself*. They are the paradigm of the ultimate effect, in cause–effect relations. But, like all things that harbor any claim upon reality, they are the products of thought. They are not mere thoughts, as though thought were incapable of reaching beyond itself to affect or effectuate anything real in a sense other than that of its own reality. But they are products of thought. The truth of God's thought is not in its correspondence to its object but in the correspondence *to it* of all that it knows. For this reason, God's thought perfectly unites the speculative and the productive, just as God's simplex identity unites wisdom and will: What God thinks *eo ipso* exists, and is just as God knows it to be.

The immediate product of God's thought is a hypostatic Intelligence associated with the outermost sphere of the heavens, but itself differentiated by the focus of its attentions. For like God it contemplates itself, but it also, as it were, gazes upwards toward its Source. Contemplating itself as intrinsically contingent (despite the timelessness of its emergence), the first Intelligence becomes the source of the first celestial body, the outermost sphere. Contemplating itself as necessitated by its Cause, it gives rise to the soul that governs the motions of that sphere and makes it a self-moving body. That is, the Mind, as object, gives rise to the Soul, whose discursive thinking is the birth of change and time. Contemplating its Cause, the first Celestial Intellect gives rise to a second hypostatic intellect, its mirror image, as it were, to use the metaphor favored by Ibn Ṭufayl. Thus the otherness of matter is a precipitate of the objectifying otherness latent in the act of thought. The life that animates the heavens and becomes the paradigm and ultimate engine or energizer of the processes of nature is the product of the rational recognition of necessity. The duality that haunts nature and that Ibn Sīnā seeks to recognize in acknowledging that all particulars are both contingent in themselves and necessitated by their causes is prefigured in emanation from the outset, its poles clearly identified with matter and thought.

The second intellect recapitulates the creative and expressive work of the first, generating another intellect, another soul, and another sphere, and so the procession makes its way, until the proliferation of simple entities is complete, and the tenth disembodied intellect projects not a single intellect or soul but the substantial forms of all natural beings, souls, ideas, and the rational principles by which all things in nature are what they are, projected not upon the simple matter of the heavenly bodies but upon the four elements, which the motions and influences of the heavenly bodies differentiate. For the tenth is the Active Intellect, identified as the Giver of Forms and the figure intended by the Scriptural image of the Angel of Revelation and Inspiration. It is thus the source of both subjective and objective rationality.

But our purpose is less to dwell on the distinctive features of Ibn Sīnā's version of Neoplatonic cosmology than to grasp what is of lasting philosophic value in his metaphysics, so we will not anatomize his world view beyond what is necessary in noting the intellectual themes that shape it. Instead, we shall focus on the single metaphysical thesis whose argument we have outlined, the synthesis of eternity with contingency, scrutinizing it in the light of criticism to appraise its vitality and usefulness in the task for which it was devised, making sense of the character of being at large.

3 CRITICISM AND RESPONSE

i

The salient and best-known critique of Ibn Sīnā's metaphysics was that of al-Ghazālī, which permanently damaged the prospects of philosophy and natural theology in Islam.[71] Al-Ghazālī's criticism, at the core of his polemical work *The Incoherence of the Philosophers*, rests on his rejection of Ibn Sīnā's claim that the idea of contingency captures the essence of what the idea of creation seeks to express. On the contrary, Ghazālī argues,[72] an eternal world like Ibn Sīnā's cannot be dependent on the act of God. By the canons of Aristotelian metaphysics, which al-Ghazālī here insists on applying strictly, it is unacceptable to claim that what has always existed need not have existed. If the world is eternal, its existence is necessary and does not need the act of God. An eternalist philosopher like Avicenna or al-Fārābī is an atheist *malgré lui*. Here is the heart of the incoherence al-Ghazālī discovers in the project of Ibn Sīnā. The Philosophers wanted to show the world's timeless dependence upon God, but the idea of timelessness demands that of self-sufficiency, and Ibn Sīnā's conception of creation as contingent in itself and necessary with reference to its cause only papers over a contradiction.

Ibn Rushd, answering Ghazālī in *The Incoherence of the Incoherence*, concedes the point, agreeing that whatever is eternal is necessary. His object is to save a more strictly Peripatetic Aristotelianism by sacrificing Ibn Sīnā's Neoplatonizing version with its provocative division of all being into the necessary and the contingent. So, after saying that Ibn Sīnā's is a fine argument and mentioning its *kalām* roots, he adds sardonically: "The only false step in it is their assumption that the world as a whole is contingent. For this is not self-evident." Averroes objects to defining contingency in terms of causality and to the assumption that all beings are either caused or uncaused, which again is not self-evident. The real outcome of Ibn Sīnā's argument, he argues, is either an infinite regress of causes and effects derived from the tautologous affirmation that whatever is caused has a cause, or the incongruous notion of a necessary contingent being, resulting from Ibn Sīnā's attempt to generalize the idea that whatever is contingent requires a cause. Taking "contingent" in Ibn Sīnā's sense is just a way of begging the question and still does not tell us that the cause inferred is Avicenna's Necessary Being; taking "contingent" in its more familiar philosophic sense, which makes no reference to causality but only affirms that a thing might or might not have been, the argument tells us only that what might not have been is still in some sense necessary.[73] And that seems to Averroes to be doubletalk.[74]

Averroes accuses Ibn Sīnā of equivocation, primarily because he still attaches to Ibn Sīnā's terms the senses assigned to their counterparts in Aristotle.[75] Like al-Ghazālī Ibn Rushd thinks it absurd to say of what is eternal that it might not have existed. He also thinks that the division of being into necessary and contingent is not a division of the existent as such. Perhaps this means that Averroes favors a nominalistic solution to Avicenna's problem, which in a way he shared, since he himself held that the *motion* of the spheres was both eternal and caused by God – thus dependent for *its* existence on God's act.[76] But such a solution is only an admission that Averroes was not as immune as he would like to have been to the problems he found most damaging in Avicenna's scheme. As I indicated, the same problems can recur in any account of causality and are resolved only through the Avicennan recognition that the same thing can be contingent in itself and necessary in relation to its causes. Realism about possibilities does draw this doctrine in the direction of creation – as in the arguments of al-Ghazālī and Maimonides; nominalism might seem to afford a means of preserving eternalism. But in either case eternalism is put on the defensive, and strict necessity is well and rightly breached.

In terms of ontology, as distinguished from cosmology, Averroes' critique seems to amount to nothing more than a complaint that Avicenna should have considered the existent as existent, as Aristotle did. Had he done so, the question of virtual being would never have arisen. In this regard, Averroes is criticizing Avicenna in effect for not begging the question about the eternity and necessity of being. Averroes clearly feels uncomfortable with the radicalism of Ibn Sīnā's approach, above all with its method of standing back from the givenness of being and considering an existent as something that might not have been. But such discomforts are not refutations. Indeed, the overcoming of such biases is essential to the progress of philosophy. If nominalism about possibility means recognizing that the same entity, even when assumed to be existent (and thought of as eternally existent) need not have existed but can be looked at (by abstracting from its causes) as not existing necessarily, then Ibn Sīnā, not Averroes, is the pioneer of the nominalistic solution to the problem of necessity versus contingency, and Averroes' solution is not an alternative to the Avicennan approach but an elaboration of it.

We can resuscitate Averroes' objections in modern terms as follows: Has not Ibn Sīnā begged the question about causality with respect to being at large? For the need for a cause does not leap out at us from the concept of being; it is not analytic to say that what is contingent in the sense that its non-existence involves no contradiction is also contingent in the sense of requiring a cause. This means that a key linkage of the argument, which Ibn Sīnā takes to be self-evident because he cannot conceive of any circumstances in the world that would warrant our abandoning causal judgments, is not analytic but requires a specific affirmation of causality. This is what Leibniz does when he makes the old *kalām* principle of the "determinant" explicit as the Principle of Sufficient reason. Yet Averroes himself will not contest such a premise. In fact, he goes to the trouble of rebuilding Ibn Sīnā's argument on that basis, transforming it into a curious reassertion of his own cosmology, although suppressing the element of contingency that gives Avicenna's proof its distinctive flavor. Post-Humean thinkers might be less generous, refusing to allow a causal postulate. Such a response clearly marks the limitations of Ibn Sīnā's framework of thought, but does not itself hold much promise for the construction of an alternative way of thinking that dispenses with the causal principle.

Even so, dialectically Ibn Sīnā seems to be hemmed in from both sides: Averroes and al-Ghazālī agree in rejecting the notion of conditional or relative necessity on which his synthesis depends. Al-Ghazālī finds incoherent the idea of a contingent effect, the world, which nonetheless never fails to exist. Averroes accepts and insists upon the eternity of the cosmos under natural laws unchanged for eternity, yet finds ludicrous the idea of a necessity that is nonetheless contingent. He rates as a failure Ibn Sīnā's attempt to naturalize and generalize the *kalām* argument from contingency within philosophy, since the linchpin of the argument, the idea of contingency, must be preloaded with the idea of causality if it is to reach even tautologously to the implication of an external cause for the object we see before us, and even then it will give us not a Necessary Being but only a necessary regress of causes. Al-Ghazālī rejects the argument from contingency on the grounds that an eternal world will never be contingent, and Averroes rejects the same argument on the grounds that it is incoherent to call the world contingent, and necessarily inconclusive to seek a cause of its being – although quite unproblematic to seek a first cause for its (eternal) motion.

To make matters worse, Ibn Sīnā's synthesis seems to bring him down squarely on both sides of some of the burning issues of his day, a sure sign of incoherence in a thinker, by many experts' standards. While Averroes, for example, judges Ibn Sīnā to have strayed into indeterminism by applying the *kalām* idea of contingency to the world at large, al-Ghazālī judges eternalist emanationism to be irredeemably deterministic. If "from one only one can come," the world will never make its way clear of the Unity of God, and the God of the Philosophers will remain hopelessly stuck in its own absoluteness. Only a will, Ghazālī argues, can differentiate Absolute simplicity or choose the moment and the features of creation, a will not bound by its own wisdom, but free to range over possibilities no one of which is more likely intrinsically than any other. It is not the case, as the eternalism of Ibn Sīnā and the Aristotelians seems to suppose, that whatever is truly possible must at some time be actual, so that the possible and the actual in the end prove coextensive. Rather, God chooses among alternatives that no external necessity preempts, and if that is not possible, there will be no finite world and no change at all, but everything will stay fixed and fast within God, as is the real, if unintended, implication of Ibn Sīnā's scheme. Here the open future, which Maimonides made the bulwark of his voluntarism with regard to man, and which al-Ghazālī prized as the bulwark of his voluntarism with regard to God, vanishes. Ibn Sīnā, as Gardet writes,

> although he affirms the essential contingency of all that is other than the Necessary Being, leaves no place for existential freedom. The emanation of the world, willed by God, is necessary emanation. The secondary causes are all determined; there is no contingent future. As the text of the *Najāt* puts it, "If any man could know all events and phenomena of earth and heaven and understand their nature, he would know with certainty how all that is to come in the future will come to be."[77]

Marmura accordingly urges that every contingent existent in Avicenna's universe is necessitated,[78] leaving us to wonder what sense there is in the philosopher's calling the effect contingent.

Most of the orientalists who make a profession of observing the outcomes of these discussions and keeping the box score of the successes and failures of the medieval philosophers seem to agree. George Hourani argues that the "Secret of Destiny," discussed by Ibn Sīnā is the truth of determinism, as stated in the very first premise in which Ibn Sīnā lays out the problem of the compatibility of predestination with divine rewards and punishments: "that in the world as a whole and all its parts, above and below, nothing is exempt from God's being the cause of its existence and coming to be, or from God's knowing it and governing it and willing it to come to be, indeed controlling and ruling it all by His knowledge and will."[79] Hourani says that "Ibn Sīnā worked out 'the secret of destiny' by upholding the divine determination very firmly and allegorically reinterpreting Rewards and Punishments."[80] But this analysis ignores Ibn Sīnā's citation of the "first premise" as part of a trilemma and his avowal, immediately after stating it, that this formulation is "general and superficial" and must be taken in the sense that is *properly* applied to God, and not in the sense familiar to *mutakallimūn.* Nor does Hourani's reading tell us why Ibn Sīnā's version of theological determinism is so unacceptable to al-Ghazālī, or why the *kalām* version is so unacceptable to Ibn Sīnā.

Al-Ghazālī's charge is that Ibn Sīnā has improperly delegated activities that belong solely to God. But clearly Ibn Sīnā's intent was to locate some of the causal efficacy and control of events within their proximate causes, whether natural or volitional, without derogation from the ultimate causal responsibility of God, properly understood. This is why he says that one must go beyond a superficial understanding of universal providence and why, at the outset of his little essay on the secret of destiny, he stresses traditions of the Prophet that warn believers away from seeking to probe that secret. He takes these as warnings against superficial understandings, saying in effect that a little knowledge is a dangerous thing. His own analysis of providence is in terms of natural law. Thus, addressing the traditional characterizations of God as knowing, governing, and exercising power, the three Stoic attributes of the Divine that the Epicurean dilemma found incompatible with evil in the world, Ibn Sīnā writes: "What we understand by these descriptions is what properly applies to Him, not what is familiar to the *mutakallimūn* but what can be evidenced and proved. For were it not the case that this world is compounded so as to give rise to goods and ills and to promote both sound and unsound actions in its denizens, the world's order would be imperfect and incomplete."[81] That is, the secret of destiny is that God governs through nature, affording both opportunities and fallibilities.[82] It is in precisely the same sense that Ibn Sīnā addresses the question of punishments and rewards, naturalizing them in Platonic fashion as consequences of the intrinsic character of our actions rather than extrinsic responses to them.[83] In other words, Ibn Sīnā argues that when freedom, naturalism, reward, and punishment are understood in a non-superficial way the apparent conflict among them dissolves. Indeed, no one can be a determinist who does not believe that events are dependent on their causes and thus *contingent* upon the natural or volitional acts that are the determinants referred to in a causal account.

As an Aristotelian, Ibn Sīnā has more confidence than al-Ghazālī does in delegated authority and relative autonomy in finite agents. What al-Ghazālī objects to and Ibn Sīnā insists on is a level of independent control under the overarching power of God. This al-Ghazālī finds contradictory, as a realist about the politics of the age might have found it contradictory to speak of autonomous rulers paying sincere fealty to the Khalif. But Ibn Sīnā had experience of just such rule and believes that the idea of relative necessity, of things made necessary by their causes but still contingent in themselves, is no contradiction but captures the real intent of the idea of divine determination and renders that intent consistent with naturalism regarding the objects in the world and voluntarism regarding human acts. Most of the modern scholarly efforts to pick apart Ibn Sīnā's synthesis are merely echoes of Ghazālī's spirited polemic against it. They are no less infected with Ghazālī's bias, even when they do not share his animus.

Ibn Sīnā does not, of course, adopt the idea that the universe is unchanging, despite the efforts of theologians antipathetic to his views to say that this is what they amount to. Nor is his version of determinism meant to exclude contingency in nature or freedom in human action, but rather to accommodate these givens of experience. The charge that nature is clasped unborn and smothered in God's bosom is at least as readily leveled at Ghazālī as at Avicenna, and when we find a modern interpreter like Michael Marmura writing, "it was the necessitarianism of his system, particularly as it pertained to the concept of divine agency" that "brought his philosophical system into a headlong clash with Islamic theology (*kalām*), more specifically with

Ash'arite *kalām*,"[84] we must place special emphasis on the "particularly." For the Ash'arite objections leveled by Ghazālī are quite selective. They do not address God's control of nature, which in the Ash'arite view is as absolute as the "literal and superficial" reading of theistic determinism would have it. The Ash'arites, in Maimonides' words, believed that each leaf "falls at the decree of God, and it is He who decrees when they will fall and where."[85] Such a view raises all the problems of predestinarianism as well as those of determinism. Its principal defect lies in its reluctance to treat causal determinations as anything but vertical and external. The Avicennan view, by contrast, assigns some level of autonomy to natural causes and volitions. The delegation does not detract from the claim that all events are determined by their causes. Nor does it detract from the ultimate causality of God to say that God made natural objects capable of acting and human beings capable of choosing for themselves. On the contrary, it would be difficult to see *what* could be meant by the idea of creation if it amounted to the claim that God made natural things in general and human beings in particular *incapable* of acting for themselves. The alternative to the external determinism of divine volitions is not and does not pretend to be some form of indeterminism. Rather it is a naturalism which does not jealously guard all power of determination in behalf of God. The God of Avicenna determines things by allowing created beings to determine events for themselves.

As for the Ash'arite claim that there is a contradiction embedded in the notion of an eternal creation, dependent upon God but not originated, this too is disingenuous. For al-Ghazālī, like most Muslim thinkers, adopted the notion of a heavenly kingdom (*malakūt*). He interpreted this idea, as Ibn Sīnā and other Philosophers had, in intellectualist, Platonizing terms. According to al-Ghazālī, this supernal realm contained the archetypes of which all objects in the natural world were mere fleeting shadows, much as the realm of becoming in Plato's myth of the cave is taken to be an ephemeral and shadowy projection of the true being of the Forms.

Traditional Muslim thinkers furnish the *malakūt* or heavenly pleroma with the Pen, the Scales, the Preserved Tablet mentioned textually in the *Qur'ān* as emblems of God's rule. Al-Ghazālī treats these as phenomenal realities encountered on the mystic quest, arising on the horizons of the imagination as the spiritual pilgrim traverses the landscape he must penetrate. They are in fact, as he explains, symbols of God's power, the Hand that holds the Pen.[86] The reality intended by *that* symbol is the Word of God, the Logos identified in

Islam as the Word of Command by which God created and continues to inspire and create. Theologically, this Word is identified with the *Qur'ān*, which every faithful and orthodox Ash'arite Muslim, who clearly opposed the Mu'tazilite heresy of a "created" *Qur'ān*, understood to be the uncreated word and wisdom of God.[87] In adopting such a view, Ash'arites saw no conflict with their radical monotheism and *ex nihilo* creationism.

Like the Christian trinitarians and exponents of Christ as the Divine Logos, whom they debated in the first centuries of Islam, and like the Hellenistic and later Jewish thinkers who devised Platonizing midrashic and later Kabbalistic, neopythagorean, readings of the Biblical references to the age-old or ageless Wisdom in which or by which God created and rules the universe, Muslims needed an intermediary between God's absoluteness and the specific manifestations of His creative power. They assigned this role to the uncreated *Qur'ān*, which became no mere book and indeed no mere attribute of God but the effulgent expression of God, distinguishable from God's absolute Identity, yet expressive of God's very will and wisdom, indeed identical with that will and wisdom. Elaborate structures of theory, ontic schematisms, delicate dogmatisms were devised by Muslim theologians to explain the relationship between God and His uncreated Word, and between that Word and the written or spoken *Qur'ān*, which orthodox theologians, even the most sophisticated, avoided calling created. It would take us far beyond our purpose here to seek to appraise the internal coherence of all such systems, or even to seek to differentiate, as Wolfson does, between what was said and what was believed.[88] For Ash'arite theologians, as Maimonides noted in their heyday, tended to stop up the gaps of belief with formulae that do not always express a clear conceptual content. My sole point philosophically is that the difficulty about a projected or emanated reality that is eternally dependent on the reality of God and yet distinguishable from Him is a problem shared by Ibn Sīnā with the Ash'arites. Abū Ṭālib al-Makkī, the admired Sufi source of al-Ghazālī, clearly distinguishes *malakūt* from divine Ipseity (*Hāhūt*). Avicenna participates in the scheme, in fact supplying al-Ghazālī with his explanation of the relation between *malakūt* as a realm of intellectual realities (sc., the disembodied intellects) and *jabarūt*, the realm of symbols that affect the imagination, the realm in which Ibn Sīnā locates the celestial souls.[89] The real objection of the Ash'arites to Avicenna's scheme is not to its logic or ontology, but to its theology and cosmology, specifically to its placement of the world in the position where orthodox theology, as they conceive it, would have placed the *Qur'ān.*

Like the Neoplatonists, al-Ghazālī too needed a hypostasis to mediate between the eternity of God and the created world. He identified this hypostasis with the Word of God and called it *al-Muṭa'*, he who must be obeyed, assigning to it such divine epithets as *al-Raḥmān*, the Compassionate. Such a move was not unprecedented in Islam, and the Platonizing tendency it represents is very old. It is certainly as old as the doctrine of an uncreated *Qur'ān*, which Muslim theologians and many western scholars believe is older than the Mu'tazilite thesis that God's speech is created.[90] Setting aside questions of dogma and looking at the matter historically and comparatively, monotheistic reliance on such a hypostasis is at least as old as the Christian idea, reflected in the Gospel of John, that God's creative Word both was and was with God, and at least as old as the idea of a primeval Wisdom which was *of* God and yet distinct *from* God. Yet al-Ghazālī's adoption of a Neoplatonic strategy in conceptualizing that hypostasis and putting it to work in addressing what Neoplatonists, by a kind of shorthand, would call the problem of the many and the One did not go unnoticed by Averroes. And as natural as resort to the conceptual apparatus of Neoplatonism would be in such a circumstance, al-Ghazālī's use of it could not fail to appear as reliance on the very conceptual schematism that he was professing to have refuted and rejected.[91]

Returning now to the central charge, of Avicenna's conceptual incoherence. Avicenna's brief is to reconcile the monotheistic doctrine of God's universal governance with the facts of nature and volition, and it is not his determinism but his deference to naturalism and (human) voluntarism that the theologians of Islam found objectionable. One of the games that *mutakallimūn* played was to call one another determinists or fatalists: Voluntarists with respect to man were called fatalists with respect to God because the delegation of human freedom seemed to tie God's hands. And Avicenna, of course, was an intellectualist, whose protestations in behalf of God's will seemed to melt away into a nugatory reduction of that will to the instrument or, indeed, the equivalent of God's understanding.[92]

The philosophic question is whether Ibn Sīnā's union of contingency with necessity was coherent. If it was, it was a major achievement in metaphysics, synthesizing the Aristotelian metaphysics of the givenness of being with the Scripturally based metaphysics that takes being and all its qualifications to be given in quite a different sense –

externally imparted rather than intrinsically presented as a *fait accompli.* I believe the synthesis was successful, and that the rival efforts to pull it apart by committed Peripatetics and sophisticated Ash'arites like al-Ghazālī, who had schooled himself in Ibn Sīnā's writings, were based on the oldest of hermeneutical errors in philosophy – insistence on taking the key terms and divisions of a rival thinker in conventional senses rather than in the sense the philosopher criticized assigned them. Naturally such reading will discover incoherence, as al-Ghazālī calls it, or equivocation, in the label preferred by Ibn Rushd.

Like certain Mu'tazilites, Ibn Sīnā believes that natural actions and indeed human choices take place by a delegated power, that our choices are in our hands and that natural events depend upon, are *contingent upon,* their causes.[93] To hold otherwise would indeed be inconsistent with his determinism, which is naturalistic in precisely this measure, and follows the Aristotelian dictum, as Maimonides will later do, that voluntary agents have more than one course open to them. That, in fact, is *their* nature.[94] But the many causes necessary and sufficient to produce an event need not actually occur. They may be waylaid by other events. The fact that causes spring ultimately from God is no qualification to this recognition of contingency. For contingency within nature is an expression of the efficacy of the causes that shunt aside what might otherwise have happened. Of course we have a logical necessity if we *posit* all the necessary and sufficient causes of a given outcome. But those causes are in fact not a posit but a complex of contingent beings and events. Their contingency is as essential to their causal character as is their necessity. For just as we say that a cause necessitates its effect, we must also say that the effect would not have occurred without its cause: Contingency is as much a feature of the logic of causality as necessity is. And we cannot say which perspective to adopt until we know (or can presume) which precise combinations of causes are given. Predestinarians like the Ash'arites do not disagree with Ibn Sīnā about any of this except in taking exception to the role of nature. For Ibn Sīnā nature is the vehicle of God's governance, and God's determinations do not rob nature of its efficacy or compete with it but impart it. If there is any quarrel here between philosophy and such traditionalist theology it is not between contingency and necessity but between naturalism and supernaturalism. For, as al-Ghazālī confesses, it is the defense of miracles that motivates the Islamic attack on Ibn Sīnā's causal doctrine.[95]

Ibn Sīnā's *Essay on the Secret of Destiny*, as Ivry shows, presumes and does not deny future contingency, when it argues that Scripture helps us mend our ways and live more wisely than we might have.[96] Marmura recognizes the dependence of the contingent upon its complex of causes, but assumes that contingency vanishes, eclipsed by necessity in the end, because Avicenna locates contingency in an effect posited as existent, and therefore necessitated on Ibn Sīnā's account. But this vanishing is an illusion of exactly the sort that made Aristotle suppose all being (sc., the species and the "principal parts" of the cosmos) to be necessary: If we start from a posit, we are confronted immediately with necessity, not ontologically but artifactually: the necessity of the given, the fact that what is must be. This does not imply that what is must have been or that anything intrinsic to its nature or to nature at large is what makes it such that it must be. It is simply the tautology that what is assumed to exist does exist that makes it contradictory to deny the existence of what we have just posited. Causality has nothing to do with it. But, as Aristotle himself urged in his discussion of the Sea Battle, and as the "Second Teacher," al-Fārābī, demonstrated all the more clearly, the fact that what we take to be given must exist does not imply that it always was the case that it must have existed and that under no alternative assumptions was any other outcome possible.[97]

To say that beings or events are dependent on their causes, whether natural or divine, is to say that they are both necessary and contingent, and the achievement of Avicenna's metaphysics in this regard was to show how such a thing could be true of the world at large, by proposing a very natural description of the world as necessary with reference to its causes but contingent in itself. To make this claim required rejecting both the Ash'arite doctrine of the world's radical contingency and the Aristotelian doctrine of the intrinsic necessity of being in the very natures of things, above all in the world at large. It would not have strengthened Ibn Sīnā's position to have allowed for some form of indeterminacy in nature. For his brief was the compatibility of determination with contingency, and the key to his argument was not to choose between the polarized views of his predecessors or to find exceptions to one view or the other but to recognize the artificiality of the polarity. This I express by saying that the necessity Aristotelians tended to generate in nature was a phantom, an artifact of the *supposition* of being and its causes. Whereas the necessity that the Ash'arites polemicized against in the Philosophers at large, including Ibn Sīnā, was a red herring, no more in fact than the image of an unwelcome naturalism that paralleled the supernatural necessity of Ash'arism itself. Ibn Sīnā linked divine and natural necessity but used the *kalām* expedient of analysis, abstracting from the givenness of the given, to overcome the notion that there was anything intrinsic about the necessity of any being but God. Later thinkers would defend or attack a natural necessity distinguishable from the necessity of logic. But Ibn Sīnā preserved the idea that all necessity is logical. He took his cue from al-Fārābī's insightful distinction of necessary implication from inherent necessity, assigning intrinsic necessity of being to God alone.

Ibn Sīnā might have offered a radical alternative to Aristotelian determinism – as the *kalām* did in positing the absoluteness of contingency in this world, insisting on the absolute freedom of God, and relegating necessity to the nexus between the world and God. But such postulational metaphysics never solves any problems. Those who are sensitive to necessities in nature or to freedoms in human action will simply allocate the modal descriptors differently, and philosophy will be none the better. It will become, in fact, a kind of dialectical shouting match, each side seeking higher ground or deeper authority from which to pitch their preconcerted conclusions. The classic conundrums – between relativism and objective truth, or between determinism, contingency, and freedom – will remain unresolved: There is still the question, even in *kalām*, of whether God's act is really free and whether its absolute determinations leave the world's events any less externally determined than the most Democritean materialism. Avicenna's achievement is not in attempting to adjudicate between determinism and indeterminism but in harmonizing a Neoplatonic/Aristotelian determination of nature with the reality of choice, change, and contingency. He does this not by a posit but by recognizing that the ideas of choice, necessity, and contingency are perspectival: From a logical point of view what is necessary depends on what is posited or assumed. The same event is necessary given the assumption of its causes, contingent in abstractive isolation from the assumption of its causes. In this regard, it is a strength rather than a weakness in Ibn Sīnā's position that he thinks of causality in intellectualist, logicist, necessitarian terms. For his argument holds even on the strongest, most logicist account of causal determinism. The more strict his determinism, the clearer is his triumph in showing that God's determinations do not dissolve the world's *intrinsic* contingency. And, of course the intellectualism of Ibn Sīnā's logicism gives him the emanationist nexus by which the emergence of a material world from

God is conceived and the compactness of God's actions with the individual identities of things, as members of their kinds, is maintained. When what is imparted from above is not only essence but existence, then it must be recognized that the contingent existent, the new existent, in creationist terms, will indeed act, and that its act, whether natural or volitional, will be its own. What is caused or created is not that act but the real being that has the power to act.

The outcome of Ibn Sīnā's analysis brought philosophy much closer to the truth and freed it from the tendentious extremes of a world that was divinized on the one hand and pulverized to a vanishing puff of smoke on the other. Ibn Sīnā's synthesis preserved and salvaged what was most right-headed in the two rival views: The world is contingent, dependent on God. Yet the facts of nature are not arbitrary or haphazard. They express the forms of things, which derive ultimately from God's wisdom.

Avicenna does not successfully anatomize the nexus between God and nature. He does not explain how God's wisdom leaves room for real alternatives, a question taken up by Ghazālī, Maimonides, and Leibniz, and in our own century by Bergson and Whitehead. He does leave miracles that violate the course of nature problematic - an outcome which not every thinker even today will take to be a virtue in philosophy. And he does fall into the Aristotelian trap of thinking that whatever is truly possible is at some time actual. The elenchus of Ghazālī against Avicennan causality and his polemic against the eternity of the world do much more for the idea of the open future than the complexity of natural interactions or even the distinction of the given from the virtual or hypothetical possibly can do. It remains problematic whether the idea that things might have been other than as they are can sustain its sense in isolation from the idea of creation that is its source. Leibniz upheld the Avicennan type of intellectualism about natural forms and causes without the full burden of the Platonizing realism that usually came, bidden or unbidden, as its price. But he needed a creationist model as the basis of the conception of alternative possible worlds before he could show that truths can be necessary and indeed analytic without thereby becoming tautologous, before he could show that *not* everything possible is actual and that existing things are necessary only with reference to their causes, and not absolutely as facts that it would be self-contradictory to deny.[98] Leibniz built here on the work of Maimonides, as I have shown.[99] But Maimonides and his predecessor al-Ghazālī built on the work of Avicenna. Without his metaphysical synthesis of a logicist naturalism with the idea of the contingency of creation, their work in restoring the credibility of the idea of creation in a form that accepted the idea of natural necessities and scientific explanations would have been impossible.

Not until Spinoza was a more adequate way found than the Neoplatonism relied on by Avicenna for integrating particulars with the wholeness of God. All Aristotelian philosophers struggled with the idea of relative self-sufficiency and the resultant ambiguity about the substantiality of particulars. Most hesitated to press the Peripatetic idea of self-sufficiency to a demand for absoluteness, lest God become the only substance and we face a choice between isolating the world from God and seeming to annihilate it or fold it into the Godhead by adopting pantheism, with its heavy baggage of ambivalences as to the divinity of natural beings or the mere naturalness of the Divine. The persistent misunderstandings of Spinoza and charges of incoherence against *him* show the wisdom of the medieval thinkers' caution on this score. Avicenna cannot be faulted for not taking a bolder plunge than he did in an age when just to be a philosopher made one suspect of heresy and when survival as a philosopher depended on finding some prince who could square one's philosophic labors with some sort of vision of orthodoxy. But the conception of being itself as both contingent and necessary, contingent intrinsically but necessary with reference to its causes, was a breakthrough for philosophy, built on and fruitfully employed by latercomers, but in its own simple terms not to be surpassed. And that was all we wanted to show.

ii

The second line of criticism we must consider comes from another age than Avicenna's and is not directed individually at him but at all theists of a type to which Avicenna paradigmatically belongs. It is perhaps best voiced in Hume's *Dialogues Concerning Natural Religion.* There Demea, the spokesman of a kind of pious fideism opposed as well to Cleanthes' rationalism as to Philo's skepticism, argues that it is not the beauty and perfection of nature but the sense of our own inadequacy that teaches us of God. "It is my opinion," he urges, "that each man feels in a manner the truth of religion within his own breast; and from a consciousness of his imbecility and misery, rather than from any reasoning, is led to seek protection from that Being, on whom he and all nature is dependent."[100] The natural source of natural religion on this account is our creaturely sense of helplessness, to which Philo adds our sense of sin and depravity, the weakness of our condition and inadequacy of our nature, the sense of the vanity of all merely human attainments and the instability of all merely natural strengths. Hume introduces these testimonies from the natural history of religion by way of prelude to the problem of evil, which he deploys as a riposte to the argument from design. But, taken together as characterizations of the religious impulse, Cleanthes' appeal to the wisdom shown in nature and Demea's appeal to the sense of creaturely inadequacy form a powerful indictment of the line of argument that Avicenna puts forward.

For religions in general and natural theologians in particular seem constantly to shift their stance, now arguing that the beauty and perfection of the world make manifest its dependence on an Author of supreme wisdom and goodness, now subtly, almost imperceptibly shifting to the denunciation of man and nature, seeking to spring up to the reality of God not from the evidence of His work but from the contrast between natural and absolute perfection, arguing from the impermanence, conflicts, inchoateness of life and all things natural, to the necessity of a counterpart to all this, a being in which consummate perfection is realized. Thus Thomas Aquinas combines the optimistic view of the world as God's handiwork with a Platonizing argument "from the gradation to be found in things." As if to add irony, Thomas' appeal from relative to absolute perfection is sandwiched between his argument from providential design and his own version of Avicenna's argument from contingency. To an unfriendly eye this may seem to say that the world both is and is not good enough to bespeak divinity. Finitude reflects divine infinity yet, at the same time somehow, by its very inadequacy, proves there is a God. The world is perfect enough to bespeak a perfect maker, but imperfect enough to need that maker's help; causes are effective enough to explain their proximate effects, but insufficient to constitute a self-sustaining system. Such apparent waffling takes many forms, from a mere wish or dialectic of the emotions in the quest for meaning, to Kant's appeal to God as the sole possible bestower of the immortality that morals to him seem to demand. The very fear of death and sense of our own mortality and unworthiness seem here to ground the claim to deathlessness and sempiternal perfectibility as a counterpart to the all too easily conceded incompleteness and unfairness of this human life in this world. Even within the argument from providence or design the same ambivalence is felt. For the suggestion is plain that nature does not care for itself, and the premise is clearly stated that it does not design or plan itself, not solely by its own means. It has even been claimed that the same dialectic underlies the appeal of the ontological argument. The same ambivalence or ambiguity is clearly present too in the Platonic drive to transcendence of change and temporality – for which read aging and death: The very absence of constancy, reality, or truth in changeable nature is taken as clear proof that these values *must* be real *elsewhere*; yet almost in the same breath it is claimed that we do have knowledge, that being itself animates the realm of becoming, that the world is beautiful and good and wisely made, despite its fragility, and that its beauty can never (as romantics might pretend) merely consist in its fragility.

Ibn Sīnā is not as wrapped up in the sense of sin and guilt as pietist Muslim and Christian authors often urge one ought to be, but he is very conscious of the changeability of things, and his appeal to a necessary being as the counterpart of the world's contingency belongs to that family of appraisals of existence that seems to project our evanescence against the backdrop of the cosmos as if to discover an alternative beyond it. The difficulty is not so much in the arbitrariness of the projection – for the denial of any absolute perfection can be just as projective. But coupled with the discovery of the marks of divine goodness in nature, the confession of nature's inadequacy rings hollow. The two claims seem to clash and compete for the same ground, as though theists had found a failsafe dialectic, pleading the world's perfection as long as the evidence or the mood holds up, then shifting their tack to argue from imperfection. When Ibn Sīnā treats being as necessary in relation to its Cause but contingent in itself, is he not just shifting his sidedrape? Where the Neoplatonists seemed to their adversaries to have made nature transparent, letting divine light shine through, and the creaturely mood of monotheistic thinkers often makes nature seem opaque, scattering God's light against nature's limitations, Ibn Sīnā seems to want to have it both ways, making nature, as it were, translucent, so that the light shines through, but not in its purity, leaving objects contingent, friable, but somehow not impervious to form, goodness, understanding.

The answer to this criticism, if it is a criticism, is that translucency models nature's relation to God better than either transparency or opacity, captures the truth more adequately than the extreme characterizations, which are indeed the products of moods. Plato, Plotinus, and Pascal all sought to express the middlingness of the human and the natural condition: We are not angels or beasts but somehow in between – neither beasts nor gods, in our natural state in human society, as Aristotle argued; neither irredeemable nor self-redeemed. The existentialists take the same appraisal from Pascal. Each being, as Ibn Sīnā states the case, bears within itself its little measure of adequacy, neither absolute nor self-sufficing, but not nugatory, not to be despised. That is the natural condition, of which the human condition is just a special case.

In Giraudoux's *Amphitryon 38*, when Hermes disguises Zeus for the seduction of the faithful Alcmene by making the god indistinguishable from her husband, Hermes tells Zeus that no mere disguise can conceal divinity; the god must dim his radiance. To appear mortal he must make himself seem to die a bit at every moment. He complies, and as the stagelights dim Hermes judges the disguise almost perfect. Just one thing is missing: Even as Zeus seems to be dying almost invisibly but continually, he must constantly think at the back of his mind, but everpresently: "I shall never die!" Then the disguise is perfect; Zeus has attained the aspect of humanity. This semi-dim light of nature is the one in which we live. The full light of God's presence, as *Exodus* teaches, is too bright for us, but we do not live in darkness either. Both ecstasy and anguish, each in their own way, seem to overstate the case. The middling condition is where we must take our start, not as a theorem to be proved but as the given to be accounted for if philosophy is to earn its bread.

False consciousness in a case like this is shown not by chiaroscuro but by the luffing of the canvas when sharp moodswings shift the sails violently from one tack to the other, now celebrating the very conditions that a moment ago were damned. It is the arbitrary transposition of moods into metaphysics – whether poetry or mysticism is its excuse – that abuses the power of abstraction to generalize our judgments; and the test of such abuse is the inner instability or momentariness of the outcomes. It is false art to gild the lily and just as false to paint bismuth on a maiden's cheek. Decadence needs no help to do the first, and death will do the latter soon enough. Truthfulness in a descriptive metaphysic will respect the mixed character of our being, and the speckled and spotted coloration of all natural projects. If there is any false or deceiving posture in metaphysics, it is equally represented by the rosy optimism of Pangloss and the dreary sourness of Schopenhauer. For the two are of a piece, dialectical counterparts, psychological and ideological moodswings that not only falsify by their hyperbole but also undermine their own credibility, and even psychologically prepare the way for one another. For who can maintain blind-eyed ebullience without eventually realizing his own ridiculousness; and who can sustain, *Angst*, anger, and alienation without eventually bursting out laughing at his own silliness? Ibn Sīnā's account means only to give us the conditionedness of being that others have acknowledged as the dependence of the *for itself* on the *in itself*, or the entanglement in embodiment of all that is finitely transcendent.

The real bite of the objection against seeking to combine contingency with an internalized necessity lies in the charge that all the bases seem to be covered, no countercase allowed for: All that we see either basks in or throws back the light. So no exception can be found to Ibn Sīnā's account. Nothing can refute it, if it constantly shifts weight from one foot to the other. And what is irrefutable is not false but vacuous, as Karl Popper taught us, if we did not intuitively sense it in confronting many an artful alibi. Shifting weight is bad faith in a case like this, counting only favorable evidence and reversing fields to a polar opposite among hypotheses when the evidence runs unfavorably. But that is not Ibn Sīnā's strategy in fact. His aspectual account finds a complementarity, *not a conflict* between necessity and contingency. Their apparent conflict is an artifact of the conventional thinking he seeks to overcome. Contingency and necessity in nature are opposite sides of the same coin. Its name is finitude.

As for Ibn Sīnā's thesis being a hypothesis for all seasons, that charge comes with the territory in any metaphysical undertaking. If the goal is a general account of being as such, then leaving more than minimal room for countercases is not a virtue but a weakness. There must be some conditions under which a theory does not hold, if the theory is to say anything and in any way distinguish the world of which it is true from an alternative in which it is not. But Ibn Sīnā's thesis meets that test. A world without events, without causality, or without beings other than God would be one in which his argument did not hold. So would a world in which nothing exists. Admittedly these are extreme alternatives, but they suffice to show that Avicenna is not speaking in tautologies or making claims that under no conditions could be false. His account of being will be true in any world that contains determinate, differentiated entities governed by causal principles. That includes most but not all possible worlds. It also gives us a very clear idea of what Avicenna's theory intends and what its limitations are. The scope of the theory is metaphysical, as its author announced from the beginning. It belongs neither to natural science nor to logic, and so it is neither corrigible in the way that empirical hypotheses are, nor irrefutable in the way that tautologies are, but applicable to all and only collections of beings whose essence does not require their existence, including any worlds that have such a system as the one that we call nature.

Comprehensiveness rather than corrigibility is the first virtue here. If rival comprehensive accounts are truly vacuous there will be not much to distinguish them. But in Avicenna's case he has resolved an apparent conflict between two such rivals, finding complementarity where partisan advocates found (and still find) only conflict and the seeds of conceptual confusion. That is an achievement that can set one comprehensive account of being apart from others.

I think the charge to be constructed from the Humean observation of the dialectic of our moods about this world and its Source would strike Avicenna if his strategy were one of playing off a kind of sublimated despondency against a kind of hyper-ventilated *Schwärmerei*, the linked emotions that Muslim mystics call elation or inflation, and its opposite, contraction, anguish, or constraint, which they typically label constipation.[101] But Avicenna's achievement is not to play upon such a dialectic but to overcome it. He does this not by the ancient Skeptics' strategy of dismissing the metaphysical impulse. He does not take that impulse as a mere symptom of one or the other all-coloring mood. Rather, his tactic is to synthesize the opposites conceptually and allow the qualifications truthfulness demands of both rival but often hyperbolic accounts. The plain intent is to qualify and mitigate them into reasonableness. The result is not the incoherent affirmation that life and the existence of all things are at once necessary and impossible, or both unutterably perfect and insupportably lacking, but that existence as we know it combines finitude with a measure of transcendence, that the claims beings make in their own names are sound, within their limits, yet point beyond those limits to a Ground of Being that utterly transcends all such limits. It is not in providing conflicting stories to account for incompatible bits of evidence that Ibn Sīnā's achievement lies, but in showing that the evidence is not really contradictory and that a single story, overcoming some of the biases of its rivals and incorporating some of their best insights, can make better sense than they did of what we see - a world that is both necessary and contingent, but in neither case absolutely so.

iii

Our third question about Avicenna's synthesis arises at a metalevel beyond that of our second. The Ghazālīan objections that we first considered take up Ibn Sīnā's theses directly, contesting their claim to truth. The Humean objections touch the very project and enterprise of attempting a comprehensive account of reality, challenging the nuances of a descriptive account on the grounds that the effort to accommodate the pied coloration of being makes any general account of it irrefutable and so empty. But a third line of objection seeks to reduce the Avicennan characterization of being to a mere projection of linguistic usage. My friend and colleague the late Angus Graham, a brilliant Sinologist, raised the issue some years ago, as a test of the Whorfian claim that "the grammatical structure of language guides the formation of philosophical concepts." Graham notes that "a verb 'to be' which serves both as copula and as indicator of existence is almost confined to Indo-European languages," that "a concept of Being combining essence and existence is confined to philosophies developed in languages of the Indo-European family," and that "although the first language of Western philosophy was Greek, its main stream passed through Semitic languages (Syriac, Arabic, Hebrew) before returning to Indo-European languages (scholastic Latin, French, English, German)." Strikingly, "in the two major philosophical traditions which developed outside this family, Arabic *wujūd* and Chinese *yu* are not 'being' but existence . . . . It was in Arabic, which sharply separates the existential and copulative functions, that the distinction between existence and essence emerged."[102] The problem here for Ibn Sīnā is that we must ask whether his metaphysical stance was not a genuine contribution to universal philosophy but a mere symptom of Arabic linguistic usage, arising from the inaccessibility in Arabic of the metaphysical concepts that seemed natural in Greek. Is Avicenna's work in metaphysics not so much a contribution as a manifestation of the inevitable closedness of all cultures and linguistic complexes to one another?

What I want to show now is that Graham's observations do not support a strictly deterministic or reductionistic account of the emergence of the Avicennan distinction between essence and existence; indeed, the origin and fate of Ibn Sīnā's metaphysics provides a clear and rather decisive countercase to the familiar claims of linguistic determinism and reduction. Graham notes that Aristotle does distinguish *what* from *whether* in the *Posterior Analytics* (89b), although "it costs him some trouble to make this plain," since he needs to make clear that he is talking about absolute existence and not just a thing's *being*, say white, and has no Greek term by which to do so. To this we can add that writers of Arabic who were committed to the Aristotelian metaphysics did not find the Aristotelian interpretation of existence in terms of essence problematic or inaccessible in the least. Thus when Aristotle says (in *Metaphysics* Zeta 1, 1028a 10 ff.) that the first among the senses of being is that which tells us what a thing is, and when he goes on to use not only the distinction among the categories but his own distinction between what and whether to argue that predicates like "sitting" and "walking" seem to imply the existence of a substance, since they cannot exist by themselves, Averroes, who was a native speaker of Arabic, an Arab by birth, a *qāḍī* and the scion of a long line of *qāḍīs* of his native Cordova, reports the passage faithfully and makes no attempt to add "existence" to the various senses of "being," where Aristotle, as Graham notes, had not distinguished such a sense.

From the perspective of Aristotle's philosophy it would be a serious error to distinguish an existential sense of the verb to be. It would vitiate Aristotle's original project of analyzing "being" to discover just what it means to say that a thing is. If there were, besides essential and accidental predication and the "being" noted under all the diverse categories, an additional *existential* sense of "being," then by Aristotle's lights that too would be subject to analysis, much like the original one, leading to an infinite regress. What I find critical in evaluating Graham's Whorfian hypothesis is that Averroes seems not at all tempted to introduce an existential sense, despite his being an Arab and having read Avicenna. He simply acknowledges the Aristotelian divisions between substance and accident, actual, and potential, one and many, and goes on to discuss the Aristotelian analysis of substance. As Ibn Rushd paraphrases Aristotle: "The word 'being' (*mawjūd*!) may indicate the essence of a given substance or the substance itself, or it may signify some accident in this free-standing particular," a quality, quantity, or other category, answering the questions "where?", or "when?", and so forth. Substance is the primary category, for it makes no sense to tell what condition a thing is in if we do not know what that thing is, and this is the question that substance terms answer, signifying the essence of a thing, assigning it to its species.[103] There is no prior existential sense.

Graham writes: "when Aristotle observes that definition shows what a thing is but not 'that it is,' which is known not by definition but by demonstration, it is convenient and sometimes hardly avoidable to translate *hoti esti* as 'existence,' although it certainly embraces not only the existence of *X* but its being in fact what it is defined as being." But this shows not that Aristotle was confined by the language he used, but quite the contrary, that he bent that language to his purposes, retaining the consistency of his conception of being even where the language he was using offered thin resources for making the distinctions and formulating the implications of theorems he had enunciated. The same is true of Avicenna. Granting Graham's claim that "in Arabic there is no convenient word" combining the existential and copulative functions, the fact remains that writers of Arabic, including al-Fārābī and the translators of Greek works, devised paraphrastic ways around that feature of the language they were using and used its resources to create such terms as "thatness" (*'anniyya*), "whatness" (*māhiyya*), and even "isness" (*huwiyya*), making the work of the scholastics who wrote in Latin much easier, by laying the basis for a flexible terminology. The need for artifice in Arabic actually supplemented the ontological resources of the Indo-European languages. But philosophers like Ibn Sīnā and Ibn Rushd use the Arabic coinages as naturally as we use terms like 'essence' and as variably with respect to their diverse metaphysical commitments.

"It is a misplaced compliment to credit al-Fārābī and Ibn Sīnā with the discovery of the ontological difference between essence and existence," Graham writes, including al-Fārābī because of the now discredited attribution of some of Ibn Sīnā's writings to him; "it was impossible for an Arab to confuse them, although he might, as did Ibn Rushd, choose for reasons of his own to identify them."[104] Now I find it a striking fact in this context that neither al-Fārābī nor Ibn Sīnā was an Arab, and neither spoke Arabic as his mother tongue. Al-Fārābī was apparently descended from an officer of the Turkic forces imported by Islamic states; and Ibn Sīnā, we have noted, was a Persian. I think a case can be made that al-Fārābī's special interest in languages and cultures does reflect his background as an ethnic outsider to the Arabo-Islamic culture into which he was assimilated. But it also reflects the fact that some of his teachers were Christian logicians, and it cannot fail to reflect the universalistic content of the philosophical materials he studied and the inner dynamic of the disciplines themselves.[105] As for Ibn Sīnā, it is tempting to attribute the synthesis he created to the hybrid Arabo-Persian culture in which he lived. But many of his contemporaries read the *Metaphysics* of Aristotle and did not make of it what he did. The emphasis Avicenna gave to contingency springs not from the Arabic language but from the dialectics of *kalām* and ultimately from the Book of Genesis, where the verb to be is never discussed and the idea of the radical contingency of being is conveyed without much recourse to abstract vocabulary.

The *Qur'ān* contains the remarkable description of God as "The Originator of the heavens and the earth, who when He decreeth a thing He simply telleth it BE, and it is."[106] But this in itself does not determine that the imperative BE is used here in a discrete existential sense, as Graham's complaints about the lack of such a sense in Greek demand. For in the same *surah* of the *Qur'ān* God also curses faithless Israelites "Be ye apes, lowly slinking";[107] and elsewhere he commands Moses, "Be of the thankful,"[108] using the same verb in the same form but with the sense of the copula, which linguists so often say is not readily expressed in Arabic. The fact is that the copula is generally suppressed in Semitic languages in the present tense indicative. But it is expressed in other tenses and moods, and when the sense of a sentence demands the present tense a pronoun takes its place wherever necessary to obviate ambiguity. In *Exodus* God says I AM THAT I AM and calls Himself I AM. This is hardly normal usage, yet no one took it to be nonsense, and the absence of a verb as copula (for here the relative pronoun *that* couples the two occurrences of the first person singular verb to be) does not prevent some readers from attempting to reduce the sense of God's self-affirmation to a predicative one, taking it to mean "I will be what (or as) I shall be," i.e., "I shall do as I please" – as though so striking an affirmation as the Hebrew presents were needed for so prosaic and self-betraying a claim.

Averroes adopted the Aristotelian metaphysical scheme because he found it convincing, despite the difficulties of expressing it in Arabic, just as Aristotle held to that scheme as consistently as he could, despite his own difficulties in expressing a conception of being that is by no means always made obvious by the usages of any natural language and that certainly was not the view of any Greek before him. Ibn Sīnā devised an alternative to that scheme, not by molding Aristotle to the usages of Arabic, nor even by following the contingency doctrine of the *kalām*, but by discovering how to redefine the terms of Aristotle's metaphysics to allow the consistency of the contingency of being with the necessity of causation. Which is to say, the metaphysics of Ibn Sīnā, like the metaphysics of Aristotle, is the product of philosophical inquiry and conviction, not of linguistic or historic accident and not of cultural affiliation.

Van Den Bergh showed in the mid-1950s that all the materials of Ibn Sīnā's synthesis were contained in Aristotle.[109] But he overstated his case for a historic reduction when he further described Avicenna's argument as "implied in Aristotle's whole system." On the contrary, Aristotle carefully avoids the notion that being at large is contingent, and his system militates (not always with perfect consistency, as Van Den Bergh showed comprehensively[110]) toward discovering an *inner* necessity in things, in their very being, which is for Aristotle their being *what* and ultimately *as* they are. Naturally in writings as comprehensive, as faithful to experience, and as sensitive to usage as Aristotle's are, the *elements* of Ibn Sīnā's theory would be present. But Averroes uses much the same materials to construct his refutation of Ibn Sīnā's argument and remains far closer to the heart of Aristotle's thinking. A more accurate appraisal is that of Ibn Sīnā himself, who held that Aristotle offered no such proof as his although such an argument was present virtually in Aristotle's writings.[111] Had Ibn Sīnā followed Aristotle's metaphysics faithfully, he would no more have derived the synthesis of contingency and necessity from those elements than Aristotle himself did when he wove them into quite a different pattern.

In clarifying the linguistic issue, Fadlou Shehadi rightly mentions the Persian Avicenna scholar Soheil Afnan before citing Graham's paper, since Afnan was a source for Graham and actually referred to "the complete absence of the copula" in Semitic languages, saying that these languages are "still unable to express the thought adequately."[112] Here the deterministic claim seems to rest on the idea that the absence of a word with a given linguistic function or combination of functions in a given language entails the impossibility of performing or combining those functions. This, of course, is fallacious reasoning, even apart from the falsity of the claim that Semitic languages lack a copula or do not conjoin an existential with a copulative function in the semantics of that word. We have seen in our Qur'anic citations that the verb to be, which is very much present in Hebrew and in Arabic, can perform copulative and existential functions indiscriminately. Al-Ghazālī can write, of his ecstatic awakening, quite naturally in Arabic:

> It was, what it was don't ask me to say;
> Think the best, but don't make me explain it away.

The fact is that many ways can be found to express existence or predication and attribution in Semitic and in all other natural languages.

But turning to the issue that most concerns Graham, Shehadi writes:

> It is often said in contrasting Greek and English that the existential-predicative distinction marks the "is" but not the "*esti.*" But

> what is meant primarily about the Arabic separation is that predication, in other than the cases of the nominal sentence, can be expressed by one set of words, while the usual way to indicate existence is with words formed from a different root. So unlike English, in the contrast with Greek, it is not a separation of functions for the same word, but an allotting of the different functions to different words. And this seems to be a more radical kind, that retains the distinction of linguistic family types. This, one might contend, makes the crucial difference since the Arabic separation yields terms for existence from the existential side, and terms for essence from the predicative side, with perhaps no promising linguistic resource for expressing the abstract 'being' which is not reducible to either essence or existence.

But, as Shehadi explains, "In Arabic . . . each of the to-be-type words can perform (or was made to perform) both the predicative and the existential functions." So were the pronouns *huwa* and *hiya*, the interrogative/indefinite *mā*, and the affirmative particles *inna* and *anna.* Shehadi concludes "it would now be too stringent to say that such Arabic philosophers (e.g., al-Fārābī and Ibn Sīnā) could not escape making the ontological distinction between essence and existence." Isḥaq ibn Ḥunayn's medieval translation of *Metaphysics* Delta 7 says that it is *huwiyya* that has multiple senses, "which could be said to derive from the copula *huwa* . . . from the copulative-essence side" of the supposed division of terms. But "Ibn Rushd in his commentary prefers the term *'al-mawjūd'*. . . and this, it would be said, comes from the existential side." In fact, "each term . . . is proposed for *all* the senses distinguished by Aristotle." And if challenged on the choice of rendering, as Shehadi rightly argues, the philosopher will answer that the prevalent or common meaning of the term may be as you say, "but in philosophy it means . . . and he would refer to the four senses of Aristotle."[113] In Avicenna's case, those senses are modified to allow for the recognition of contingency at the very root of being, which Aristotle himself had so assiduously excluded. Like most philosophers, Ibn Sīnā followed the practice so well stated by Humpty Dumpty in *Through the Looking Glass*: "When *I* use a word it means just what I choose it to mean – neither more nor less . . . . The question is which is to be the master – that's all."

What distinguishes natural languages as such from the formalism of artificial languages is the protean flexibility we enjoy in invoking (and discarding) categorial schemes, using alternative strategies to set our categorial foundations where we please. As I have argued elsewhere, natural languages do not bear with them a uniform and mandatory structural framework or system of metaphysical axioms, let alone an ideology or "world view."[114] Averroes, a native speaker of Arabic, adopted the metaphysics of Aristotle and gave it in some ways a clearer exposition than it ever had in Greek. Ibn Sīnā, who was not a native speaker of Arabic, could combine the *kalām* metaphysics of contingency, which many Arabic writers rejected, with a modified Aristotelianism that many Aristotelians and *mutakallimūn* assumed to be inconsistent with it. It took an al-Ghazālī to articulate just where the incompatibility might lie and how deep it went. More conventional thinkers saw simply a hostility and suspicion between two traditions; or, if they were philosophically inclined, perhaps sought a vague accommodation that drank at both fountains but paid little attention to the deeper issues of coherence and synthesis. Avicenna saw the issues clearly but did not accept the purported inconsistency of necessity with contingency – provided that one did not use metaphysics to paint over the very conception of being with the *postulate* of necessity.

Historically speaking, Avicenna's synthesis did not hold up, at least not in the form he gave it. The reason for its ultimate failure of widespread acceptance was the same as the reason for its philosophic/scientific reputability in its more immediate intellectual environment, the fact that it was coupled with a rejection of the world's temporal creation. As a matter of policy or politics, this rejection was a mistake in the longer run. Creation was a symbol essential to all three monotheistic faiths and more capable than Ibn Sīnā knew of sustaining those faiths and of being sustained by them. Even philosophically, Ibn Sīnā's decision to jettison creation may have been an error, since it was the idea of creation that gave meaning, as Maimonides argued, to the philosopher's idea of contingency, and thereby gave content, as al-Ghazālī argued earlier, to Ibn Sīnā's theism.[115] But if it was a mistake, it was a principled mistake, part of Avicenna's determination to follow where he thought he saw the argument lead and not to reduce philosophy to ideology or *kalām*. What counted most for him in this regard, ironically enough, was the determination not to exclude matter from the absolute creative act of God. For Ibn Sīnā saw matter as an eternal counterpart of eternal form; to make creation temporal would have meant reverting to *formatio mundi* rather than absolute creation. Formless matter would lie warehoused in indeterminacy for unmeasurable eons, awaiting an arbitrary decision of God's to act. And God's role would have been reduced to that of a mere starter of the race rather than a continually active sustainer of being in all its aspects. It was such reasoning that led Avicenna to formulate his version of the cosmological argument in a manner that proved perturbing and unacceptable, although fascinating to his successors. Yet, in a form other than the one he gave it, rejoined with the idea of creation, Ibn Sīnā's idea of the world as contingent in itself but necessitated through its causes, all the way back to the highest Cause of causes, did survive through the work of al-Ghazālī, Maimonides, and Thomas to become the cornerstone of monotheistic philosophy in the west.

NOTES

1 Abū 'l-Ma'ālī al-Juwaynī, *Kitāb al-Irshād*, ed. J.-D. Luciani (Paris: E. Leroux, 1938) 2.

2 *Irshād*, chs. 3, 4, 8.

3 See L. Johnson, "God or Nature? Philoponus on Generability and Perishability," in R. Sorabji, ed., *Philoponus and the Rejection of Aristotelian Science* (Ithaca: Cornell University Press, 1987) 179–96.

4 *Galeni Compendium Timaei Platoni*, ed. P. Kraus and R. Walzer (London: Warburg Institute, 1951) Arabic, 3–5, quoting *Timaeus* 28C.

5 See H. Davidson, *Proofs for Eternity, Creation, and the Existence of God in Medieval Islamic and Jewish Philosophy* (New York: Oxford University Press, 1987) 154–212; Wm. Lane Craig, *The Kalām Cosmological Argument* (London: Macmillan, 1979).

6 *Dāwūd al-Muqammiṣ's Twenty Chapters*, ed. S. Strousma (Leiden: Brill, 1989) 92–122.

7 *A Muslim Philosopher on the Soul and its Fate: Al-Āmirī's Kitāb al-Amad 'alā 'l-Abad*, ed. E. Rowson (New Haven: American Oriental Society, 1988) 78.

8 Jerusalem Letter, ed. Tibawi, *IQ* 9 (1965) 80 ll. 24–9.

9 Al-Fārābī writes:

> some bodies, like animals, are observed to have an origin, and the mind transposes 'having an origin' from plants and animals and concludes that the heavens and the stars have an origin . . . if it is known that the animals are originated and that they are like the heavens in being contingent and it is true that everything contingent is created then the shift is sound . . .

See K. Gyekye, "Al-Fārābī on the Logic of the Arguments of the Muslim Philosophical Theologians," *JHP* 27 (1989) 135–43, esp. 140–1, citing al-Fārābī's *Kitāb al-Mukhtaṣar al-Ṣaghīr fī 'l-Manṭiq 'alā ṭarīq al-mutakallimīn*, "A Brief Exposition of the Logic of the Philosophical Theologians," ed. M. Turker, *Revue de la Faculté des langues, d'histoire, et de géographie de l'Université d'Ankara* 16 (1958) 266 ll. 16–

20; cf. N. Rescher's tr., as *Al-Fārābī's Short Commentary on Aristotle's Prior Analytics* (Pittsburgh: University of Pittsburgh Press, 1963) 94 and A.I. Sabra's review in *JAOS* (1985) 241–3. Al-Fārābī's concern is that the theologians take scriptural poetry too literally, reading the metaphor of artisanship into the metaphysics of nature. His discontent with the idea of contingency in the elements of the cosmos is evident as well in his polemic against Philoponus; see M. Mahdi, "Alfarabi against Philoponus," *JNES* 26 (1967) 233–60.

10 *Qur'ān* 6:1, 7:54, 9:36, 15:27, 15:85, 16:17, 22:5, 23:14, 27:60, 35:11, 36:80, 37:150, 39:6, 40:67; 43:9, 55:15, 75:38, 77:20, 96:2, etc.

11 See The Presidency of Islamic Researches IFTA, eds., *The Holy Qur'ān* (Medina: King Fahd Holy Qur'ān Printing Complex, 1410 A.H.=1989) 114–15; cf. *Qur'ān* 3:2, 20:111.

12 *Kalām* theorists made a dogma of continuous creation, sometimes relying on *Qur'ān* 2:255, "He sleepeth not, nor doth he slumber," as a proof-text validating God's eternal activity, and making the idea of God's sabbath rest theologically problematic; see Roger Arnaldez on al-Ṭabarī in "Influences Juives dans la Pensée Musulmane," *Recherches de Science Religieuse* 66 (1978) 580. It is doubtful that the Qur'anic "protestation" is "the origin of the doctrine of continuous creation." For that doctrine, like *kalām* ideas of an eternal *Qur'ān*, responds to the challenge voiced in arguments like those of Proclus and Simplicius that if God is a Creator essentially creation must be eternal. Muḥammad was innocent of such arguments, but the thinkers of the *kalām* were much taken up with them; and they had counterparts in Jewish and Christian ideas of God's eternal wisdom/word/act, ideas that go back at least as far as Philo.

13 *Dalālāt al-Ḥā'irīn* I 76, ed. Munk, 1.127b ll. 8–18; see my *Rambam: Readings in the Philosophy of Moses Maimonides* (New York: Viking, 1976; reissued Los Angeles: Gee Tee Bee, 1985).

14 See Joseph Owens, *The Doctrine of Being in the Aristotelian Metaphysics* (Toronto: Pontifical Institute of Medieval Studies, 1978); Daniel Frank, *The Arguments 'From the Sciences,' in Aristotle's* Peri Ideon (New York: Peter Lang, 1984); cf. Edward Booth, *Aristotelian Aporetic Ontology in Islamic and Christian Thinkers* (Cambridge: Cambridge University Press, 1983) and my review, *PEW* 37 (1987) 191–201.

15 See *Posterior Analytics* I 2, 71b; cf. *Generation of Animals* II 6, 742b 18–33.

16 See *Metaphysics* Alpha, 984a–85a, *De Anima* I 2, 405a 14–17; *Poetica* 15, 145b 1.

17 See S. Sambursky, *Physics of the Stoics* (London: Routledge, 1959) 1–48.

18 The Greek is *prohodos, Enneads* V 2.1.

19 See D.B. MacDonald, *EI* 1.305 and the discussion in Emil Fackenheim, "The Possibility of the Universe," in A. Hyman, ed., *Essays in Medieval Jewish and Islamic Philosophy* (New York: Ktav, 1977) 48.

20 Cf. Charles Kahn, "Why Existence Does not Emerge as a Distinct Concept in Greek Philosophy," in P. Morewedge, ed., *Philosophies of Existence: Ancient and Medieval* (New York: Fordham University Press, 1982) 7–17: "existence in the modern sense becomes a central concept in philosophy only in the period when Greek ontology is radically revised in the light of a metaphysics of creation: that is to say, under the influence of Biblical religion" (p. 7). Kahn answers the question of his title by analyzing "the" Greek idea of being in terms of truth. But Plato, although Greek, does not share Aristotle's views about the locus and character of being, as Paul Seligman's trenchant essay in the same volume

(pp. 17–32) rightly argues. Ironically, Plato does tend to identify being with truth, and Van Den Bergh even blames Aristotle's understanding of being in terms of truth for Avicenna's very *un*-Aristotelian linking of existence with contingency, *TT* 2.102–3. The crucial difference between Aristotle and Avicenna, of which Greek references to truth and knowledge are only symptomatic, is that Aristotle starts from the world as it is, as a given, whereas Avicenna (like Plato) looks at the world also in terms of its virtuality. It is this sense of contingency that the scriptural accounts foster.

21 See Saadiah, *ED* III 2, ed. J. Kafih (Jerusalem: Sura, 1970); cf. Spinoza, *Ethics* I, Prop. 5, ed. Carl Gebhardt (Heidelberg: Carl Winter, 1972).

22 See Maimonides, *Code, Hilkhot Teshuvah*, 5.1–4; *Guide to the Perplexed* III, 17.5, ed. S. Munk (Paris, 1856–; repr. Osnabrück: Zeller, 1964) 3.35a; cf. my "Determinism and Freedom in Spinoza, Maimonides and Aristotle," in F. Schoeman, ed., *Responsibility, Character and the Emotions* (Cambridge: Cambridge University Press, 1987) 107–64.

23 See, for example, Saadiah, *ED*, tr. Rosenblatt, 21, 130, 176, 270, and esp. 337–40, 348–9.

24 See my "Rāzī's Myth of the Fall of the Soul and its Function in his Philosophy," in G. Hourani, ed., *Essays in Islamic Philosophy and Science* (Albany: SUNY Press, 1975) 25–40.

25 See M. Mahdi, "Alfarabi against Philoponus," *JNES* 26 (1967) 233–60.

26 See my "Three Meanings of the Idea of Creation," in D. Burrell and B. McGinn, eds, *God and Creation* (Notre Dame: University of Notre Dame, 1990) 85–113; "The Rational and Irrational in Medieval Jewish and Islamic Philosophy," in S. Biderman and B. Scharfstein, *Rationality in Question* (Leiden: Brill, 1989) 93–118.

27 See Farhang Zabeeh, tr., *Avicenna's Treatise on Logic*; Part One of *Danesh Nameh Alai* (The Hague: Nijhoff, 1971) 38–9.

28 In Plotinus and Proclus too the highest causes are responsible for the existence and not merely for the motion of what lies below them, but never is it claimed that lower existence is contingent in the sense that in absolute terms it need never have existed. It is here that Ibn Sīnā parts company with the Neoplatonic tradition in a direction defined by the *kalām* reverence for the Scriptural idea of creation.

29 See *Shifā'*, Ilāhiyyāt I 6, ed. I. Madkour (Cairo: Organisation Général des Imprimeries Gouvernementales, 1960) 37–9, A. Hyman, tr., in Hyman and Walsh, *Philosophy in the Middle Ages* (New York: Harper and Row, 1967) 240–2; *Najāt*, ed. M.S. Kurdi, (Cairo, 1938) 224–7, excerpted in A.-M. Goichon, *La Distinction*, 159–67; *Risāla al-'Arshiyya*, in *Majmū' Rasā'il* (Hyderabad: Dā'irat al-Ma'ārif, 1935); and *'Uyūn al-Masā'il*, ed. M. Cruz Hernandez, *Archives d'Histoire Doctrinale et Littéraire du Moyen Age* 25 (1950–1) 303–23; the texts are collected in G. Hourani, "Ibn Sīnā on Necessary and Possible Existence," *Philosophical Forum* 4 (1972) 74–86. Cf. *Ishārāt*, ed. Forget, 140–57; tr. Goichon, 354–93.

30 Davidson argues (300–2) that Ibn Sīnā's denial of an infinite causal regress is unnecessary and forms in effect a corollary rather than a scholium to his argument. Perhaps what Davidson has in mind is Crescas' claim, so important to Spinoza, that even an infinite series or system requires a cause. But we must be careful not to confuse the causal infinity that Ibn Sīnā excludes with the infinite temporal sequence which he finds innocuous. It is critical to the success of Ibn Sīnā's claims that one not envision, say, an infinite series of gods or

celestial intelligences, each producing what lies below it but itself produced by some higher being. Such a series would never reach an absolute being, i.e., one necessary in itself. Ibn Sīnā himself makes the bold move of *summing* the hypothetical infinite series and arguing that it too, like any conditioned reality, stands in need of a cause. Davidson, like Crescas, thinks that this move goes far enough; one need not argue further against an infinite causal regress. But Ibn Sīnā sees that this last cause too must be shown to be uncaused and not contingent. So he adopts as a scholium the assumption that a causal sequence cannot be infinite if it is at any stage to have an actual effect.

31 Achena and Massé *Le Livre de Science* 1 (Paris: Les Belles Lettres) 179–216; cf. Davidson, 293–8; al-Fārābī, *K. Mabādi' ārā' ahli 'l-madīnati 'l-fāḍila*, edited and translated by R. Walzer as *Al-Fārābī on the Perfect State* (Oxford: Clarendon Press, 1985) 14–17.

32 R. Popkin, "Spinoza, Neoplatonic Kabbalist?" in L.E. Goodman, ed., *Neoplatonism and Jewish Thought*, n. 61.

33 See *Metaphysics* Delta 5, 1015b 9–15: "Some things owe their necessity to something other than themselves; others do not, while they are the source of necessity in other things. Therefore the necessary in the primary and strict sense is the simple; for this does not admit of more states than one . . . . If, then, there are certain eternal and unmoveable things, nothing compulsory or against their nature attaches to them." Here multiple "simples" are not deemed problematic, and reality as a whole is not treated as the effect of a cause, precisely because it contains multiple self-sufficient constituents.

34 *Ilāhiyyāt* 2.357; Achena and Massé, 1, 56; cf. M. Fakhry, "The Subject-Matter of Metaphysics: Aristotle and Ibn Sīnā," in M. Marmura, *Islamic Theology and Philosophy Studies in Honor of George Hourani* (Albany: SUNY Press, 1984) 140. Cf. Spinoza, *Ethics* I, Prop. 18, "God is the immanent, not the transient cause of all things." Spinoza uses a spatial metaphor in his proof: Nothing is outside God. Ibn Sīnā uses a temporal model: Nothing succeeds God; God continues active through all events.

35 Juwaynī calls God "the Cause of causes." This language, which al-Ghazālī echoes, is vacuous if causes are unreal. See Abū 'l-Ma'ālī al Juwaynī, *Kitāb al-Irshād*, J.-D. Luciani (Paris: Leroux, 1938) 84, al-Ghazālī, *Ihyā' 'Ulūm al Dīn* 4 (Cairo, 1967) 187; cf. M. Fakhry, *Islamic Occasionalism and its Critique by Averroes and Aquinas* (London: Allen & Unwin, 1958) esp. p. 78.

36 See Nelson Goodman, *Fact, Fiction and Forecast* (London: The Athlone Press, 1954).

37 Not only are species in Aristotle eternal and unchanging, but the universal quantifier bears existential import. This is as it must be, for the necessary truths of science are not mere truisms or tautologies for Aristotle but facts about the world and the laws of nature, rooted in the essential natures of things. For similar reasons, a proposition that will never be true is classified by Aristotle as impossible, so there is no realm of pure virtuality for Aristotle – at least not when he writes in a cosmological vein.

38 See, e.g., G.E.M. Anscombe, "Aristotle," in *Three Philosophers* (Oxford: Blackwell, 1963; 1961) esp. 22–3; cf. E.A. Moody, *The Logic of William of Ockham* (London, 1935) 263.

39 Kant's point that existence is not a "real" predicate, i.e., not an informative, determinative or differentiative one, at least not a predicate that enhances our

knowledge of the *character* of a thing, was anticipated by al-Fārābī in his answers to questions posed by students; see his *Risalah fī jawāb masā'il su'ila 'anhā* no. 16, ed. F. Dieterici, in *Alfārābī's Philosophische Abhandlungen* (Leiden: Brill, 1890) and the discussion in N. Rescher, *Studies in the History of Arabic Logic* (Pittsburgh: University of Pittsburgh Press, 1963) 39–42. Al-Fārābī insists that for naturalists, who assume (as Aristotle does) that the existence of a thing is the thing itself, the proposition "Man exists" has no predicate. They assume that a predicate must tell us something *about* what we have before us. But for logicians (since it makes an assertion about man, which may be true or false), the same proposition has a predicate. From here it is only a short step or two to Ibn Sīnā's recognition that Aristotelian naturalists take for granted the existence of the objects they study (species like man), whereas the metaphysician willing to admit the contingency of all determinate things must take existence to be "a notion superadded to the essence of a thing."

40 *Posterior Analytics* II 7, 92b 4–15.

41 Spinoza, *Ethics* I, Prop. 11, Dem.: "posse existere potentia est."

42 See *Enneads* VI 2.1, 2.8, 3.6, 3.7. As A.-M. Goichon noted, the distinction between essence and existence is latent in Plato's distinction of forms from particulars, *Phaedo* 74A, *Republic* 509B, *Timaeus* 50C; see her *La Distinction de l'essence et de l'existence d'après Ibn Sīnā* (Paris: Brouwer, 1937) 132; Aristotle rejected it when he rejected the hypostatic forms.

43 J. Trouillard, "The Logic of Attribution in Plotinus," *IPQ* 1 (1961) 133, 135; cf. 131–2.

44 *R. fī 'l-'Ishq*, ed. M. Mehren, *Traités Mystiques d'Avicenne* (Leiden: Brill, 1894) Arabic, 2–3; the translation here is my own; cf. Emil Fackenheim in "A Treatise on Love," *Medieval Studies* 7 (1945) 208–28; G.E. von Grunebaum, "Avicenna's *Risāla fī 'l-'Ishq* and Courtly Love," *JNES* 11 (1952) 233–8; F. Rundgren, "Avicenna on Love," *Orientalia Suecana* 27–8 (1978–9) 42–62. Al-Ghazālī implicitly criticizes Ibn Sīnā's Neoplatonic reasoning here when he argues in the *Iḥyā' 'Ulūm al-Dīn* that love cannot be imagined in the lifeless; see Simon Van Den Bergh's discussion, "The 'Love of God' in Ghazālī's *Vivification of Theology*," *JSS* 1 (1956) 305–21.

45 In *De Interpretatione* 9. Like al-Fārābī in his commentary on the famous Sea Battle passage, Ibn Sīnā inveighs against the reduction of actuality to necessity – ironically, since that is the offense with which he is most often charged. Specifically, he protests the reduction of potential or capacity to actual performance. Madkour (Introduction, *Shifā'*, 13–14) identifies the doctrine criticized by Ibn Sīnā as Megarian; and in terms of its distant origin that is sound. But nearer to hand were the Ash'arites, who strenuously argued the confinement of powers to the very moment of their execution. Al-Fārābī aims at the Ash'arites when he says that the denial of contingency in events is "a view repugnant to any religion and very very harmful for people to believe." *Sharḥ fī 'l-'Ibāra*, ed. Kutsch, 98; F.W. Zimmerman, tr., *Al-Fārābī's Commentary and Short Treatise on Aristotle's De Interpretatione* (London: Oxford University Press, 1981) 93; cf. my "Al-Fārābī's Modalities," *Iyyun* 23 (1972) 100–12; Ghassan Finianos, *Les Grandes Divisions de l'Être «Mawjūd» selon Ibn Sīnā* (Fribourg Suisse: Éditions Universitaires, 1976) 198.

46 "Philosophical Analysis and Ibn Sīnā's 'Essence-Existence' Distinction," *JAOS* 92 (1972) 432.

47 *Danesh Nameh*, Achena and Massé 1.178. How interesting that Kant should preserve this insight in distinguishing the *ding an sich* from an object of consciousness but suppress it with regard to the distinction of an actual from a possible 100 *thalers*.

48 Averroes noted the *kalām* roots of Ibn Sīnā's argument in *The Incoherence of the Incoherence*:

> This proof … was first brought into philosophy by Ibn Sīnā, as superior to the approach of the ancients, for he held that it starts from the very essence of being, whereas the methods of others work from accidents of the First Principle. Ibn Sīnā took the approach from the *mutakallimūn*, for they thought it self-evident that reality is divided into the necessary and the contingent, and postulated that the contingent must have a cause and that the world as a whole, being contingent, must have a cause that exists necessarily. This was the conviction of the Mu'tazilites, before the Ash'ariyya, and it is a fine argument, except for their assumption that the world as a whole is contingent, which is not self-evident.

M. Bouyges, ed., Averroes, *Tahafot at-Tahafot* (*L'Incohérence de l'Incohérence*) (Beirut: Catholic Press, 1930) 276. Cf. the description of Mu'tazilite argumentation at *TT* 320 ll. 13–14; and Ibn Rushd, *K. al-Kashf*, ed. M. Mueller (Munich, 1859) 39; tr. Mueller (Munich, 1875); Davidson, 292. In a private communication, my friend Nicholas Heer writes, "I don't know any *mutakallim* before al-Ghazālī who used a proof of God based on *imkān*," that is, based on the pure idea of the contingency of finite being. "Their proofs are all based on *ḥudūth*," the originatedness of the temporal world. Now in al-Ash'arī, the argument we find for creation is (almost self-consciously) primitive and undeveloped, based on the Qur'anic suasion (22:5, 23:14, 56:58–9) that it is God, not man, who takes responsibility for the creation of semen and indeed for the subsequent development of the embryo; see *K. al-Luma'*, ed. R.J. McCarthy, 6–8. But in the post-Avicennan *kalām* of al-Juwaynī (d. 1085) and al-Shahrastānī (1076–1153) the arguments from "preponderance" and "particularization" come to the fore. These arguments are based on the idea that if a thing might or might not have been so (including existent or non-existent), but *is so*, then there must have been some determinant of its being so. This is the line of argument that Maimonides takes to be paradigmatic of the *kalām* approach deemed by its advocates in his time to be the most advanced (see *Guide to the Perplexed* I 73, methods 5 and 6; but al-Ash'arī's approach is also summarized nearly verbatim, as method 1); see Harry Wolfson, *The Philosophy of the Kalām* (Cambridge: Harvard University Press, 1976) 435–52. Al-Juwaynī ascribes the line of argument that Maimonides' *kalām* contemporaries deemed advanced to Mu'tazilites of Basra. These are identified by Wolfson as followers of Abū 'l-Hudhayl al-'Allāf (ca. 750–841/2), who was called by Nyberg "the first speculative theologian of the Mu'tazila," *EI*, 1.127. Abū 'l-Hudhayl's arguments in behalf of creation appear to be influenced by the views on contingency that were preserved from late antiquity under their spurious attribution to Empedocles, and which we have already found cited in the work of al-Āmirī. The "advanced" method does seem to have been influenced by Ibn Sīnā's formulations. Yet I believe Ibn Rushd is right in holding that Ibn Sīnā's approach is ultimately that of the *kalām*. The metaphysics of the *kalām*, particularly the reduction of substances to atoms in the early, occasionalist *kalām*, was a metaphysics of contingency. That was its theme. As Maimonides sees it, partly with the aid of Ibn Sīnā's own analysis, the *mutakallimūn* wanted to show that creation was necessary. It was in the interest of that goal that they conceptualized being as radically contingent, each atom dependent at each instant on the creative act of God. That was the approach pioneered by Abū 'l-Hudhayl; see Richard Frank's study, *The Metaphysics of Created Being According to Abū 'l-Hudhayl al-'Allāf: A Philosophical Study of the Earliest Kalām* (Istanbul: Nederlands Historisch-Archaeologisch Instituut in het Nabije Oosten, 1966). It is ironic that it took an Ibn Sīnā to formulate the theme of the early *kalām* in its purity, and that the impact of his formulation could not be appropriated within the *kalām* itself until atomist occasionalism had become a historical dead letter for the advanced (sc., post-Avicennan) *mutakallimūn*.

49 For the efforts of Neoplatonists to find Aristotelian roots for the proof that the world's *existence* depends on God, see Proclus, *On the Timaeus,* ed. E. Diehl, 1 (Leipzig, 1903) 266, 295; Proclus *ap.* Philoponus, *De Aeternitate Mundi contra Proclum*, ed. H. Rabe (Leipzig, 1899) 238–9; Simplicius, *On Aristotle's Physics*, ed. Diels, 10 (Berlin, 1895) 1360–3.

50 H. Brown, "Avicenna and the Christian Philosophers in Baghdad," in S.M. Stern *et al.*, eds, *Islamic Philosophy and the Classical Tradition . . . in Honor of Richard Walzer* (Columbia: University of South Carolina Press, 1972) 45. Brown quotes a passage in which Avicenna berates the dead Abū Bishr, demanding to know what role is left for the First Cause if the heavens move by a necessity of their own; he charges the Peripatetics with being so preoccupied with the motion of the spheres that they fail to distinguish between relative and absolute necessity and thus to develop a metaphysical proof for the existence of God.

51 Zabeeh, 47. Ibn Sīnā here pinioned the most vexed assumption of Aristotelian physics, that of the immanence or transience of the motive force.

52 See Dimitri Gutas, *Avicenna and the Aristotelian Tradition* (Leiden: Brill, 1988) 71.

53 Avicenna rejected the claim that the dependence of the world's existence upon God could be drawn from the Aristotelian Prime Mover argument, but he acknowledged that the eternal subsistence of the world and its continual motion are equivalent for Aristotle. See Avicenna *On Metaphysics XII* in A.-R. Badawi, *Arisṭū 'inda 'l-'Arab* (Cairo, 1947) 23, 26; Davidson, 282–3.

54 See *Shifā'* 1.6 and Davidson, 281–7; cf. M. Mahdi, "Alfarabi against Philoponus," *JNES* 26 (1967) 234; M. Marmura, "Avicenna on Primary Concepts in the Metaphysics of his *al-Shifā'*," in R.M. Savory and D.A. Agius, *Logos Islamikos: Studia Islamica in Honorem G.M. Wickens* (Toronto: Pontifical Institute of Medieval Studies, 1984).

55 Anselm writes: "I began to ask myself whether there might be found a single argument which would require no other for its proof than itself alone; and alone would suffice to demonstrate that God truly exists, and that there is a supreme good requiring nothing else, which all other things require for their existence and well-being." *Proslogium*, Preface, tr. S.N. Deane (La Salle: Open Court, 1968; 1903) 1.

56 "A Third Version of the Ontological Argument in the Ibn Sīnian Metaphysics," in Morewedge, ed., *Islamic Philosophical Theology* (Albany: SUNY Press, 1979) 188–222.

57 G.M. Wickens wrote that Avicenna's distinction between essence and existence, "made it possible to circumnavigate the morass of pantheism" and "may well

have opened the way, moreover, for St. Anselm's formulation of the ontological proof," in Wickens, ed., *Avicenna: Scientist and Philosopher: A Millenary Symposium* (London: Luzac, 1952) 53–4. Simon Van Den Bergh dismissed the claim on the grounds that the elements of Ibn Sīnā's argument are present in Aristotle; see his review of Wickens, *BSOAS* 16 (1954) 401. But Ibn Sīnā's thesis about existence is incompatible with a strict Aristotelianism, as Ibn Rushd saw clearly. More important to the case is that Avicenna's writings were translated into Latin a few years after Anselm's time. I would not be surprised if a path were one day traced from Avicenna to Anselm's door. But for the moment that door remains shut, and to open it is clearly not a prerequisite to understanding Anselm. The underlying concept and even the need for an ontological type of argument are deeply entrenched in any form of Platonism, in the recognition of divine absoluteness. Indeed, a Platonic, Augustinian reading of the concept of being could have sufficed to guide Anselm both to his cosmological proof of the *Monologium* and to his ontological proof of the *Proslogium*. Augustine laid a meditative basis for Anselm's argument in a critical turning of his own thought arising in a Platonizing, anti-Manichaean argument of his friend Nebridius: "since most truly and certainly, the incorruptible is preferable to the corruptible . . . I could not in thought have arrived at something better than my God" (*Confessions* VII ii–iv 3–6; cf. *De Moribus . . . Manichaeorum* 12; *Contra Secundin. Man.* 20; *De Fide contra Man.* 18, 35; *Disput. 2 contra Fortunat. Manich.* 5, *ad fin.* and above all, *De Civ. Dei*, 8.6, 12.2, where Augustine says of God, "est per essentiam suam.") It is a short step from the corruptible to the contingent, or from the incorruptible to the Necessary. Plato himself distinguished essence from existence, both explicitly and implicitly, as we have seen. So did Philo, in *De Posteritate Caini* 48, 169. What is important is not the distinction *per se* but what is done with it. What Ibn Sīnā does is to find in the sharp contrast of Necessary from contingent existence his own distinctive answer to Aristotle's question about being. The central distinction of Avicenna's metaphysics is thus of the greatest relevance to Anselm, although his is not at all a prototype of the ontological argument, or even a sign of willingness to accept such an argument. Anselm is emphatic, both in his Preface and in his correspondence with his teacher Lanfranc, in identifying Augustine, and especially Augustine's writings on the Trinity, as his philosophical source for the *Monologium*; but he names no such source for the *Proslogium*, where the ontological argument appears. His open worry about the unaccustomed form the *Monologium* took was that it would seem to have no anchor at all in authority. Lanfranc seems to have objected to it on just that ground, despite the blanket reference to Augustine. His cool response led to a rupture in the intellectual intimacy between him and his philosophically more penetrating disciple. Yet, despite the actual avoidance of an appeal to authorities, Anselm was no philosophical naïf. The metaphysical starkness of his meditations (like the starkness of some medieval or modern architecture) is not the mark of a primitive but the achievement of a master. Born in Aosta, Anselm found the direction of his life at the monastery of Bec in Normandy, in the teaching of Lanfranc (1005–89), who was famed not merely as a monastic administrator but as the restorer of logical studies in Europe, and who preceded him as Archbishop of Canterbury soon after the Norman invasion. Lanfranc's polemics on transubstantiation were based on a sophisticated analysis of categorical propositions, "one of the first" of the "many triumphs" that appeal to Aristotelian grammar and the doctrine of the *Categories* was to have "in the next two centuries," as Southern writes. But in a way, Lanfranc's adversary Berengar may have influenced Anselm still more deeply, when he argued that the *hoc* of *hoc est corpus meum* must still refer to the *actual* flesh of Christ even as the sentence ends, if the affirmation it makes is to be true. Anselm never wrote on transubstantiation, but his earliest work, *De Grammatico*, is a philosophical reading of the *Categories* that could readily lead an Augustinian to the affirmation that no perfection of a Perfect Being can in any way be lacking to it. See R.W. Southern, *Saint Anselm: A Portrait in a Landscape* (Cambridge: Cambridge University Press, 1990) esp. 17–20, 29–30, 43–50, 60–6, 70–2.

58 The direct theological affinity of Anselm to Avicenna is thus in the argument for a highest and best cause of all goodness, which Anselm develops in the *Monologium*. Like Avicenna's contingency argument, this argument (which Aquinas accepts as one of the five ways) is a posteriori. It begins from the premise: "Since there are goods so innumerable, whose great diversity we experience by the bodily senses and discern by our mental faculties . . .," a premise which Anselm believes opens the "easiest" and most obvious route to establishing the existence of God for the most ordinary, untutored, or unspiritual inquirer; see S.N. Deane, tr., *St Anselm: Basic Writings* (La Salle: Open Court, 1968; translation first published, 1903) 35–6.

59 N. Kemp Smith, tr., *Critique of Pure Reason* (New York: St Martin's, 1965; translation first published, 1929) A603–14/B631–42.

60 "Essence and Existence in Ibn Sīnā: The Myth and the Reality," *Hamdard Islamicus* 4 (1981) 3–14.

61 *Ishārāt* (Istanbul, 1894) 302, tr. after Rahman.

62 *Shifā', Ilāhiyyāt*, VI 2.

63 Rahman, 13.

64 See *Ishārāt* 3.19, and Ian Netton, *Allāh Transcendent: Studies in the Structure and Semiotics of Islamic Philosophy, Theology, and Cosmology* (London: Routledge, 1989) 151; A.-R. Badawi, *Histoire de la Philosophie en Islam* (Paris: Vrin, 1972) 2.631–2.

65 See *The Holy Qur'ān: English translation of the meanings and Commentary*, ed., The Presidency of Islamic Researches, IFTA (Medina: King Fahd Holy Qur'ān Printing Complex, 1410 A.H.= 1989) 114.

66 The Psalmist's language was not lost on the Islamic prophet, but the modern glossator ignores it, instead contrasting Psalms 78:65, whose imagery seems to him to compare disadvantageously with the words of the *Qur'ān*. Since depth of meaning is gained in part through added layers of interpretation, partisan provincialism will miss the very depth it seeks.

67 Cf. E. Fackenheim, "The Possibility of the Universe in al-Fārābī, Ibn Sīnā, and Maimonides," *PAAJR* 16 (1946–7) 39–70.

68 Thus *Guide* I 2, II 17.

69 Al-Fārābī on *De Interpretatione* 9, ed. Wilhelm Kutsch and Stanley Marrow (Beirut: Catholic Press, 1960); F.W. Zimmermann, tr., Al-Fārābī's Commentary and Short Treatise on Aristotle's *De Interpretatione* (London: Oxford University Press, 1981); see my "Al-Fārābī's Modalities," *Iyyun* 23 (1972) 100–12, Hebrew with English summary. It was formerly thought that the distinction between essence and existence was the explicit work of al-Fārābī. Gilson, following Max Horten, even refers to al-Fārābī's "epoch-making distinction of essence and

existence in created beings," noting the affinities of the distinction to the occasionalism of the *kalām* and ascribing its motivation to al-Fārābī's "profoundly religious spirit," his "capability of adapting the overwhelming richness of Greek philosophical speculation to the nostalgic feeling for God that Orientals have," and "to his own mystical experience." Étienne Gilson, *History of Christian Philosophy in the Middle Ages* (New York: Random House, 1955) 185–6. But the *Gems of Wisdom*, which Gilson quotes as the basis for attributing to al-Fārābī the distinction we find in Ibn Sīnā, has been shown by the work of a succession of scholars including Leo Strauss, A.-M. Goichon, Paul Kraus, Khalil Georr, and Shlomo Pines to be the work not of al-Fārābī but of Ibn Sīnā himself. See S. Pines, "Ibn Sīnā et l'Auteur de la *Risālat al-Fuṣus fī'l-Ḥikma*," *REI* 19 (1951) 121–4.

70 See my "Context," *Philosophy East and West* 38 (1988) 307–23; "Determinism and Freedom in Spinoza, Maimonides, and Aristotle," in F. Schoeman, ed., *Responsibility, Character and the Emotions* (Cambridge: Cambridge University Press, 1987) 107–64.

71 It is true that philosophy continued in Islamicate lands after the impasse between al-Ghazālī's *Incoherence of the Philosophers* and Ibn Rushd's *Incoherence of the Incoherence*. Indeed, I would maintain that the human impulse to philosophy cannot be eradicated as long as there is thought at all. But the injection of philosophy in the Avicennan mode *into* Ash'arite thinking preserves Avicenna's themes at the cost of muting their explicit self-identification *as* philosophy and fettering the philosophic method, which even among the later Greeks had become very traditional and now relinquishes the claim to radical intellectual independence and risk taking, that is, following where the argument may lead. In the Islamic East, original philosophic work continues to be done, again *within* and in response to the Avicennan tradition, specifically by the Sufi theosophists of the illuminist tradition. But here mystic gnosis takes the lead, again channelized by tradition; and metaphysics becomes a framework of axioms, some quite challenging and fascinating, but not an enterprise conducted for its own sake and answerable to its own standards.

72 *TF*, discussions 1–4.

73 *TT*, 276–7.

74 *TT* VIII, 395; *Long Commentary on Metaphysics* XII, item 41, ed. Bouyges, 1631–2; cf. *De Substantia Orbis*, V.

75 As Davidson writes (335), "Averroes' objections are based on incorrect information and misunderstandings" — especially on a projective and unsympathetic reading of Ibn Sīnā's key terms.

76 See Ibn Rushd, *De Substantia Orbis* VII and BM, Hebrew MS 27559, 305a–9b. Averroes saw Avicenna's initiative not as an original contribution to metaphysics but as a compromise with the vulgar in the area of cosmology. Ibn Rushd's response is to restore the Aristotelian identification of God with the first mover of the outermost sphere, to do away with the idea of the world's existential dependence upon God, and ultimately to reject emanation in favor of the more primitive conception of God as the prime mover that derives from Book VIII of Aristotle's *Physics*; see Arthur Hyman, "From What is One and Simple only What is One and Simple Can Come to Be," in L.E. Goodman, *Neoplatonism and Jewish Thought* (Albany: SUNY Press, 1992) 110–12.

77 L. Gardet, "L'Humanisme Gréco-Arabe: Avicenne" *Journal of World History* 2

(1954–5) 829, quoting *Najāt*, 302, *ad fin.*; cf. his *La Pensée Religieuse d'Avicenne* (Paris: Vrin, 1951) 45–61 for a more nuanced reading: there Gardet tracks Avicenna's seeming ambivalence to a frustrating reference of Ibn Sīnā's to the lost *Oriental Philosophy*, but Gardet also finds a suggestive remark of Ibn Sīnā's as to God's creation of contingent beings *as* contingent.

78 M. Marmura, "The Metaphysics of Efficient Causality in Avicenna," in *Islamic Theology and Philosophy*, 179.

79 *R. fī Sirr al-Qadar* (Hyderabad: Dā'ira al-Ma'ārif al-'Uthmāniyya, 1354 A.H.=1935) 2.

80 G. Hourani, "Ibn Sīnā's 'Essay on the Secret of Destiny," *BSOAS* 29 (1966) 27–48, repr. in *Reason and Tradition in Islamic Ethics* (Cambridge: Cambridge University Press, 1985) 239.

81 *R. fī Sirr*, 2. Hourani misses Ibn Sīnā's emphasis on argument and indeed misses the force of his argument, rendering "there would have been no completion of an order for the world," *Reason and Tradition*, 229; he also narrows Ibn Sīnā's focus (233–4), which is the general problem of evil; the issue of rewards and punishments is just a special case.

82 Saadiah and Ibn Ṭufayl are among the authors who pursue a comparable naturalistic reading of providence, in *The Book of Theodicy* and *Ḥayy Ibn Yaqẓān* respectively. Maimonides similarly argues that if natural means were not necessary to the attainment of God's ends, many things would have been created in vain.

83 Ibn Sīnā acknowledges his Platonic inspiration here, and Hourani rightly cites *Phaedo* 80–2, *Phaedrus* 246–56, and *Republic* X 613–20 for the doctrine, yet slights the content of these passages, which might have aided in clarifying Ibn Sīnā's thesis. Hourani seems eager instead to score Straussian points by finding a cryptic denial of predestination and affirmation of determinism. He similarly slights the Mu'tazilite commitment to natural retribution, a doctrine Ibn Sīnā supported in his reflections on history. Hourani seeks to deny the relevance of Ash'arism as a target of Ibn Sīnā's, preferring to set him into a polemic against the Mu'tazilites. But the *Danesh Nameh* shows that Ibn Sīnā was well aware of Ash'arite "orthodox" doctrine (as Saadiah was before him) and keenly sensitive to its challenge. The *Shifā'* shows that Ibn Sīnā preferred to rationalize predestination in terms of (his contingent version of) determinism, rather than, as Hourani suggests (238), to deny it in favor of determinism – just as he rationalizes requital in terms of the natural visiting upon the soul of the consequences of its acts instead of dismissing the idea of reward and punishment "in the usual sense of requital for deserts imposed by another person." Why should a philosopher (as opposed to an ideologue) confine himself to the usual senses of terms, when analysis reveals such senses to be shot through with uncritical, unsupported, or incompatible suppositions?

84 Marmura, "Efficient Causality," 183.

85 *Guide* III 17.3, cf. 17.5.

86 See al-Ghazālī, *Mishkāt al-Anwār (The "Niche for Lights")*, tr., W.H.T. Gairdner (Lahore: Ashraf, 1952; London, 1924) 135. See also *Ma'ārij al-Quds* (Cairo, 1340 A.H.) 149, 203–4; *Iḥyā' 'ūlūm al-Dīn* XXXV *Tawḥīd*, Shaṭr 1, bayān 2; and the discussion in A.J. Wensinck, *La Pensée de Ghazzali* (Paris: Maisonneuve, 1940) 79–101.

87 See A.J. Wensinck, *The Muslim Creed* (London: Cass, 1965; 1932) 77, 150–1.

88 See Harry Wolfson, *The Philosophy of the Kalam* (Cambridge: Harvard University Press, 1976) 235–303.

89 For the notions of *malakūt, jabarūt, hāhūt, lāhūt*, etc., see *EI* 1.350–2, s.v. *'Ālam*$_2$; Thomas Hughes, *A Dictionary of Islam* (Lahore: Premier, 1965; repr. of the London, 1885 edn) 169, s.v. *Ḥaẓarātu 'l-Khams*; and the very committed essay in Cyril Glassé, *The Concise Encyclopedia of Islam* (San Francisco: Harper and Row, 1989) 128–32, s.v. Five Divine Presences.

90 For a detailed exposition of this view in the thinking of a later Mu'tazilite, see J.R.T.M. Peters, *God's Created Speech: A Study in the Speculative Theology of . . . 'Abd al-Jabbār* (Leiden: Brill, 1976).

91 See *Mishkāt al-Anwār*, Gairdner's introduction, 16–21 and his "Al-Ghazālī's *Mishkāt al-Anwār* and the Ghazālī-Problem," *Der Islam* 5 (1914) 121–53. For Ibn Rushd's response, see *TT*, Discussion 1 ad fin., Bouyges, 117; cf. Ibn Rushd's *Kashf 'an Manāhij al-adillā'*, ed. Mueller, 21.

92 See William Montgomery Watt, *Free Will and Predestination in Early Islam* (London: Luzac, 1948) 48–9, citing al-Ash'arī, *K. al-Ibāna 'an Uṣūl al-Diyāna* (Hyderabad, 1321 A.H.) 73; tr. Walter C. Klein (New Haven: American Oriental Society, 1940) 113. Many views have been proposed about the basis of the term *Qadariyya* before and since C.A. Nallino's "Sul nome di 'qadariti'," *Rivisti degli Studi Orientali* 7 (1916–18) 461–6, but I take the passage from al-Ash'arī to be decisive: The Qur'anic usage of *qadar* was with reference to *God's* determination of events (2:19, 20:42, 30:53, etc.), but those who made man the determiner were opprobriously called "determinists," and the term stuck, in spite of their understandable desire to attach the label to their adversaries. As al-Ash'arī explains,

> The *Qadariyya* suppose that *we* deserve the name of *Qadar* (fate), because we say that God foreordained (*qaddara*) wrongdoing and misbelief, and whoever affirms predestiny (or fate) is a predestinarian (or fatalist), not those who do not affirm it. The answer is that the *qadarī* (determinist) is he who affirms that the *qadar* (determination) is his own and not his Lord's, that he and not his Creator determines his own acts. This is the proper usage. The goldsmith is the man who does goldsmith's work, not the man who has goldsmith's work done for him . . . we do not say that we rather than God determine our own acts but that He determines them for us.

Harry Wolfson offers an alternative explanation in *The Philosophy of the Kalam* (Cambridge: Harvard University Press, 1976) 619; but, although he gives a good explanation of the origins of the sense of the term and its apparently opprobrious connotations, he does not adequately explain, as al-Ash'arī does, why the term was applied to both sides of the free-will–predestination dispute, or why it stuck to those whom we would call the voluntarists. What we must remember is that a voluntarist with respect to human choices was thought by his adversaries not to be a sufficient voluntarist with respect to God. The Ash'arites, like the *minority* Bolsheviks, who called themselves the *majority*, vanquished their adversaries and survived to do the naming.

93 Two Mu'tazilites credited with such views were al-Mu'ammar and al-Naẓẓām; see Maimonides, *Guide* I 73, Wolfson, *Kalām*, 559–78. Maimonides follows the view attributed to Naẓẓām to the extent of echoing the illustration associated with it; see Ash'arī, *Maqālāt al-Islāmiyyīn*, ed. H. Ritter (Wiesbaden: Steiner, 1963) 404 ll. 4–9.

94 Cf. Marmura, "Efficient Causality," 180–3.

95 *TF* Discussion 17, *ad init.*, Bouyges, 2nd edn, 191–2: "The first point is their thesis that the connection observed between causes and effects is one of necessary implication . . . It is only so far as the support of miracles that breach the customary is built upon it that we must contest this first point." Van Den Bergh's translation suppresses Ghazālī's emphatic "only so far as" and substitutes "the familiar course of nature" for the Ash'arite "the customary."

96 Alfred Ivry deferentially corrects Hourani's bias in "Destiny Revisited: Avicenna's Concept of Determinism," in M. Marmura, ed., *Islamic Theology and Philosophy: Studies in Honor of George Hourani* (Albany: SUNY Press, 1984) 160–71, esp. 169.

97 *De Interpretatione* 9 and al-Fārābī op. cit.; cf. Gilbert Ryle, "It was to be," in *Dilemmas* (Cambridge: Cambridge University Press, 1962; Tarner Lectures of 1953) 15–35.

98 For a corrective to Russell's familiar view of Leibniz as freezing all events in windowless monads (paralleling the charges against Ibn Sīnā) see H. Ishiguro, "Pre-Established Harmony versus Constant Conjunction," in A. Kenny, ed., *Rationalism, Empiricism, and Idealism* (Oxford: Clarendon Press, 1986) 61–85. See also my "Leibniz and Futurity: Was it all over with Adam?" in M. Dascal and E. Yakira, eds, *Leibniz and Adam* (forthcoming).

99 For the Maimonidean background of possible worlds, see my "Maimonides and Leibniz," *JJS* 31 (1980) 214–36.

100 *Dialogues Concerning Natural Religion*, X, ed. Norman Kemp Smith (Indianapolis: Bobbs-Merrill, n.d.; Nelson, 1947; first published posthumously, 1779) 193.

101 See Qushayrī, *Risāla*, ed. Z. Ansari (Cairo, 1948) 32–3, in R.C. Zaehner, *Mysticism, Sacred and Profane* (Oxford: Oxford University Press, 1961) 85, 227.

102 A.C. Graham, "'Being' in Linguistics and Philosophy," *Foundations of Language* 1 (1965) 223–31.

103 *Tafsīr Mā Ba'd aṭ-Tabī'āt*, Bouyges, 2.744–6.

104 "'Being' in Linguistics and Philosophy," 229.

105 See my "Islamic and Jewish Philosophies of Language," in Kuno Lorenz *et al.*, eds, *Handbuch Sprachphilosophie* (Berlin: De Gruyter, forthcoming), and "Morals and Society in Islamic Philosophy," *Encyclopedia of Asian Philosophy* (London: Routledge, forthcoming).

106 *Qur'ān* 2:117; 3:47, 16:40, 19:35, 36:82, 40:68; cf. 3:59. The Qur'anic remark reads like an induction from *Genesis* 1:3, 6, 9, 11, 14, 20, 24.

107 *Qur'ān* 2:65; 7:166.

108 *Qur'ān* 7:144.

109 He cites *De Generatione Animalium* 731b 24, *Nicomachaean Ethics* 1139b 24, *De Generatione et Corruptione* 338a 1, *Metaphysics* 1015b, 1050ab, and 1072b 10. See *TT* 2.102–3.

110 *TT* 2.215.

111 Ibn Sīnā, *On Metaphysics Lambda* and *Mubāḥathāt*, both in A.-R. Badawi, ed., *Arisṭū 'inda 'l-'Arab* (Cairo, 1947) 26, 180.

112 S. Afnan, *Philosophical Terminology in Arabic and Persian* (Leiden: Brill, 1964) 29–30. In his *Avicenna: His Life and Works* (London: Allen and Unwin, 1958) 125, Afnan resists a linguistic reduction:

> We have followed Avicenna's reasoning in order to show the manner in

which he draws the distinction between the necessary and the possible being and the relation between the two. It might be thought that the differentiation, with its logical origin and form is more linguistic than real, but he has arguments for what makes a necessary being really necessary.

113 F. Shehadi, "Arabic and the Concept of Being," in G. Hourani, ed., *Essays on Islamic Philosophy and Science* (Albany: SUNY Press, 1975) 147–57.

114 See my "Six Dogmas of Relativism," in M. Dascal, ed., *Cultural Relativism and Philosophy* (Leiden: Brill, 1991).

115 See Maimonides, *Guide* II 19–21; al-Ghazālī, *TF*, Discussion 4.

3

IDEAS AND IMMORTALITY

If God is absolute, then God cannot be known empirically. All that we know empirically is temporally conditioned and therefore contingent and complex, a compound of essence and existence in Avicenna's terms. From an Avicennan standpoint, such contingency in all finite things seems to be recognized implicitly in the Aristotelian analysis of all bodies as complexes of matter and form – the divinely derived principle of actuality linked with the virtuality of a material substrate. But God transcends such complexity; divine necessity of being places God above the mere contingency of some wired-together system whose nature we discover by taking it apart, physically or conceptually, to uncover the conditions of its existence and operation.

If God cannot be known empirically and God is known, then rationalism must be true in a rather strong form: not merely the modest claim that the world is intelligible, but the access of intelligence to the pure principles of being. Such rationalism joins forces with the more modest kind by regarding our intellectual access to the Divine as affording us access to the a priori conditions of understanding. God, as the unconditioned ultimate explanatory principle, is then known not through any process but immediately and directly. All other understanding takes place with the help of God, in the sense that the idea of divine absoluteness conditions and informs all our most general concepts. To put the idea in Spinozistic terms: Conceptual knowledge is possible only *sub specie aeternitatis*. Medieval Neoplatonists found the approach clearly voiced in the Psalmist's (36:9) words: "For with Thee is the fountain of life. By Thy light do we see light."

One might suppose that so pure a rationalism as Avicenna's excludes mysticism. There is, after all, a traditional rivalry between the mystic notion that the Ultimate transcends intelligibility and the rationalist thesis that the more real a thing is the more intelligible it is in itself. And the experiential claims of mysticism are readily set aside. No mere encounter is self-validating in its claims. So it would seem that the allegations as to the absolute made in the name of immediate experience are unsubstantiated, and the idea of God, as a pure concept, can be reached only as an asymptote, the logical extreme subtended or demanded by some train of reasoning. Yet even in such a case one must ask what concept or value guides the extrapolation and how the content or even the direction of any ultimate term is to be apprehended. If the idea of God is not to remain an opaque virtuality, it must be the object of thoughts which a syllogism merely frames and to which a progression merely points the way, but which are grasped not discursively at all but in a pure intuition, the very intuition that orients any such progression and anchors any such syllogism. An irenic stance, then, is more fruitful than the polemical or dismissive: Rationalism, as Plato understood, must fuse with mysticism, linking the processes of dialectic and experience itself with the pure intuition of reason. Reasoning will validate and describe, sensory and emotional experience will hint and lead the way to what pure rational intuition reveals directly, seemingly timelessly - not by the invasion of eternity by human temporal consciousness, nor even by the viewing of eternity from afar, but by the incorporation in our very temporal awareness and discursive reasoning of a priori elements whose operations we can understand only by reference to the eternal and absolute.

Like all rationalists, Ibn Sīnā sees that no pure concept can be derived empirically. Thus he posits that the ideas of being and necessity are primitives, given to the mind by the hypostatic Active Intellect.[1] No process can discover them. They cannot be learned. For they are presupposed in any mental process that would lead to them, and any effort to build them out of simpler constituents would come to ground rapidly in circularity. In defining its elements it would presuppose the very categories it was intended to account for. Such primitives as these, Ibn Sīnā reasons, must therefore be givens in the nature of the case. The two that he singles out as ultimates, being and necessity, are, of course, foundational to our idea of God, the Necessary Being, in whose unity their distinctness is lost, and whose ultimacy encompasses all that is constitutive in the traditional ideas of divine perfection. For, where essence is identical with existence, necessary being is not a dyad but the mere furthest extension of the idea of reality; and where being is perfection, the ultimate reality is also the highest good.

But even in contingent things, where the concepts of being and necessity do not naturally resolve to a single concept, they are to be discovered only by the timeless act of the mind - or, as we would prefer to understand it, the casting of the mind's eye toward timelessness, when it recognizes natural necessity (and the goodness/aptness or perfection) in things and so glimpses the God-rootedness of all things in nature. Just as Plato held that unity or goodness in anything is the hallmark of the Divine in everything, and just as Aristotle held that scientific knowledge is the understanding of why things must be as they are and interpreted that question in terms of the aims all things pursue, so Ibn Sīnā found in the conditioned necessity of each contingent being that is made necessary only by its causes, the anchor point of the dependence of all things on God. The concept of each thing reflects and refracts in its own specific way the purity, goodness, and absoluteness of God.

Consider the propositions that we call laws of nature. Empiricism is pleased to label them generalizations. But they make higher claims than mere summaries of observations. They profess to be true not only of all cases observed but of all that might be observed. Some modern philosophers call them "lawlike," hesitant to speak of natural objects "obeying" laws. But, despite the hesitancy, the classic claims reemerge: *These* generalities have predictive and explanatory force. They intend not only coverage of the past but application to the hypothetical. Thus they are analyzed in terms of counterfactuals: Implicitly they make claims about what would happen if things were done that might never be done; they tell us what we would experience if we performed certain actions that only very rarely do we actually perform.[2] We do not claim only that all observed electrons have a mass with a certain ratio to the mass of a proton, but that all electrons and protons whatever under comparable conditions will be found to preserve the same ratio.

Hume, by a genial fiction, ascribed the element of necessity that we embed in our predictive and explanatory judgments to a projection by the mind, the Lockean outcome of the constant association of one idea with another. But that is only the good natured Tory admitting, in the spirit of his contemporary, Henry Fielding, that a bastard progeny can be as sound of character as legitimate offspring. It is not to render causal or other lawlike judgments legitimate. This Kant sought to do by showing that the a priori elements of judgment correspond exactly with the abstract determinants of sentential form. But that is only to anatomize the presumptiveness of the understanding as articulated in the deep structure of the very language that is its product. It is not to discover a warrant but only to follow Hume in seeking to *make* a warrant out of usage.

Ibn Sīnā's program is more ambitious, although founded on the same critical recognition that guided Hume, the recognition that we cannot make a silk purse from a sow's ear, or universal, necessary judgments out of fragmentary sense data. He too links the objective, conditional necessities of nature with the subjective recognition of those necessities by the mind – but not to reduce either to the other, as is so often done by philosophers who account for natural necessities as mental projections, and for those projections in turn as outcomes of a natural necessity, in the framing of the mind by evolution, or experience, or socio-linguistic custom. Rather, as we shall see, he derives the necessary concepts from the supernal world, as Muslim theologians called it – or, in the language of the Philosophers, from the Active Intellect.

An immediate strength of Ibn Sīnā's approach, beyond the consistency it gives his epistemology by scotching the quest for empiric discovery of elements that are not to be empirically acquired, is the Platonic haven it affords to Ibn Sīnā's quest for a rational basis of the claim to immortality. For the access of the mind to pure rational concepts is taken by Ibn Sīnā, as it was taken by Plato, as clear proof of immortality. But, like all philosophic answers, this one comes at a cost, here to be noted in the coin of compactness. The *Qur'ān* calls for physical resurrection, not merely spiritual or intellectual immortality. And, even setting aside the question of squaring the discoveries of philosophy with the demands of dogma, an enterprise which might be relegated to the theatre of *kalām*, there remains the disparity between intellectual and moral claims upon (and by) the hereafter.

Plato's argument in the *Phaedo*, ultimately, is that we can expect immortality only insofar as the intellect assimilates itself to the Forms through knowledge of them, becoming like to what it knows and thus realizing the timelessness that was its underlying being all along. But where, then, is accountability? Setting aside questions as to the becoming of what has always, *timelessly*, been the case, there is the stubborn fact that the Platonic ideas are universals. The soul, as intellect, attains their timelessness only to the extent that it attains their universality and so loses the individuality of personhood. Plato figures this fact in the suggestion (*Republic* X 621) that the River Lethe, "whose waters no measure can contain," washes us in forgetfulness. Which is to say that in the afterlife we lose individuality. For personhood depends on memory. Of the wicked it can be said that dissoluteness is also their dissolution: To the extent that they are drawn down by the inferior horse of the *Phaedrus* myth, toward physicality and the sensuous, they fail to knit together those threads of thought that might have bound them to the eternal. For the wise and sound it can be said that their intellectual integration is the transcendence of otherness and physicality and is thus their linkage into unity with all that is divine. But then there is no individual bearer of deserts to reap the consequences of virtue or of the discipline of wisdom.

Al-Fārābī reasoned that the hundreds of Qur'anic verses of promise and threat portend a deeper accountability which the images of Heaven and Hell only visualize poetically. But in the withering light of argument, the *object* of the imagery seemed at risk of dissolving into poetry as well. Ibn Ṭufayl reports that in his lost commentary on Aristotle's *Nicomachaean Ethics* al-Fārābī went beyond dismissal of eternal punishments for the wicked and held that all hopes of happiness beyond this life are "senseless ravings and old wives' tales."[3] Davidson attributes al-Fārābī's equivocal commitment to immortality to a change of heart or loss of nerve,[4] but I suspect that al-Fārābī's statements simply reflect the equivocal character of the Platonic arguments themselves: If there is immortality, it is not for individuals, and the rest of what is said of punishments and requitals is what must be dismissed as old wives' tales.

Ibn Rushd, emboldened by his predecessor Ibn Bājjah, seems prepared to pay this price, dissolving individual identity and arguing that *qua* man we are all one; only accidents distinguish us. In the hereafter (that is, in our essential being) there is but one soul. For it is only insofar as we are embodied that we are discrete. But Ibn Sīnā balked at such a resolution. He did so not only out of deference to a dogma of Islam (for had such concerns moved him decisively he would have held to temporal creation and physical resurrection), nor even solely out of a human desire to preserve the moral nexus between the attainments of this life and the purchase of immortality, but also, critically, for a philosophic reason that is an abiding reference point of his philosophy from its inception: the sense that individual human consciousness bespeaks a transcendence which the arguments of philosophy must acknowledge. Thus, despite his Platonism, Ibn Sīnā maintains the immortality of individual rational souls.

The key to his approach is that he does not, like Plato, regard the human soul as uncreated. Individual human souls have an origin and are individuated by the fact of their creation. Their distinct histories give them an individuality that they can never shed. Even when disembodied, an Avicennan soul retains consciousness and the individuality of its history. An individual soul cannot *predate* its embodiment. Thus it must be thought of as created: physicality is the condition of its individuation and of its temporality. For Ibn Sīnā it is evidently an ontological mistake to speak of the existence of a non-individual soul, much as we might argue that it is nonsense to speak of the same soul as different persons, or as being now a person and "in a later life" an animal.[5] Ibn Sīnā's premise, clearly, is that the intellectual soul that is subject to immortality is thought or consciousness, and thought must be focused and individuated: focused objectively, individuated subjectively. Only embodiment gives us the perspective that enables us to objectify, and only temporality allows us the unity of apperception (as Kant called it) that imparts subjective identity, i.e., subjecthood. Thus our existence as persons begins with our individuation in (and *by*) the bodies that differentiate us. But our experience, which is the product of the temporality that physical living renders necessary, provides us with an identity, Ibn Sīnā argues, that is no longer dependent on that body and is thus capable of surviving its dissolution.[6]

A corollary of Ibn Sīnā's view, emblematic of his rejection of the incarnationism of the extreme (*ḥulūlī*) or drunken Sufis, is the recognition that the soul's assimilation to the eternal disembodied intellect and universal forms which are the objects of its knowledge is never complete – just as the assimilation of the higher disembodied intellects to those above them is never completed by their contemplation. Distinctness of the individual subject is maintained, even in the fulfillment of our contemplative and mystical outreachings. Thus, just as there is no monopsychism in Ibn Sīnā, there is no pantheism or monism.

Al-Ghazālī will take the philosopher to task for generating (over the putative infinite eons of cosmic time) an infinitude of living souls,[7] an infinity that seems paradoxically to be augmented as the spheres continue their eternal revolutions. But Ibn Sīnā does not take refuge in metempsychosis or in collapsing all minds into a single consciousness or meta-consciousness. He stands by the discreteness of disembodied souls as a corollary of their very consciousness. Each mind is conscious of its own discreteness, and that is the basis of its self-identity and distinctness from all other things. This Avicennan appeal to self-consciousness as the foundation of identity will become the basis of al-Ghazālī's own response to the threat of monopsychism. He will argue that your mind is not mine, and never can be, since you and I know different things. Our discrete identities are defined by a consciousness which is indissolubly distinct between your subjecthood and mine.[8] The same argument, whose history can be traced back to the phenomenology of consciousness in the psychology of Philoponus,[9] will ground Descartes' existential claims in the *cogito*. Indeed, the celebrated Floating Man argument of Ibn Sīnā[10] is an ancestor of the Cartesian *cogito*.

1 THE POSSIBILITY OF KNOWLEDGE

Conventional wisdom, which often proves to bear a striking resemblance to the thoughts of Locke, and perhaps to their polemical vindication in the thinking of Mill, would have it that all ideas reach us through the senses. General ideas are treated as abstractions; and the most general, as higher-order abstractions. Thus I am said to acquire the general idea of "cow" or "bovine" from repeated sightings or images of cows, linked by association and blurred in memory to a single, less determinate image upon which the conventional name is stuck like a label and to which subsequent data are assimilated in a cumulative, gradual, or occasionally radical fashion. Notions such as "like" and "unlike" are higher-order abstractions, ideas of ideas: I note an affinity not only among various images of cows, but also among such affinities themselves. My idea of likeness is nothing more than the generalized relation of my images of cows, horses, dogs, and many other images that I have been in the habit of linking together. Our most basic notions, such as that of "existence," are yet higher-order abstractions, linking in some way all or most of the ideas already formed by conjoining sensory data into objects, or cobbling together lesser abstractions into larger ones.

The difficulties that this model confronts on critical scrutiny have been noted since the time of Plato,[11] although often swept under the carpet, ignored, restated, and repeatedly revived or reinterpreted. One obvious difficulty is that the model rapidly loses touch with the sensory base it professes to find unproblematic, locating in abstractions a mode of thought that it cannot so readily describe as images. For the universal term "cow" to be accounted a blurred image it must be blurry enough to have little if any determinacy of size or shape, color, or aspect. The higher-order universal "animal," or very high abstractions like "good" or "complex" are only very tenuously related to any image at all. Empiricists may posit a residual after-image as a sort of point of mental contact for such notions, or rely on words or other symbols as the presumptive cynosure of thought when it addresses such an idea. But ghost-images have *at best* a genetic relationship with the relevant ideas, and neither residual images nor words contain or explain what it is we understand when we grasp such an idea, but only what it is we may be thinking of *as* we think the idea, or perhaps in some cases as a condition of our mental access to it. This is to confuse the file label, or the occasion of a file's logging in, with the contents of the file itself. After all, general concepts are not blurry but crisp and sharp, not visually but conceptually.

Equally troublesome for the notion that universal ideas are higher-order abstractions of sense impressions is the circularity of the familiar empiricist account: Memory is said to link diverse images that I associate, allowing them to form a single composite. That has been the story from the blurred signet seal mark spoken of by the Stoics all the way down to Locke and beyond. It is problem enough to see how the many heterogeneous sounds and smells and moving planes of light that I am to denominate a cow can be linked together associatively, especially once they are stripped of the determinacy of their particularity. But, as Plato, Leibniz, and Kant, all recognized, my ability to link such images presupposes (on the empiricist model) such higher-order concepts as likeness, which accordingly cannot consistently be derived from the very experiences they make possible. It is purportedly because of some family resemblance among sightings of cows that I conjoin them in a single blurry image, rather than, say filing one sighting of a cow with one sighting of an aeroplane, a sip of beer or milk, and three bad dreams. To make the associations necessary to the formation of the most primitive general concepts, then, presupposes a higher-order operator, the functional equivalent of "like." And this, by the approved account, is a notion derivable only by higher-order abstraction from abstractions already attained.

Language and instruction, of course, step in to fill the gap, abetted, on some accounts, by bio-genetic predispositions of the brain, archetypes, or operators that foster or foment appropriate match-ups. But, Avicenna argues,[12] instruction itself must rely ultimately on insight. And, we may add, even preprogrammed "recognitions" will be no more than arbitrary unless they are given some (pragmatic) foundation in nature and thus made conceptual at least in intension – i.e., given some real reference to objective natural kinds and natural forms and features of reality. Avicenna anticipates this last line of argument when, following al-Fārābī and a long line of predecessors, he speaks, in almost Epicurean terms, of the lamb's proleptic apprehension of the "intentionality" of the wolf.[13] But in such a case, of course, we are not yet speaking of understanding.

Aristotle, with his great respect for sense experience as the food of curiosity and the starting point of wisdom, is often, mistakenly, taken as the hero of an imaginary battle with Plato over rationalism, partly because of his rejection of Plato's hypostatic Forms. But Aristotle himself found forms, unchanging, pure, and intelligible, where Plato never dreamed of looking for them: in ordinary natural objects and their species, and in the fleeting reflections of human thought. Like Plato, Aristotle was convinced that to treat ideas as mere figments of human intelligence is to invalidate the discoveries of that intelligence and sever its hold on nature. The skeptical outcome of any such nominalism, he agreed with Plato, would be a relativism that would be powerless to extricate its exponent from solipsism and would render impossible any coherent judgment about the world. Aristotle's "rejection" of Plato's Forms is as much a protest against their exile from nature as it is a reaction to the ontic prodigality of their hypostatization.

Aristotle's handling of the conceptual, epistemic problem is creative, instructive, and foundational to the approach of Kant, and perhaps Peirce, in seeking a middle ground between radical empiricism and Platonism. He treats concepts as constructs, not derived *from* the matter of experience, but not wholly alien to the sensory givens either: Pure concepts (even including the "higher-order" concepts like those of *being*, *good*, and *unity*, which by Aristotle's own account are systematically ambiguous and in each case bear no common notional content and so *cannot* be abstracted from the common elements of *any* common experiences) are derived, evidently by a kind of back-reasoning analogous to Peirce's abduction, from the very process of judgment itself. That is, one looks back at a judgment made and asks, in effect, what conceptual terms or operators were necessary to the production of this thought or the making of this inference. We learn and perhaps even understand such concepts not by pure Platonic intuition but by detection of their functions in a judgment. If it is objected that terms and their conceptual contents are, by Aristotle's own account, presupposed in the synthesis of sentences and judgments, the answer is that this is so, but that the terms of one judgment can be extricated from the analysis of another.

Aristotle has the advantage of his holism and realism here. His approach is analogous to what our own contemporaries call bootstrap epistemology. It has much to recommend it, especially to those whose suspicions of "foundationalism" are not merely symptomatic of a disposition toward negativity. No Cartesian, Aristotle abstracts away from no extant knowledge but the single desideratum of a particular inquiry. He allows himself all the rest of thought, materially and formally. Thus he elicits *being*, in its diverse senses in the *Categories*, from the judgments in which it is posited; and, to legitimate a concept like that of "vertebrate" in zoology or "virtue" in the *Ethics*, he assumes that we know all that we do know when we use such concepts. In quite *un*-Euclidean fashion, the sum of all knowledge is brought to bear on the resolution of each single point that for the moment is treated as unknown. But if that sum were to be organized in Euclidean fashion, as the young Ibn Sīnā sought to do in his card file, the undefined elements clearly emergent would be those named by the words: *being*, *necessity*, *simplicity*, *goodness*, *oneness*. These primitives Avicenna must regard as a priori givens. And so he does.

In context, Aristotle can give definition to these most general or abstract terms by the reverse of the analytic method: Such terms as these do not break down into conceptually differentiated parts, genera, and differentia, but their senses are seen by their impact, the ways they can be used in organizing other terms – just as any "simple" is understood not by analysis but by contextual location and grasping of its role and action in an environment. If we consider now the lesser challenge of concepts like *man*, or *horse*, or *chair*, which in their purity are never encountered by the senses and indeed never exist in their fullness at any one particular moment in history, the same technique is used. That is, there is an appeal to usage and experience. But experience here is not an array of sensa, and usage is not reduced to the mere dance of stimuli in dialectic with our biological requirements, or of individual needs with social desiderata. For there is, it is assumed, a structured and intelligible world outside our consciousness, and our needs are intellectual, not merely practical: We want to understand that world, not simply to adjust to it or secure its adjustment to our wishes.

Aristotle traces the genesis of basic concepts in a striking Homeric simile:

> out of sense-perception develops what we call memory, and out of frequently repeated memories of the same thing comes

> experience. For multiple memories make up a single experience. From experience in turn, the universal, now stabilized in its fullness within the soul, the one standing over and against the many, as a single identity running through them all. Here arise the skill of the craftsman and the knowledge of the scientist – skill in the realm of what comes to be; and knowledge, in that of what is. In short, these states of knowledge are neither in us in their determinate form, nor derived from prior, higher states of knowledge. Rather, they emerge from sense perception – as in a battle a rout is stopped if one man makes a stand, and then another, until the company is regrouped. And the soul is so constituted as to be capable of this.[14]

As Kant explains, the conceptualist account pioneered by Aristotle suffers neither from the innatist apriorism of Plato, analogous to biological preformationism, nor from the *ad hoc* innovationism of the empiricists, which seeks, in effect, to derive something from nothing, as if by spontaneous generation. The conceptual account is like epigenesis. There *is* a genuine development, but also a genuine pattern. The process is not self-validating but is tested by the adequacy of its product: There *is* a workable pattern, corresponding to the objective rationality of nature. This the mind does not invent or impose, or discover in the roots of consciousness, but constructs, as it were, using perceptions, memories, experience, as materials, building more ambitious subassemblies from each simpler order of the given, and arranging the resultant higher-order constructs to fit the appearances as they are given in nature, or taken from it. Aristotle is pleased to couch his account in empirical terms, emphasizing, against Plato, that it is from sensory givens that the mind works. But it is not *toward* sensory outputs that it verges. The outcome and the endpoint of the process here described is an idea, not imparted or innate, but constructed, developed by the working of the mind itself, according to its own nature and capabilities, and according to the patterns found in nature, which are themselves ideas or forms in an objective sense.

Aristotle speaks of a flexible, leaden rule used at Lesbos that can be conformed to a given curve in stonework and then used to select stones to fit its contours, so that each new stone is fitted to the next and finds its place in a desired pattern without the need of being cut to fit.[15] Like the Lesbian rule, concept formation, by Aristotle's account, involves the simultaneous, or reciprocal, shaping of the molding or rock wall *and the rule*. It is here that Platonism reemerges:

In linking one memory to the next of the relevant type, in capturing and stabilizing an image to transform memory to experience, or in focusing and perfecting an idea for art or understanding, one has constant reference to higher-order elements of the very universals that the account is meant to rationalize or warrant. Conceptually, these are the building blocks and formal mortar, the joists, lintels, hinges, timbers, and plans out of which concepts will be composed and theorems put together and prepared for testing against the phenomena – which include not only appearances in the empiricists' sense, but also opinions, hypotheses already on the ground, in keeping with the method approved by Plato and employed regularly by Aristotle as well.[16]

For Aristotle our reliance on notions that cannot be warranted without circularity seems quite unproblematic. Since only one concept need be justified at a time, all the rest are assumed, often taken for granted as an outcome of instruction. This is the pedagogic fact behind the formidable "esotericism" of Aristotle. A mere distaste for Plato's (mathematical) brand of foundationalism combines in Aristotle with a healthy openness to all the categories we actually use and is legitimated by a dynamic epistemic model that envisions the coalescence of our basic categories and concepts out of experience. The presupposition of any term, for Aristotle, is not unwholesome question begging but a concrescence of relevancies, the onsite improvisation or appropriation of tools that prove their worth by being put to work the very moment they are taken up. And, although tools can and should be modified to the task at hand, the fact is that normally they *are* taken up and need not be invented or improvised from scratch. For it *is* a teacher normally that guides us to the recognition of the concepts by which a straight line or a right angle can be constructed, not only on paper but in the mind. That is why we normally learn grammar before we learn logic in any formal sense; and that is *how* we are capable of learning logic *by* learning grammar.

But, as Avicenna insists, behind all such pedagogy, regardless how comprehensive, must lie insights, one's own or those of the original conceptualizer, elemental to the very processes of recognition by which each conceptual step is taken: If discovery is a construction of concepts new to the mind, as prompted by experience, then such construction is possible only through employment of primitive concepts which the mind itself cannot construct. Even if primitives are to be derived by back-projection, to be recognized as elements, teased out analytically from the syntheses in which they are presupposed, they must meet with some answering affinity or propensity in the mind.

In a more radical context than that presumed by Aristotle, then, the givenness of formal elements in the very process of rational, Socratic induction is fatally damaging to empiricism. The radical empiricist can avoid the problem only by denying the very relevance of pure concepts (even while using them to universalize his claims). The true conceptualist must fall back on his Platonic roots, as the Aristotelian tradition in fact did, when Alexander of Aphrodisias identified the active intellect, as Aristotle called the conceptually constructive aspect of the mind, with the supreme divine Intelligence, and when Muslim thinkers called on that intellect, now identified with the disembodied intelligence of the lowest of the spheres, our own, to provide the ideational content necessary to all conceptual thought. The hypostatic Active Intellect, assured of its own reality by Aristotle's arguments for a highest Intelligence that would be pure actuality, became the haven of the Platonic forms, providing Neoplatonists a viable response to Aristotle's compelling arguments that the Forms could not exist in themselves. It afforded as well a means of explaining divine knowledge and governance over nature, since God's self-knowledge no longer need seem empty of material content or causal efficacy if the Wisdom or the Word of God, identified with the Active Intellect, could be equated at the same time (through the identity of conceptual knowledge with its object) with the forms that are the reality and source of all particulars.

Epistemologically, the Active Intellect was the natural place to turn for the linkage of our scientific thought with nature. Since it informed the human mind as well as the natural species of all things, it could be relied upon for the match-up between our ideas and the structuring forms in nature: Both the subjective and the objective ideas of things were approximations projected from the Platonic realities that formed the content of that formerly divine and (under Islam) still angelic Intelligence. Avicenna writes:

> We argue that the human soul is rational potentially and then becomes actually rational. But anything that emerges from potency to act does so only on account of some cause that is already actual. So here we have a cause that brings our souls from potency to act in regard to conceptual ideas, the objects of rationality. It is in fact the same cause that bestows intelligible forms. Thus it must be an intellect that is rational in act, that

actually *has* the disembodied conceptual forms of things. *Vis-à-vis* our souls it plays the role of the sun in relation to our eyesight. For just as the sun is visible actually, by its own nature, and by its light renders visible what is otherwise not actually visible, so this intellect renders ideas intelligible to the soul.[17]

Avicenna offers two lines of argument against the adequacy of the senses to supply us with real, scientific knowledge.[18] The first is based on the same considerations that skeptics use in setting out the problem of induction, although Ibn Sīnā does not conclude that the situation warrants skepticism. The second is based on a problem about locating conceptual knowledge in any part of our anatomy, or in any physical body whatsoever.

(i) Knowledge, as Aristotle showed, is at its best when its contents are general and necessary. Naturally, knowledge is assumed to be comprised of propositions; for only propositions make truth claims. Even the knowledge of acquaintance is cognitive only insofar as it involves judgments about the one with whom we are acquainted (e.g., that this is she, that he is a friend, that they are trustworthy, etc.). Scientific knowledge is identified not by the physical character or sensory appearance of its object, but by the universality and necessity of its general claims. When our judgments are not only universal but necessary, we have the sort of cognition that allows explanation and prediction, rather than a mere collocation of facts. This is the sort of understanding that is the goal of the quest for knowledge from the outset.

Necessary conclusions can be reached in a train of syllogistic reasoning, but only if the initial premises include propositions of comparable strength. Such universal and necessary starting points are themselves the outcomes of our grasping the essences of things, so that we not only know but know how and why we know and why the things we have understood must be as they are. Such an assumption is crucial to Ibn Sīnā's distinction of experience from mere sensation: To know that a pattern is stable we must know not only that it is repeated but that what is constantly repeated has a cause; *when* we know the cause we know *why* the pattern is constant and then can make predictions from experience (buttressed by understanding) to the future. To understand causes is to recognize forms. Avicenna must then ask how we come to know the forms or essences of things. Plato thought it was by immediate acquaintance with the hypostatic Ideas which exist timelessly in themselves as the conditions of all becoming, and innately in the soul, as the conditions of all knowing. Their presence is the proof of immortality. For Plato it is a given that scientific, conceptual knowledge does exist: If all cognition were sensory, all judgments would be mere opinion, and there would be only the sheer incoherence of Protagorean subjectivism and Cratylean phenomenalism in place of science. For even opinions could not be affirmed as true if opinion were all there is; and even appearances could not be discriminated, named, or described if there were not the ontic stability of some realia to which appearances make reference. Thus, Plato reasons, the Forms are prior to appearances, bodies (the objects of opinions and beliefs), or even selves; they are primary, not only epistemically but ontically.

Ibn Sīnā will not accept that answer, because, in violation of Aristotle's arguments against the independent existence of the Forms, it treats them as free-standing hypostases. "Reason," Ibn Sīnā insists, "the intellectual faculty, is what abstracts conceptual ideas (*al-ma'qūlāt*) from any determinate quantity, place, position, or any other of the previously mentioned [categories]. . . . It is absurd to say that such a concept exists externally; we must say that it exists divorced from all spacial location only when it exists in the mind."[19] Yet clearly Plato was right in holding that conceptual knowledge cannot come from sense experience alone. For the senses always show us particulars, never what is universally the case. They do not distinguish what is essential or necessary from what is accidental (or even rare). And at best they show us only what is so, never that it must be so or could not be otherwise. "Forms imprinted on corporeal matter are mere phantoms of particular, divisible things, each part of which is related, actually or potentially, to a corresponding part of their image."[20] But lawlike judgments govern more than any possible accumulation of experience can govern. As Ibn Sīnā writes, "the objects of conception stipulated as falling within the province of the power of reason to understand seriatim are potentially infinite. And we know that anything capable of dealing with a potential infinity cannot be a body or any power or force within a body."[21]

Like Aristotle, and like Socrates for that matter, to whom Aristotle ascribed the self-conscious discovery of induction, Ibn Sīnā attributes our awakening to general concepts to a process of induction. He is in this sense an empiricist, as is Aristotle himself. We would never know what a dog is if we had never seen a dog. But induction on Avicenna's account is not the mere leaping to conclusions about the general presence of unit traits or sense data in sensory particulars that stronger and, say, post-Humean forms of empiricism tend to make of it. As in Aristotle's reconstruction of Socratic induction, it is rather the mental discernment of an intelligible pattern.

Avicenna follows Aristotle's reconstruction of Socratic induction as the piecing together of experience out of the scraps of sense, imagination, and memory, rather than the mere accumulation of rationally unrelated data. Accordingly, he argues that *experience*, as distinguished from bare or enumerative induction, can differentiate causally related phenomena from coincidences. In the Persian work he wrote for Alā' al-Dawla, Ibn Sīnā lists "the givens of experience" among the premises of sound reasoning:

> These are the assumptions which are warranted neither by reason alone nor by the senses alone but which can be known by the two working together. Thus, when the senses always find the same behavior in a given thing, or see the same state always having the same outcome, reason can recognize that this is by no means the result of chance. Otherwise the same pattern would not always be repeated, and the observed pattern would not be the commonest. Examples are the burning of fire and the purging of bile by scammony.[22]

In the book of the *Shifā'* corresponding to Aristotle's *Posterior Analytics*, which the Arabic tradition calls The Book of Demonstration, recognition of a causal connection is taken in turn to warrant drawing a universal conclusion from (finite) experience.[23] The induction here is not enumerative: It can be sound although incomplete, and unsound although seemingly complete, if relevant differences of *kind* were overlooked among the examples studied. The causal understanding necessary in (rational or Socratic) induction rests on (rational) intuition (*ḥads*), of the sort used, for example, in framing the true hypothesis that the light of the moon comes from the sun. Introduction of such (a priori) principles as (causal) necessity or (species-wide) universality requires the aid of the Active Intellect. Differentiating such informed or thoughtful induction from the merely enumerative kind, Ibn Sīnā caps the critical lacunae of the Aristotelian account, that is, the Homeric simile of the rout, with a demand to name the rational basis of linkages among percepts, and thus with a Platonic recognition that what is empirical can only *suggest* the pure ideas, whose absolute content lies beyond the empiric sphere.

Aristotle, we have seen, relies upon the capabilities of the mind (aided by culture, language, and instruction) to construct the appropriate concepts to fit the phenomena. The trouble is that in the process he either relies surreptitiously upon Platonic forms, or falsifies the analysis by "discovering" formal elements in, or "from" sensory experience that are never really there: perfect circles, straight lines, and other such regulatory notions. When we "round off" a circle out of the rough approximation we behold, or "complete" any other sensory pattern, we are adjusting the empiric presentation to meet or approximate a formal conception that is only notionally present, proposed in our minds but not present in the given, not derived from it, suggested by it, perhaps, but only to the mind that is primed to see. It is here that Ibn Sīnā finds a necessary role for the hypostatic Active Intellect.

(ii) As for the locus of rational knowledge, Ibn Sīnā argues that conceptual ideas cannot be stored as images are, in the brain, since such ideas have no parts. The idea of equality, for example, cannot be tucked away in any part of the body, or in any way laid out in matter, since such an idea is complete and unitary in itself. It cannot be divided and thus does not occupy space:

> One thing of which there is no doubting is that a man has something in him, some substance responsive and receptive to conceptual ideas. And we argue that the substance which is the seat of these ideas is not a body and does not depend for its existence on a body, even though in a certain sense it is a power in a body, or a form to a body. For if the locus of our concepts were a body, or any sort of extended thing, such ideas would have to be located either in a single, indivisible part of it, or in some divisible part. But the only thing that is indivisible in a body is a point . . . and a point is the final limit of a line, or of an extended body in a particular location; it cannot be separated from that line or body, allowing something else to exist in it, as opposed to existing in that body[24] . . .
>
> So suppose now that conceptual ideas were located in some divisible body. It would follow that they would be divided when that body was divided, and their parts would be either homogeneous or heterogeneous. If homogeneous, how could they be conjoined to form something different from themselves, for the whole as such is not the same as its parts unless it is the sort of whole that is augmented by mere addition to its measure or its number, not by a specific form. If a concept could be formed in this quantitative way, it would be some figure or number. But

> not every idea is a mere shape or number. That would make concepts nothing more than images and not conceptual at all. Concepts, in fact, as you know, cannot be treated as formed of homogeneous parts. How could they be, when one part of a concept implies another, and is in turn implied by a third.... Obviously ... the parts of a concept cannot be heterogeneous unless it is as the parts of a definition: genus and differentia.... And since every portion of a body is in principle infinitely divisible, genera and differentia would have to be so as well, if ideas were materially embodied.... But it is well established that genera and differentia, the components of the definition of a single thing, do not go on forever but are finite in every sense – and if they were not, they certainly could never be gathered up in a single body![25]

At first sight the argument may appear naïve, a primitive counterpart to Ibn Sīnā's subtle proof that imagination (since it is involved with projecting and displaying images of sensory, extended, divisible things) must be a physical faculty, so as to be capable of mapping what it displays (or stores in latency in its retentive backroom).[26] But Ibn Sīnā's argument is subtler than may at first appear: Of course we may store images or symbols, words perhaps ideally, to aid us in re-accessing our conceptual thoughts. But, without the act of understanding, such cues would be opaque: To remember a conceptual idea, as opposed to remembering its mark, is to think and understand it all over again. Ideas cannot be stored.[27]

Biogenetic structuralists should take particular note of the difficulty Avicenna's argument poses for them: Appeals to an evolved, innate capacity of the mind to operate with formal symbols and relations may provide a model for describing certain developmental achievements critical to our ability to generate linguistic structures, but they do not explain our ability to grasp or use concepts that are even in part a priori.[28] Even if the symbols or the means of cuing or manipulating such concepts are innate (whether in Plato's or in Chomsky's sense), the understanding of such cues and apprehension of the conceptual values they mark or symbolize, in the very nature of the case cannot be.

For our own purposes, we might wish to formulate Ibn Sīnā's conclusion in terms of a recognition that conceptual ideas are a process rather than a mark or impression. We might have difficulty with his claim that there is a (non-physical) locus for the reception of such ideas. The model may seem too spiritual, too mystical. It is certainly too compromised by the very imagery it is trying to escape – Plato's ancient imagery of the signet ring and wax tablet. But it is very clear that, if there is conceptual knowledge, then the objects it intends are not objects of the senses. And a powerful undertow of Ibn Sīnā's argument pulls us toward recognition that there is conceptual knowledge in precisely the sense that would require such knowledge to be non-sensory in intension, regardless of what hints may prompt its discovery, or of where the symbols of those hints may be stored.

Avicenna's solution to the problem of conceptual knowledge will be appreciated only by those who recognize that there is indeed a problem to be solved. Those who deny that we possess or need conceptual knowledge will find no charm in Platonism. Those who think that pure concepts can indeed be back-projected onto the empirical manifold will see no need for recourse to a hypostatic intellect to impart them. But it falls to those who propose such back-projections to account for the source from which the mind is enabled to propose such ideas. I am myself quite sympathetic to the effort and to the project that demands it, whether in behalf of naturalism and empiricism, or in behalf of the allied (and quite authentically Aristotelian) recognition of the immanence of what is active in human intelligence (regardless how one settles the question of its rootedness in the Divine). But, even if one does not trace the activity of the human rational intellect *ontologically* back to God, I suspect that *epistemologically* one might find such a journey necessary. For I have serious doubts whether the necessary categories or the elemental operators that are required to give thought its start can be warranted without reference to intensionalities that rise far beyond the empirical and contingent. Such reference would be a counterpart to Ibn Sīnā's assignment of an active, causal role to the hypostasis that he calls the Active Intellect. A comparable reference to the Transcendent may prove to be unavoidable in all human knowledge that reaches the level of the scientific.

Clearly Avicenna's solution to the problem of conceptual knowledge is radical and costly – not quite as costly ontologically as might appear at first blush, if we think of the Active Intellect as paid for ontologically by its role in informing nature and therefore regard its epistemic function as a bonus, but costly beyond the reach of all but the most committed Neoplatonist. On the other hand, in the context of Avicenna's established commitment to Neoplatonism, the move has definite advantages. One of these can be expressed in terms of what might be called the rationalist's problem of tautologous explanation.

Consider the Socratic induction that any rationalist must use to grasp the nature of any natural object. Such understanding will be achieved by intuiting or constructing the essential character of the particular as a member of its kind, understanding its properties and their relations to one another in defining, expressing, and preserving that individual's being. Explanation will consist in reducing phenomena to the essential properties they express – behavior to dispositions, for example. But the dispositions are discovered only in the behavior and most often are defined (for good pragmatic reasons) only by reference to it. As a result, explanations verge toward the tautological and predictions begin to sound like truisms. Undergraduates are often taught to laugh at the scholastics for their *virtus dormitiva*, by which medieval ignorance of the pharmacological effects of opium was masked in an exotic expression that simply named the effect while pretending to identify a cause. But the problem is structurally endemic in rationalism: If we understand things in terms of properties that constitute their essences, will not *every* explanation have the same form? What will prevent every account from reducing simply to the tautology that things are what they are and do what they do? That outcome, of course, is a perversion of the Aristotelian quest for specificity in explanation and a product more of reductionism than of essentialism. But it is difficult to see how it can be forestalled if explanations always go back, as in fact they should, to what things are.

The problem is not relieved but only exacerbated by the operationalist expedient of reducing properties, including dispositions, to their observable, or ultimately, their observed features. For now we find that explanation is in fact impossible. The property to which causal reference might have been made is now nothing but the (observed) effect itself. Mechanism may paper over this collapse of causal attributions, by assigning causal primacy to the arrangements and motions of bodies and their parts (and formalism follows by directing the mind away from causal questions altogether, to the mathematical beauties of pure pattern). But, as Leibniz recognized early on, there is no efficacy in bodies as such, unless we *assign* them some dispositions (however passive and inert these may seem) – whether mass, or other physical or chemical powers of matter, or the sheer ability to exclude another particle from the same space. But then these powers or dispositions are properties, and explanation by reference to them again becomes tautological.

Avicenna's approach can in a way forestall such a conclusion and help to obviate the confusion on which it is based. For Avicenna avoids the assumption that it is a necessity of logic that things must be what they are. The essences of things, like their existence, are imparted, through a train of natural causes that runs back temporally to infinity, and through a train of metaphysical causes that runs back ontically to the primal volition of God.[29] So the necessity of each thing's being what it is is not logical but causal, and the activity of a thing is not tautologous but synthetic, since each thing's essence, like its existence, is necessary with reference to its causes but contingent in itself. Here we see a basis for discriminating logical from causal necessity. And we see in turn how explanatory statements can be informative. For they tell us not just that things must be what they are but that specific causal factors, both internal and external impart specific characters to things, by virtue of which those things behave as they do.[30]

Of course a thing must be what it is, but that does not imply that such a thing must have existed, as a necessity of logic. It is self-contradictory to deny that a thing is what it is, but there is no contradiction at all in affirming that it need not have been at all, or need not have been as it is. Contingency allows for the differentiation of the world out of God's Self-contained and necessary being. And contingency, dependent ultimately on the latitude of divine volition and the interplay of causes, is what leaves room for the syntheticity of human judgment. Our discoveries, predictions, and explanations, then, are not just our having access to the essences of things to find that things must be as they are and do as they do. They are synthetic apprehensions of the specific essences of things, in which we grasp why things are as they are and behave as they do behave, by reference to the causes that enable a thing to be what it is and do what it does.

Ibn Sīnā's approach to knowledge addresses the question as to how discoveries can take place, how reasoning can be informative, in a way that is quite different from the formalist's method of distinguishing sense from reference, as in Frege, and relying on our ignorance of logical or semantical connections and on referential opacity to mark the difference between the analytic and the synthetic. Ibn Sīnā's model allows for a realist distinction between the two: Events may be causally connected that are not logically connected (except in the trivial sense that one might *posit* their connection). The same considerations that make possible genuine discoveries thus leave room for an open future, as many a strictly formalist account does not. Ibn

Sīnā's account, of course, is much closer than the tautologistic parody to Aristotle's naturalistic intentions. And it helps to make clear why empiric study is necessary even within the heart of rationalism. For what we understand when we understand why things work as they do (and why they must) is not a relationship of logical implication but a pattern of reasonableness whose structure can be formalized mathematically but whose relations become deductive only by the positing, i.e., *postulation*, of specific contents and significances for its material terms. Causes for Avicenna do entail their effects; essences, crucially, *act* in the dispositions of things. But the givenness of these causes and essences is not an axiom of logic but a contingent fact; their effects, accordingly, are contingent, although they can be inferred deductively from a formal scheme that postulates the relevant causes as givens.

Perhaps the most damaging criticism one can make of Ibn Sīnā's epistemic scheme is that it leaves too much to the Active Intellect. The human body is realized as human by the imparting of the soul, which is in fact the distinctive form of humanity. The soul itself is realized by the imparting of the intellect, whose lowest form is the passive, potential, or material intellect. Just as the human form, the soul, comes to us from outside, the gift of the *Dator Formarum*, or Imparter of Forms, that is, the Active Intellect, so the informing of the soul with intelligence, even with rationality, which is potential intelligence, is the work of that self-same Form Giver.[31] And the realization of human intelligence in each individual, the informing or enlightenment of the material or potential intellect by the attainment of concepts, involves its transformation by the Active Intellect into what is called the Acquired or Derived Intellect, a designation which gives emphasis to the externality of the action. It is as though Aristotle's differentiation of the work of human intelligence into active and passive phases were subverted here, since whatever is active or actually intellectual in us is separated off and ascribed to an external agency, the same external agency that imparts form to matter in any event.

We should not overstate the case. It is not the case that the imparting of actual intelligence, or understanding, is on all fours with any other imparting of form, so that we had just as well been given knowledge from birth, in the manner, say that our species or our eye color was determined. Knowledge is not just another form. Its attainment depends on the presence of prior forms which are to it as matter is to form in general. Thus it is not the case, as certain *mutakallimūn* proposed, that any matter can receive any form and that intelligence could therefore reside, if God so willed, in an undifferentiated atom, or a corpse. Only the human soul can be the substrate of human understanding: The life of a specific kind of organic body, and the proper functioning of that body are necessary prerequisites.[32] What this means epistemologically is that understanding and discovery remain human acts and, indeed, achievements. They are not simply passively received or implanted.

For a philosopher like Alexander of Aphrodisias, who developed the theory of the external Active Intellect, the immanent action of such a divine principle was quite unproblematic. Pagan philosophers in the tradition of Aristotle did not sharply and jealously distinguish actions that were locally initiated from those that were external, i.e., divine in origin. Witness Aristotle's theory of motion, which made the highest cause of motion to be God, conceived of as the Aim of all directed action, yet saw each individual agent as its own miniature prime mover, operating by its own natural or voluntary action to pursue its own self-constituted aim. But in the monotheist Avicenna the overlap of responsibilities is preserved: God's responsibility for all events does not exclude the individual responsibility of each agent, as it might in the occasionalist *kalām*. God still acts through the actions of all beings and in that sense sustains them. There is Qur'anic warrant for such a view in the oft cited verse: "When you shot, it was not you who shot but God."[33]

Thus in Ibn Sīnā's theory of knowledge the soul organizes sensory images, as received, integrated and perhaps rearranged by the imagination, assigning them pragmatic significance as notions (*ma'ānī*, cf. the Latin *intentiones*). Retained in memory, these become hints or cues that guide the individual intellect to the relevant universal ideas. "Intentions" function, then, analogously to schemata in Kant's epistemology, mediating the seeming incommensurability between sense impressions or images and pure intellectual concepts, answering a question that Plato's innatism left unresolved: If knowledge is by acquaintance, how can anything be learned, how can we recognize what we do not already know? Plato's claim was that we do not genuinely acquire new knowledge; rather, all real knowledge belongs eternally to the eternal soul. In that case, as Aristotle saw, there is no real discovery, but only uncovering of what was always present in us from the outset. Such a conception of knowledge not only obviates or trivializes the act of learning but also refocuses the attention of the would be learner away from nature and toward the realm of the eternal. It is no accident that Aristotle, who defended the reality of discovery against the a priorism of Plato, partook of every empirical science – and no accident that the one science Plato took most seriously (and Aristotle least so) was mathematics.

Ibn Sīnā's contribution here is to argue that although sense data can never give us concepts, they can, when properly worked up into images (by a capability that even non-rational animals share), provide us the material clues to concepts. Such notions or intentions make clear the relevance of specific formal concepts to particular experiential situations. The appropriate concepts can then be noted or intuited (or constructed) by rational beings, beings that do have access to pure, or intellectual, concepts. We construct the simulacra and then identify the concepts proper to them. Here all the work of Aristotle's phenomenology of rational consciousness, the relevance (but not omni-sufficiency) of experience and memory, are salvaged and made compatible with a Neoplatonic epistemic scheme that does away with Plato's innatist elenchus, his argument (*Theaetetus* 199–200) that knowledge can never be acquired (hence, must be innate), since what is unknown will be unrecognizable, and what is recognized (and so understood) must already be known. We can recognize concepts (and orient ourselves toward those that are appropriate) not because we already know them, but because experience gives us notions that are suggestive of them, sufficiently that if we have access to an appropriate concept, we can recognize its relevance (and the irrelevance of others) to a problem we confront, and thus, as it were, pluck down the appropriate concept from the repertoire that the Active Intellect holds in readiness.

Aristotle can say much the same thing without the intervention of a hypostatic Active Intellect, relying on the mind itself to construct the relevant concept fictively, as an element in a trial hypothesis. But the difficulty in this approach is that an Aristotelian construct, if indeed it is grounded in the materials of experience, seems to be no more than an Avicennan notion or schema. It lacks the purely formal characteristics that sensory experience cannot provide. Whereas a conceptual idea could not be grounded in the senses, except in the way that the thought of dinner takes its rise from the sound of the dinner bell, by association and suggestion. We may give up the claim to conceptual knowledge so as to preserve strict empiricism. But genuine concepts will require more than sensory foundations. Aristotle himself acknowledges as much, when he treats the divine as the "Prime Mover" of thought in the *Eudemian Ethics*:

> One does not deliberate as a result of deliberation – which itself presupposes deliberation, but there is some starting point; nor does one think as a result of thinking that one should think, and so *ad infinitum*. So thought is not the starting point of thinking, nor deliberation of deliberation. What then can be the starting point except chance? Thus everything would come from chance. Perhaps there is a starting point with none other outside it, and this can act in this sort of way by being such as it is. The object of our search is this: What is the commencement of movement in the soul? The answer is clear: as in the cosmos, so in the soul, it is god. For in a sense the divine element in us moves everything. The starting point of reasoning is not reasoning but something greater. What then could be greater even than knowledge and intellect but god.[34]

It is clear to Ibn Sīnā, at any rate, that, if we are to sustain conceptual claims as such, we must aid empiricism with intuitions that are uncompromised by temporality. These are what the Active Intellect provides for Ibn Sīnā. The fact that they can come to us only from above in no way diminishes the human need for experience in discovering their empiric roles and in no way diminishes the active role of human thought and understanding in grasping up for them and teasing out their myriad significances.

It is in this sense, I think, that we should understand Avicenna's saying, in the *Compendium on the Soul*, that the intelligible Forms come to us either (a) by divine inspiration (*ilhām ilāhī*) "as is the case with the primitive concepts" (sc., those we would have to presuppose in the construction of any others), which come to us "without any process of learning or dependence on the senses," or (b) through syllogisms. The latter, as I would understand it, means that the pure concepts necessary to the workings of a syllogism are reached abductively, by examination of the ideas we must have had available to make our reasoning rigorous. But even these concepts, Avicenna argues, since they are perfect expressions of the divine idea, can be reached by minds of exceptional alertness (*yaqẓa*, the term that Ibn Sīnā and Ibn Ṭufayl will employ in their allegories of the perfect human mind) without the necessary intervention of syllogisms, or of any process of discursive reasoning (*rawiyya*), through contact (*ittiṣāl*) of the properly endowed human intellect (*fiṭra*) with the Univeral Intelligence of the Active Intellect. This last is the sanctification properly understood as the domain of prophets.[35]

Whether we see our general knowledge as coming from above or as constructed from below now becomes a matter of emphasis and perspective: The individual human contribution remains indispensable, but the basis for it is itself a gift of God. The flowing of the forms of things into the mind is indispensable as well. The Ikhwān al-Ṣafā', like Avicenna reflecting on the epistemology of al-Fārābī, did not hesitate, even in the most mundane cases, to call it inspiration.[36] But such inspiration would be wasted on a rock. Sensory inputs are necessary, to provide the matter upon which concepts are projected, or from which they are elicited; but sensory data are never sufficient to thought.

On Avicenna's model, as on Plato's, empirical observations give the mind the cues it needs to find the relevant formal principles. But we can see more clearly on Avicenna's model than on Plato's, why such cues are needed. As Aristotle said, knowledge of the Form of the Good is too general, too non-specific to tell us what the human virtues are or how we ought to act in concrete situations. The same is true in the natural sciences: The Platonic Forms are too general to specify the particularities of events. But why is this so, if the Form of the Good is supposed to encompass all the forms and lie at the root of all being? The answer, again, is grasped in the idea of contingency. If Platonism is right in calling the Form of the Good the *fons et origo* of all things, then all knowledge in principle could be a priori - should be a priori at its best. Only human ignorance, lack of acquaintance with particular (innate!) intuitions would forestall complete deductivism, and the attendant reduction of all truths to tautologies. But if creation is not the mere emanative specification of the intellectual/ontic fullness of the good but somehow involves contingency and choice, then knowledge is not deductive and explanations are not tautologies.

The creationist critics of Avicenna faulted him for rejecting the temporality of creation and for not seeming to share their own idea of divine volition. They saw that Ibn Sīnā's commitment to a full universe and his intellectualist necessitarianism about divine choices committed him to a view of nature that compromised his crucial thesis as to the world's contingent essence and existence. But they followed where he led on the issue of contingency, seeing that human freedom, the open future, and even the differentiation of cause from effect depend upon contingency. Their disagreements with Ibn Sīnā were over whether he had gone far enough in pressing the point of principle, that the world does not simply *follow from* divine perfection as corollaries follow from geometric theorems, but rather must be chosen, causally determined, differentiated from its alternatives, *ab initio* and at every step. Only so is its utter undifferentiation avoided, the explanatory program of rationalism preserved from vacuity, and knowledge preserved from tautology. It is not simply because we do not know the inner being of God that our knowledge is contingent and incomplete, but rather because, apart from the determining choice of God and the action of all the ontically consequent causes in their delegated roles (whose action is not fixed in facticity until it is complete), there would be no determinacy to be known.

2 THE SUBSTANCE OF THE SOUL

In a famous argument at the outset of the *De Anima* of the *Shifā'*, the Floating Man argument, Ibn Sīnā undertakes "to establish the existence of the thing that is called the soul." He begins from observation: "We observe that certain bodies sense and move voluntarily. We observe, moreover, that some take nourishment, grow, and reproduce their kind." Like other Aristotelians, Ibn Sīnā understands ensoulment in functional terms. He argues that such functions as these

> do not arise in these bodies by virtue of their physicality. Rather, they have in their essences principles other than physicality that are responsible for these actions. And whatever gives rise to such actions (and, likewise, in general, whatever acts as an initiating source of actions) cannot be devoid of will and is therefore called "soul." This expression is the name of that entity not because of its substance but in regard to its relation to the body, i.e., insofar as it is the source of these movements.[37]

These definitional thoughts are a little slippery. Ibn Sīnā partitions bodies, in classical Aristotelian manner, into a material and a formal aspect. He relies on the mere virtuality of the material aspect (deprived as it is of all determinate dispositions) to entail its utter passivity and inertness. The reduction of all that is physical as such to the bald and overly general character of "physicality" leaves behind no physical basis for the energizing of any natural bodies, animate or inanimate. All motion, then, would need soul as a prime mover – a major theme, of course, in Aristotelian physics. If we assign intrinsic motions to the various sorts of matter (e.g., upward motion to fire, on an Aristotelian model; or, say, some more complex electrochemical actions to acids and bases on a more modern model), Avicenna's claim would be that such motions do not express the sheer physicality of the bodies involved (since not every body shares them) but rather reflect the organizational structure of the matter in question and so express not its material but its *formal* character, analogous to soul in the human case, and derived (on Neoplatonic assumptions) from the overarching Worldsoul.[38]

The Newtonian discovery that all matter, *qua* matter, does have certain properties in common, specifically those connected with mass, damages Ibn Sīnā's Aristotelian framework here by tending to break down the sharp dichotomy between what can be attributed to materiality and what must be ascribed to form, essence, or "principles." But the analysis of such primal functions as gravitational attraction or electromagnetic radiation into structural expressions of diverse kinds of particles might help in some measure to rehabilitate or at least render accessible to us Ibn Sīnā's basic theory here – not his hylomorphism, but the broader and more interesting claim that something analogous to a soul underlies any initiation of action in a physical thing. The inseparability of form from matter, which was itself an Aristotelian doctrine, is not unhelpful. For it allows us to project what a twentieth-century Avicennan might understand by an intrinsic property. Clearly this would be a characteristic inseparable from the object. But the *virtuality* of its separability, our mental capacity to abstract a property and suppose, say extension without mass or mass without extension, not in a context thick with the suppositions of our actual knowledge, but in the abstract realm of hypotheses, shows us that in absolute terms even such intrinsic properties are contingent. Kant expressed a related idea by saying that (in a Cartesian framework) the proposition "All matter is extended" is analytic, whereas the proposition "All matter has mass," although equally true and universal, is synthetic. Newton's discoveries were necessary before we could affirm with confidence that whatever is extended also has mass. Ibn Sīnā would say that the intrinsic properties of matter are imparted, just as the elements of any composite (even one whose decomposition is to be attained only in the analytic laboratory of the mind) are only contingently connected and must be externally supplied to one another, i.e., brought together by causes, leading back ultimately to the Self-sufficient Cause.

Al-Ghazālī, in his critique of the philosophers, uses Ibn Sīnā's affirmation that something analogous to a will must initiate any action or motion, to undermine Avicennan naturalism. Taking as a paradigm the kindling of a piece of cotton, he argues that mute matter can initiate no change:

Fire is an inert body (*jamād*) and so has no action. So what evidence is there that it is the active cause of the burning? None except the observation that the kindling of the cotton takes place on contact with the flame. But such observation proves only that it happened when the contact took place, not because of it, or that there was no other cause. For there is no disagreement that the influx of the vital spirit and the powers of sensitivity and motion to the sperm of animals does not stem from the natures of the elements, which are confined to heat, cold, moistness and dryness. Nor do we disagree in saying that the father is not the maker of the child merely because of his depositing sperm in the womb; we agree that it is not he who gives it life, sight, hearing or any other traits. It is well known that these begin at that point, but we do not say that they exist *because* of it. Rather, we ascribe their existence to the agency of the Ultimate, either directly, or through the mediation of angels entrusted with such temporal concerns. This is a point on which those philosophers who affirm an Author of nature are perfectly clear, and it is with them that we are conducting our dispute.[39]

Al-Ghazālī here exploits Ibn Sīnā's Neoplatonism and rejection of mechanistic reductionism to place the philosopher in a difficult position. Alexander of Aphrodisias relies on the complexity of the organic body to make credible the role of the soul as a living principle. But, on Aristotelian principles, all physical complexity resolves to the four elemental qualities, hot and cold, wet and dry. Surely, al-Ghazālī argues, a philosopher like Ibn Sīnā would not find sufficient richness in these to generate the complex motions of living beings. On the contrary, Neoplatonic philosophers in fact rely on the imparting of spirit from above to explain the miracle of life. What the philosophers call "principles" the traditional texts call angels, but the meaning is the same:[40] Life derives from above, not from inanimate physicality, but from the realm of spirit, ultimately, from God. By the same token, al-Ghazālī implies, even the elemental qualities and actions, on the Neoplatonic account, stem from above. Fire, water, earth, and air, in themselves, are inert:

Philosophers committed to the Truth are therefore unanimous in holding that these incidents and events that occur when bodies come in contact with one another or shift their relative positions simply flow forth from the Giver of Forms, which is

> an angel or angels. They even hold that the imprinting of an image in the eye stems from the Form Giver, and that daylight, clear vision, and an object that is not transparent are mere preconditions, predisposing the substrate to receive this form. They press this theory in regard to every event. And this refutes the claim of one who professes that the flame is what makes the kindling take place, that bread is what sates us, or medicine what gives us health – and so for all causes.[41]

Avicenna would certainly not treat physical events and material predispositions as irrelevant, say, to the formation of an image in the eye; nor would he attribute the formation of such an image to the direct action of the Active Intellect. But his hylomorphism, his allocation of all definiteness and definition to the formal aspect of reality, and his corresponding assignment of mere passivity and inertness to matter as such play into al-Ghazālī's hands. Matter as such does not think, and by strictly Aristotelian principles it does not act either. Bodies, on Avicenna's scheme, act in specifiable manners on account of the forms that organize them and give them a definite character. And the forms do come from above. Thoughts too come from on high, insofar as they are thoughts. And even the shapes perceived by the eye, insofar as they are shapes, come from the Active Intellect, not through its action on the eye directly, but through its imparting of the forms to the objects which the eye beholds.

Al-Ghazālī's criticism seeks to damage Ibn Sīnā's naturalism by assimilating natural causality to the work of some spiritual principle. The presumption is that souls and their cosmological counterparts are more easily understood than matter – and that the notion of action in matter is simply a confusion, since all action is an expression of form. It works to al-Ghazālī's advantage that among those committed to "the Truth" the operations of the soul seemed to be uncontroversial and that matter had been reduced to mere passivity, otherness, and inertness. But the net effect of this criticism of al-Ghazālī's on Avicennan psychology is to underscore the functionalism of that psychology: The soul in any creature is what makes possible the activities of life – the growth and reproduction of plants, the sensitivity and motility of animals, the consciousness and rationality of human beings. If there is a psychological basis for rebutting al-Ghazālī's criticism, it is through the recognition that living and non-living beings do not achieve the same levels of activity because living beings do not have the same form as the non-living. That form is the soul, and indeed it is obvious on this basis why, say, plants are not said to have souls in the same sense that animals are. For, in a very real and very Aristotelian acceptation, they are not alive in the same sense, i.e., they do not live in the same way; there is an essential difference between these two kingdoms in what it means to say of any member of them that it is alive.

Avicenna certainly does not believe that all events are the direct work of God. Particulars act by the natures imparted to them; and it is because things have such natures that we can refer to them as bodies and expect them to behave, as we say, true to form. Nor is it acceptable to suppose that just because matter (as a pure and abstract virtual nature) is conceived to have no efficacy it therefore follows that bodies do not act, or that the funding of Avicennan nature from a spiritual or intellectual source implies the impossibility of mechanics. On the contrary, Aristotelian, Neoplatonic, and Avicennan bodies *are informed* and *therefore do* exist and act. The inanimateness of fire does not imply that it does not express the nature it is given. The fact that matter qua matter is, on Aristotelian principles, inert implies only that such actions as we need bodies to engage in would not take place were it not for the imparting of form. Form here *is* analogous to soul. But a better way to put it would be to say that soul is a special case of form, one whose actions, in the human case, are polyvalent rather than monovalent. But the virtual inertness of matter, the inaction of the abstract matter which represents the outcome of analysis, mentally subtracting all that gives definition to the specific sorts of bodies, only shows that the bodies we know would not exist and function (as we see they do) without the presence of something analogous to soul.

What is important psychologically in Ibn Sīnā's account here is that it draws an analogy between the soul of a living thing and any source of movement. Avicenna himself stresses the limitations of the analogy: "All we have proved thus far is that something exists which is responsible for the effects cited." We have not shown *what* the soul is or what category it belongs to, but "we have established that something is there, in terms of its manifestations. Now we must follow up these signs to discover the true nature and character of their cause, as when we know that one thing has been set in motion by another, but do not know by what."[42] Just as Ibn Sīnā's analogy does not directly tell us much about what a soul is, it does not contribute much to our understanding of natural movements in general, as though we already knew what souls were and now discovered that all movements are initiated in much the same way that our own voluntary actions are.

For, as Spinoza explains, to understand a cause solely in terms of its effect is not to grasp the essence of the cause itself.[43] The analogy tells us only that when Aristotelian philosophers use the word "soul" they are referring in the first instance to whatever it is that differentiates living from non-living beings.

Avicenna's notion that whatever initiates motion in matter must be soul or soul-like is altogether too fraught with suppositions (about the passivity of matter and the intellectuality of causes, an artifact of their conceptualization!) to be of much use to us here. But his conception of the soul as a formal principle that initiates motions which bodies would not otherwise exhibit remains helpful nonetheless, if only because it helps to exorcise visions of the soul as a ghostly substance whose physicality is denied in the same breath that assigns it location, spatio-temporal dimensions, and even a misty, almost palpable presence to imagination. Such quasi-physical conceptions of the soul were commonplace in antiquity and enjoy a curious metamorphosis and rebirth in the *kalām*. Many early *mutakallimūn* held that the soul was an atom to which the accident of life attaches, a doctrine Ibn Sīnā took pains to refute when he argued at length that rational consciousness could no more subsist in an atom than it could in a fully extended and differentiated body.[44] And as late as the fourteenth century, the theologically irredentist and romantically reactionary Damascus theologian Ibn Qayyim al-Jawziyya (1292–1350) defined the soul as a body "differing in essence from a sensory body, a body that is luminous, supernal, living, and moving." He went on (oblivious to Alexander of Aphrodisias' refutation of the Stoic doctrine of *krasis*, which had allowed one body to pervade or perfuse another, putting one body in the same place as another) to say of the soul: "It permeates the substance of the bodily organs and flows through them as sap flows in roses, oil in olives, or fire in charcoal."[45] Ibn Sīnā's Aristotelian and functionalist working definition of the soul is breath of fresh air by contrast.

Having laid out his working definition of the soul, Avicenna argues strenuously, using Aristotelian terms, that the soul is no ordinary form but an entelechy: it makes a thing, in this case a living thing, what it is, makes it capable of action *as* what it is. He argues further that the human soul is itself a substance. Ibn Sīnā is disagreeing here with the tradition of Alexander of Aphrodisias, who had treated the soul strictly as a form and argued that it is a substance only in the way that any form is a substance, as that which gives reality to the matter it informs, by making it a specific sort of thing –

in this case, a living thing. What motivated Alexander, as his *De Anima* shows,[46] was the concern that Stoic and similar efforts to conceptualize the soul as a substance had encouraged its treatment as a physical thing. Ibn Sīnā's concern is quite different. Alexander's battle against materialistic images of the soul had been fought and won (among "those committed to the truth") centuries before. It could be won again, whenever the need arose, by repetition of the Avicennan arguments against the inhering of human, rational consciousness in matter. But the notion that the soul was somehow a mere expression or characteristic of the body, even if not a body itself, remained a serious challenge among philosophers inclined to naturalism. Accordingly, Ibn Sīnā follows Aristotle in emphasizing that some entelechies are mere forms, while others are substances: The soul that simply animates an organic body is its form. Here soul is to body as seaworthiness is to ship. But the rational soul, the human mind or consciousness, does more and is more. It is a substance and in principle separable from the body. This is Avicenna's Aristotelian thesis to be proved. Here (*pace* Alexander) soul is to body as pilot is to ship.

The argument on which Ibn Sīnā rests his case depends, as he puts it (and as Roger Arnaldez and Thérèse Druart have rightly emphasized[47]), on introspection and a kind of focusing or awakening of attention (*al-tanbīh wa 'l-tadhkīr*).[48] It asks us to perform a thought experiment, which Ibn Sīnā says anyone can perform:

> One of us must suppose that he was just created at a stroke, fully developed and perfectly formed but with his vision shrouded from perceiving all external objects – created floating in the air or in space, not buffeted by any perceptible current of the air that supports him, his limbs separated and kept out of contact with one another, so that they do not feel each other. Then let the subject consider whether he would affirm the existence of his self. There is no doubt that he would affirm his own existence, although not affirming the reality of any of his limbs or inner organs, his bowels, or heart or brain, or any external thing. Indeed he would affirm the existence of this self of his while not affirming that it had any length, breadth or depth. And if it were possible for him in such a state to imagine a hand or any other organ, he would not imagine it to be a part of himself or a condition of his existence.[49]

The argument is ancestral to the familiar modern arguments about brains in vats; even more so, to Descartes' *cogito*,[50] since the cogency of the thought experiment rests upon what we can and cannot abstract: If the self, the identity or essence of the individual is conceivable without the body, if consciousness can be affirmed while not affirming (or in Descartes' epistemological turning of the point, while doubting, that is, entertaining the denial of) the existence of a body or of any external object, then clearly no such notion is constitutive to our essence as conscious beings. As Ibn Sīnā himself concludes:

> But you know that what is affirmed is distinct from what is not affirmed, and what is implied is distinct from what is not implied. Thus the self, whose existence he affirmed, is his distinctive identity, although not identical with his body and his organs, whose existence he did not affirm. Accordingly, one who directs his thoughts to this consideration has a means of affirming the existence of the soul as something distinct from the body, indeed, as something quite other than the body, something which he knows through his own self-consciousness, even if he had overlooked it and needs to be alerted to it.[51]

Avicenna is fond of this argument and repeats it toward the end of the *De Anima* of his *Shifā'*, arguing there[52] that the unity of consciousness provides the answer to the question why it does not need a body. He calls the Floating Man "an argument of my own (*lanā*) for the existence of the soul that makes its case by awakening the mind and calling attention squarely to the point, for one who has the capacity to mark the truth itself without needing elaborate instruction, rattling of his cage, or protection from captious notions."[53] Its function he says, once we know what the word "soul" means, is to tell us what sort of thing it is that deserves the designation, i.e., what sort of thing can provide the functions assigned to the soul; here specifically, that of consciousness. Since the positing of consciousness does not depend on the positing of a body, the subject of consciousness, which is the true self, the human rational ego or intellectual soul, does not depend for its existence on the existence of a body.

Where Descartes argues from the immediate self-presence of consciousness and our capability of doubting all external objects, to the indubitable existence of that consciousness (*res cogitans*) and its distinctness from all other things (since they, simultaneously *are* doubted), Ibn Sīnā argues similarly, using a fictive hypothesis rather than a supposition of doubt, to abstract all that is non-essential from the conception of the self. In either case one is left with the pure fact of self-consciousness, and the fictive abstraction shows that its conception, and so its essence, depends on that of no external body. Kripke uses similar argumentation against the mind-brain identity thesis, resting his case on the (ultimately Avicennan) claim that it is logically possible for a brain state to exist without the corresponding state of consciousness.[54]

In the *Book of Hints and Pointers* Avicenna elaborates his argument:

> Reflect upon your self and consider, if you were in good health, that is of sound intellect, but differently situated than you are, could you be unaware of your own existence? Could you fail to affirm the reality of the self? I do not think that any rational person could deny such a fact. Even if he were asleep or drunk, self-awareness would not be completely absent, even though one would not be consciously representing his own existence continually to himself.
>
> Suppose your being to have been just begun. You are of sound and capable intelligence, but your bodily parts are so disposed that you cannot see them or touch your limbs or organs; they are separated from one another and suspended for the moment in thin air. You would find that you were conscious of nothing but your own reality.
>
> By what means would you be conscious of your self at that moment, or at the moment just before or after it? What would it be in you that had such awareness? Do you find any of your sensory faculties that could play this role? Or would it be your mind, a power quite other than the senses or anything connected to them? If it is your mind, and it is a faculty distinct from the senses, is its awareness mediated or unmediated? I don't see how, in this particular moment, you would need anything to mediate your awareness. Rather, your consciousness at this moment is unmediated, and it follows that you can be conscious of your self without reliance upon any other power or the intervention of any other faculty. . . . Does it occur to you to ask whether the vehicle of your awareness is not the skin that you can see with your own eyes? It is not. Even if you shed your skin and acquired another, you would still be you . . .
>
> You might say, "I affirm my own reality only through awareness of my own actions." But, if so, you must have some action that you affirm in our illustration, some motion or some

> other act. But we excluded that, by hypothesis. And even though you speak of an action in the most general terms, this action of yours, if you posit an action categorically, must have a subject categorically. And that precisely is your self.[55]

Kant calls the outcome of the Cartesian approach we find anticipated in Avicenna, "problematic idealism," because its treatment of the conscious subject as in principle independent of any body, whether its own or that of any external thing, renders the knowledge of external bodies dependent on our knowledge of the reality and veracity of the mind. Problematic idealism is a form of realism, since in the end it does accept the reality of external bodies. But Kant was sensitive to charges of idealism against his own system and therefore sought to rebut "problematic idealism" and vindicate what he took to be a more wholesome realism. This he did by appealing to his own analysis of the pure forms of sensibility (time and space) to argue, that it is a delusion to suppose that human consciousness is possible without awareness of an external world, since consciousness is always temporal, and temporality presupposes, as a point of reference, an external permanence, i.e., that of a body. Thus "The mere, but empirically determined, consciousness of my own existence proves the existence of objects in space outside me."[56]

What this means for Ibn Sīnā is that, if Kant is right in holding that consciousness is *always empirically determined*, one cannot, as Avicenna's thought experiment purports to show, posit consciousness without simultaneously positing a body. The one *does* presuppose the other, and neither is, in Cartesian terms, to be conceived solely in terms of itself; or, in Avicennan terms, to be affirmed without the affirmation of the other. Kant's claim against Avicenna would be that the consciousness projected in the thought experiment, minimally would be temporal, and that its temporality in turn would necessarily be marked by some sensory or otherwise physically grounded event, rhythm, or sequence, whether consciously differentiated or unnoticed but nonetheless presupposed.

Kant's argument is an improvement over Hume's bald and argumentative assertion that one simply never sees the "self" – a fact that Avicenna and others in the tradition he represents readily acknowledge and can as readily account for simply in the terms by which they describe the phenomenology of self-consciousness. The strength of Kant's argument is in the premise that all human consciousness is temporal, a thesis that some varieties of pure rationalism may be reluctant to adopt, but one which we conceded at the outset of this chapter. The assertion that the scope of conceptual thought extends beyond the bounds of temporality does not in my view depend on the (Quixotic) denial of the temporality of all human consciousness. For we can designate conceptually (and keep tabs on nominally, or mathematically) notions that we can in no way encounter experientially. I think the heart of what unites Plato's interest in the mathematical with his interest in the mythic and symbolic is the capacity of both these realms to intend what experiential, i.e., temporal consciousness cannot compass. But if we can, intellectually, intend what we do not experientially encounter, we need not rely on troublesome descriptions of the timelessness of mystic experience, conceptual apprehensions, or dreamless sleep to allow ourselves to recognize that we have knowledge of many things that are not temporal (mathematical and logical knowledge being paradigm cases among them), although the awareness we have of them, and our avenues of reaching it are entirely temporal.

Ibn Sīnā will be loath to grant Kant's claim that all consciousness is temporal. For him both conceptual knowledge and mystical experience are foretastes of the timelessness of immortality - even if both are somewhat tainted by temporality in our access to them and egress from them. Thus Ibn Sīnā rejects the (ultimately Platonic) recognition that all individual consciousness is temporal.[57] But even granting such temporality, weaknesses remain in Kant's criticism. The assumption that the permanence presupposed by temporality cannot belong, say, to the soul itself, rather than to some external thing, is highly tendentious. And the supposition that the external thing in question must be a body seems circular to me. It presumes that, in order to explain the experience of temporality, we must make reference to the very bodies whose existence is in question on the Cartesian model, or not affirmed on the Avicennan model. Plotinus, for one, makes the life and discursive thought of the Soul the condition of time and change, rather than treating body *per se* as their necessary basis.

A psychologistic counterpart to the Aristotelian assumption that time is the measure of motion underlies Kant's argument, allowing him to infer from the mere awareness of time to the reality of bodies. The argument is undergirded by the assumption that awareness of time must express physically grounded sensory or apperceptive events - that our sense of the passage of time is the marking of physiological processes, of noticeable (even if backgrounded or unnoticed) changes in the sensory field, or of constancy in that field relative to changes in our apperception. Since the Kantian criticism rests on a psychologistic revision of Aristotle's relativistic definition of time, Ibn Sīnā's acceptance of that definition, which takes time to be the measure of motion, may damage his claims for the purity of consciousness. A theory like that of al-Rāzī, who held time to be an absolute,[58] might have served him better here. But such a theory would probably have unglued Ibn Sīnā's commitment to an ageless (i.e., perpetually enduring) universe, and so was not available to him.

Ibn Sīnā clearly needs time to be relative to consciousness if he is not to say that disembodied consciousness transcends the temporality that once gave it individuation by giving it a history. For acceptance of the claim that disembodied minds are atemporal would be a major concession to the Platonic dissolution of their individuality which Ibn Sīnā hopes to avoid. A mind without matter to individuate it seems to flutter too freely over the abyss of eternity if the only thread that holds fast its individuation is the tenseless fact that once it had a history of its own. Ibn Sīnā finds attractive the claim that pure conceptual thought is timeless, but that undermines the homeliness of his thought experiment (the consciousness of the floating man is *not* atemporal) as well as compromising his resistance to Platonic absorption (or quasi-absorption) of the self within the All – the path that Ibn Bājjah, Ibn Ṭufayl, and Maimonides were to take.

The strength of Kant's criticism, which I think strikes Ibn Sīnā as hard as it does Descartes, is in exposing the artificiality of the abstraction of consciousness from what may or may not be its (material) conditions. Here I think Ibn Sīnā's argument is fatally hit. Such abstractions as those employed in Ibn Sīnā's Floating Man argument can tell us what consciousness is. The clarification of such matters of definition is indeed the purpose of analysis, and both the Cartesian *cogito* and the Avicennan Floating Man are tools of analysis. But such abstractive devices can never tell us *what* consciousness is, i.e., that it is a substance, that such a substance as the soul exists – which it was Ibn Sīnā's hope to demonstrate.

For such reasons as this and because I believe that more is at stake in Ibn Sīnā's argumentation for the substantiality of the soul than the mere assertion of the *separability* of the human rational soul from the body, I have argued that Ibn Sīnā's defense of substantiality should be read in terms of his own functionalistic conception of the soul.[59] Ibn Sīnā does use his arguments for the substantiality of the soul to prove its immortality and incorruptibility, but in so doing, he argues from the essential independence of the soul.[60] He holds that intellectual apprehension would be impossible if the soul's action were wholly dependent on the body,[61] that self-knowledge would be impossible if rational consciousness were dependent on an organ (just as sense perception and imagination cannot see the organs they employ), that the understanding, unlike the senses, is not worn down by constant use, damaged by focusing on powerful objects, or eroded by age. On the contrary, wisdom improves with maturity, even as the senses have begun to wane. And, if it is argued that forgetfulness also takes hold with age or illness, the philosopher answers that it is only increased care for the needs of the body that distracts the souls of the elderly or ill from intellectual functions.[62]

Now I would not say that the independent action of the intellectual soul is the entire cash value of Ibn Sīnā's affirmation of the substantiality of the soul. Separability is central among the philosopher's commitments. Still, his commitment to immortality leads him to articulate a doctrine of the substantiality of the soul whose central content is the thesis that the soul is not dependent wholly on the body, is not a mere quality or activity of a material thing or expression of its material properties. The soul for Ibn Sīnā does not exist in the body as a mere form in a substrate; and this idea has a significance for us far beyond the question of the soul's putative separability. It means that human actions are not to be conceived solely in terms of the behavior of the body, are not reducible to physical terms or explicable wholly and solely by reference to mechanical (or electro-mechanical) events. The soul is not a mere function of the body. Its actions are not always to be conceived as passive or dependent variables. They are independent as well. Souls can affect bodies; it is not always a case of bodies affecting souls. Ideas, beliefs, and volitions can have consequences and can, indeed, be self-governing. This thesis (unlike the idea of a disembodied soul) is crucial to our ability to maintain or restore the idea that a *person* is an agent, that human thought, action, and experience are not adequately described or explained in mechanistic terms. Thus, to say that the soul is a substance is not merely to make a soteriological claim; it is to claim that human beings are subjects, that we can and do act and are not simply acted upon. Freedom and autonomy, the inadequacy of reductive mechanism, rather than immortality in a traditional sense, here become the critical issues regarding the substantiality of the soul.

The key claim for us here is that regardless of the intimacy and complexity of the relationship between consciousness and the body, the relationship is not simply that of effect to cause.[63] Bodies act (for

Avicenna) insofar as they have specific forms; but souls act as well. Their states are not strictly determined by those of the bodies they belong to, even if it proves to be the case that for every mental state there is a corresponding physical state in the body or the brain. Consciousness itself may be a determinant of the states of the body – as, for example, when we discover or develop an idea or come to a decision, and consciousness itself determines the conformation of the brain and the resultant operations, say, in committing the relevant words, images, or symbols to memory, or effectuating an overt action.

Freedom may seem at first to be just as problematic a thesis as separability or immortality, but we have a wealth of phenomenological data in the one case that are simply unavailable in the other. The same or very similar physical circumstances apparently do not invariably produce the same ideas, practical or emotive responses. And, even when all the physical or physiological "givens" in a situation have exercised their effect, we find phenomena such as changes of heart, spontaneous decisions, creative discoveries, and inventions in the sciences and the arts, spur of the moment notions, whims, and caprices, which make it hard to deny some measure of functional autonomy to the mind.

What Avicenna's arguments for the substantiality of the soul portend for us, as I put it years ago, is that,

> The peculiar nature of self-consciousness is that it is self-constituting. It is not the consciousness of the brain, or of the body, or of anything but itself and the objects put before itself. It is unique, non-transferrable, indivisible, non-combinable. It need not conceive itself as occupying space or taking up place. It can readily put anything before itself as an object, but is present only to itself as a subject.[64]

Where Plotinus argued that bodies cannot think, Ibn Sīnā found *mutakallimūn* urging that there are no logical grounds for excluding such a possibility. To explain why bodies cannot think he did not minimize the intimacy of the nexus between the physical and the mental dimensions of psychology, but focused on the character of thought itself, conceptual thought, to bring home to us (regardless of how physically rooted we may find the elements or the matter of thought to be) the extent to which conceptual thinking and the purity of consciousness transcend the physicality which is their precondition. What cannot be denied, phenomenologically, is that bodies are not thought. Nothing but consciousness itself is self-conscious. Regardless of what consciousness depends on (and here I am more than prepared to part company with Avicenna), there is an aspect to the idea of the substantiality of consciousness which cannot be gainsaid: Once constituted, consciousness is not an accident, not a function of any other thing, as a dependent variable would be. It acts, construes, conceives the world and itself, creates the world conceptually and categorially, as vision projects its own miniature and manageable image of the world. Consciousness seizes autonomy for itself, and by acting and projecting makes itself a subject and neither an object nor any sort of mere reflection of or reaction to its surroundings.

The barest phenomena reveal (at least as clearly as they reveal temporality) that consciousness is not (to borrow Spinoza's trenchant image) a mere picture painted on a screen. It is invariably active, engaged, participatory, reflexive, and self-transparent (i.e., containing no referential opacity save what insincerity or bad faith erect). These are phenomenological givens well known at least since the time of John Philoponus to the tradition Ibn Sīnā represents.[65] Besides arguing for the unifying effects of consciousness, Ibn Sīnā expresses his conception of the self-transparency and self-instigated activity of the mind through the image of a body illuminated – and thus heated and made transparent – by the sun. He argues that when the soul, in due measure, supplies its own activity, the case would be as when the sun not only warms or illuminates an object but in fact sets it aflame. The active or functional autonomy of the human rational consciousness is the incandescent object, which receives its power from the sun, yet by that power gives light as well as receiving it.

3 THE SUBSTRATE OF IMMORTALITY

Ibn Sīnā argues at some length for the immortality of the soul. The core of his argument is the claim that, since the soul does not depend for its existence on that of the body, it cannot be presumed to be destroyed with the body's destruction.[66] For our own purposes, the functional rather than ontic autonomy of the soul seems to be what is most valuable and enduring in Avicenna's arguments here. Yet Avicenna's distinctive – Hall calls it "idiosyncratic"[67] – doctrine of individual (as opposed to collective) immortality (as opposed to physical resurrection) itself bears a significance quite beyond the grasp of animal appetite eager for longer, richer, or more trouble-free existence.

In all three of the monotheistic sister faiths, Islam, Christianity, and Judaism, we know our obligations and the nature of the good life as the will of God, specified in Revelation and interpreted in tradition. We know God as the Ideal of Perfection; and perfection, as relevant to our obligations, through human nature. What prevents the scheme from collapsing into circularity is our intuitive, Platonic knowledge of the Good Itself, our scientific knowledge of nature, and the junction of the two in our knowledge of the self. As Alexander Altmann showed some years ago, monotheists recast the Delphic maxim KNOW THYSELF into a powerful epistemic tool. The ancient meaning of the motto inscribed at the Pythian oracle of Apollo, was a warning to acknowledge our mortality, to know that we are human, not divine. The same message underlies the ancient Oedipus tragedy: that man, in seeking to escape his destiny, is ignorant of all that mortality portends, and so, despite his seeming understanding, ignorant of the most elementary fact about himself, graphically represented in the riddle of the Sphinx, that man grows old and dies. But for Plato and for later thinkers in his tradition the Delphic maxim formed the clew to an elaborately woven tissue of glosses and conceits that philosophers cast at higher game.[68]

Ibn Sīnā finds in the maxim an invitation to profound self-scrutiny. The motto, he says, is shared by philosophers and saints – scientists and mystics alike. For it was passed down among the ancients in one of their temples,[69] but it had also entered Islamic tradition as the saying: "He who knows himself knows his Lord." By Avicenna's time this saying had become a favorite *ḥadīth* of "intoxicated" – i.e., pantheistic[70] – Sufis, for its suggestion of the soul's identity with God. But philosophers and theologians of more sober stamp shied away from the idea that the inner self is divine, preferring another Platonic suggestion, that the mind knows God through an inner likeness.[71] Ibn Sīnā understood this likeness in terms of the realization of the human intellect, its perfection as an intellect through assimilation to and contact with the Active Intellect. It is through such contact, as we have seen, that we know the forms of things, i.e., know things as they really are, as God knows them; and it is through such assimilation that we know God.[72] For God is the cynosure of the Active Intellect. As Philip Merlan shows, Alexander of Aphrodisias laid the groundwork for the theory when he argued, in a Peripatetic, intellectualist gloss of Plato's *homoiosis theoi*, that man's "material intelligence" is like the unwrittenness of a slate; when it is transformed into active intelligence it achieves a likening to the divine.[73]

The idea of intellectual contact with the Divine does seem to open the door, however, not merely to a likeness between man and God but to their identity. After all, matter is the Aristotelian principle of individuation. Once our embodiment is transcended, no membrane, it would seem, remains to divide a disembodied, or wholly en-*formed*, soul from its Source. The mind for Aristotle *is* what it knows, so to know God seems tantamount to *being* God. Describing the state of the fulfilled human intelligence on such a model, Merlan writes:

> in lieu of the cloud of unknowing, we have in rationalistic mysticism the flood of sheer light . . . absolute transparency . . . self-knowledge. In an ordinary act of knowledge the object of knowledge is something opaque which knowledge illuminates and makes visible. But in the ecstatic act of knowledge nothing opaque is left, because what is known is identical with what knows . . . Omniscience is the ultimate goal . . . to know god and to possess divine omniscience coincide . . . Aristotle meant literally what he said: there is a kind of knowledge which is in some way all-comprehensive. God possesses it – man should try to acquire it. . . . Man desires and is able to divinize himself.[74]

Plato's playful references to Empedocles' associative model of the knowing of like by like here become the foreplay to perfect mystic union. But that consummation is not devoutly wished by every exponent of the tradition. Where pagan thought could freely speak of the indwelling of *a* god or of union with some divine being, strict monotheism must rely on Neoplatonic hypostases, which are nothing apart from God, yet are not simply identical with God, if anything is to be distinguished from the Absolute. The preservation of individuality becomes critical here, if the world is not to collapse into the undifferentiated monism of Parmenides. And the preservation of human individuality is critical to Ibn Sīnā in particular, lest the immortality he sought so single mindedly collapse into the all-encompassing unity of the Godhead.[75]

Avicenna recognizes and values the access to divinity and the forms of all things that the Neoplatonic theory of assimilation to God affords. But by preserving the subject–object distinction he reaps a benefit of rational mysticism that might not have been expected, preserving the individuality of the disembodied soul and protecting his Neoplatonism from a pantheistic reduction. Ibn Sīnā shares al-Fārābī's thought that through contact with the Active Intellect we know (to the extent that this is humanly possible) as God does and thus know God and indeed all things. On Platonic principles it is possible to know anything scientifically only if one knows as God does. But it is crucial for Ibn Sīnā to preserve individual identity as the locus of this knowledge. The immortality of assimilation would come at too high a price if it meant loss of the very identity that is to enjoy the beatific state.

Innocent of Stace's dogma of the ineffable and oceanic character of all ecstatic experience, Ibn Sīnā preserves the rational mind even (or especially!) in the height of ecstasy, securing consciousness against an emotive identification of its finitude with God's infinitude and ensuring the continuum between knowing all things in their specificity and knowing God. For without that continuum, mystic experience is made to foster the illusion of the absoluteness of the merely contingent I, and the promised omniscience is evacuated of all concrete content. As Majid Fakhry writes of Ibn Sīnā's scheme:

> The whole process of human cognition thus becomes a gradual progression or ascent from the lowest condition of potentiality to the highest condition of actuality, or the apprehension of those intelligibles stored away in the active intellect. The name that Ibn Sīnā and his successors gave to this progression is not union with, or even vision of, but rather conjunction or contact (*ittiṣāl*) with the active intellect.[76]

It was the schematism of the Active Intellect that allowed Ibn Sīnā to frame the logic behind the inference "he who knows himself knows his Lord."[77] To render that inference cogent, articulate its terms and discover their logical relations was an achievement that all natural theologians could treasure, especially because Avicenna set aside the potential for pantheism in the Socratic idea that there is a god within us. He criticized Porphyry for upholding the *union* of the soul with the Intellect, taking this clearly to imply the loss of individual identity, defeating what Ibn Sīnā took to be the very goal of rational mysticism, the attainment of individual immortality. Nor did he accept Plotinus' teaching of the divinity of the soul.[78] Rather, he used the full rigor of Neoplatonism to discipline the idea that the fulfilled human intelligence is (in the language of the more sober mystics) in contact (*ittiṣāl*) with Divine.

This term too, like so much of the language of mysticism, is found in Plotinus.[79] His word is *aphe*, a term used for the kindling of a flame, contact with a contagious disease, the touching of harpstrings, the contact of a wrestler in a grip (cf. *Genesis* 32:25), the intersection of two lines or surfaces in geometry, or any point of juncture. Contact allows direct apprehension. At the surfaces contiguous figures do become one. But each retains its identity. Neither is reduced to the other. So in knowledge or in ecstasy, as Ibn Sīnā understands it, the individual is still present as a subject, to receive the higher understanding that gnosis makes possible. And God too does not vanish, swallowed up into the illusory ocean of human consciousness in what the Sufis call its "expansive" mode.

In a passage that profoundly influences Maimonides' opening discussion of the *Guide to the Perplexed*, where the human rational soul is identified as the referent in the Biblical affirmation that man was created in God's image and likeness, Ibn Sīnā identifies what is spiritual or intellectual with what is immortal in man. But he is careful in so doing not to speak of any fusion that would merge or submerge individual human identity:

> The work of the human rational soul is the noblest of tasks, since it is the noblest of spirits. Thus its office is to contemplate reflectively on the marvels of God's art, its face turned toward the higher world. For it does not love this lower realm and meaner station. As the guardian of higher things, preserving the thought of the Primal Realities, it has no interest in food or drink and no need for kissing or coupling. Rather its task is to await the unveiling of realities and focus its perfect intuition (*ḥads*)[80] and unsullied consciousness (*dhihn*) on the apprehension of the subtlest of principles and read with the inner eye of insight the tablet of God's mysteries, combatting with every device at its command the pretensions of vain fancy.
>
> It is distinguished from all other spirits by its perfect rationality, its comprehensive and articulate intellectuality; and its object, throughout life, is to purge the sensory and grasp the conceptual. God gave it a power specific to it, the like of which no other spirit shares: the power of reason. Reason is the tongue of the angels, which have no voice or verbal language but through this gift apprehend without sensation and impart understanding without words. It is reason that orders man's relation to the supernal world (*Malakūt*), and speech itself merely follows after. For one who does not know how to reason is powerless to set forth the truth . . .
>
> The activity most distinctive to the human soul is knowing, consciousness. It has many uses, including acknowledgement, recognition, and worship of God. For when a person knows his

> Lord in thought, apprehends His Identity in the mind, sees His grace mentally, by way of reason, he ponders the very essence of God's creative act: One sees the perfection of the Truth Itself in the celestial bodies and supernal substances, recognizing that they are the most perfect of all created things, in view of their transcendence of all corruption, turbidity, and compounding of conflicting natures; one sees in one's own rational self a being akin to the very eternity and rationality of the heavenly bodies, and one rises in thought to the Commanding Word of the Unseen and recognizes that command as well as creation are His, as He says: "Are not creation and command His?" (*Qur'ān* 52:7). For the flowing forth of creation is entailed by His Command.
>
> As a result one yearns to apprehend all the levels of their hierarchy, one is aroused to enter into relation with them and to share in their exaltedness, and so one ever humbles oneself and meditates stedfastly, praying and fasting constantly, thereby attaining abundant reward. For it is the human soul that receives a reward, since it survives the perishing of the body and is unmolested by the passage of time. It is the soul that is brought back after death. By death I mean the sundering of soul from body, and by resurrection, the linking (*muwāṣila*) of the soul with those spiritual substances, and its reward and bliss is this resurrection.[81]

God's command here is the Word or *logos*, understood Qur'anically as the imperative BE, by which God created. It is assimilated Platonically to the supernal world of the intellectual realities or pure, disembodied intelligences. The celestial bodies, because of and despite their perfectness as bodies, bespeak the divine Command or Word or Wisdom, from which they flow and by which they are necessitated, precisely because they are not necessary in themselves. Perfect as they are, there is no contradiction in denying their reality. They are contingent in themselves, necessitated only by their Cause. The pretensions of vain fancy, which one must combat even in the penumbra of the beatific experience, are the pantheistic delusions that might lead one speciously to identify oneself as one of the supernals. And the resurrection promised in the *Qur'ān* is none other than the eternity and imperturbability that the rational soul enjoys once sundered from the body, a joy proportioned, as Ibn Sīnā argues in the sequel, to the degree in which the inner spiritual and intellectual nature of the mind has indeed successfully disengaged itself from its physicality. It is neither the physical resurrection hoped for by the literal minded, nor the fusion with the supernal expected by the less sober of the Sufis. Arberry casually renders *muwāṣila* as "union," but Ibn Sīnā is careful to say "linkage," using the same root, with the same semantic force as is present in his carefully chosen use of the term *ittiṣāl.*

Merlan fuses Avicenna's *ittiṣāl* with the more monistic *ittiḥād,* union with communion. But Avicenna insists on the distinction, for good reason. His argument is that, if the human mind actually *became* the Active Intellect, that hypostasis would be divisible. Otherwise, the mind that knows anything would know everything. Here Avicenna relies on the primary datum of individual consciousness, its privileged self-access, privacy, and inviolability, laying the groundwork for the Cartesian *sum res cogitans,* just as his Floating Man argument lays the groundwork for the Cartesian *cogito.* The nub of the argument is that there is no consciousness for the intellect, higher or otherwise, without individuality.

Ibn Sīnā underscores this argument in the *Book of Hints and Pointers,* arguing against the claim that conceptual knowledge involves the identity of the mind with its object, a theory he ascribes to "certain writers." As Goichon points out, Ibn Sīnā himself used such (Aristotelian) language in his earlier works, but abandoned it when he came to see its implications. How, he demands, can a subject know anything if in the very act of knowing it loses its own unique identity? Does a mind that knows first *A* and then *B* remain the same mind that knew *A*? If the communion of the mind with the Active Intellect, by which knowledge is agreed to occur, amounts to union with the Active Intellect, and that hypostasis is not rendered divisible by this fusion with human particularity, then surely the finite mind would become omniscient, since it would now contain every intelligible form, the pattern and plan of all creation.

Porphyry, who is blamed for the doctrine that the knowing mind unites with the Active Intellect, is reported to have written a book on the subject highly praised by the Peripatetics but "dried up, fleshless dates," in Ibn Sīnā's estimation. Porphyry's admirers, he adds, feared that they did not understand his book, but the fact is, Ibn Sīnā insists, Porphyry did not understand it himself. The vituperative tone of this treatment, near the end of Avicenna's most mature and considered work, leaves no doubt about the the earnestness of the arguments it caps, aimed vigorously and concertedly against the union of knower with known and the fusion of the mind of the human knower with the Active Intellect, which is the condition of its knowing.[82]

Yet Merlan chastises Goichon for projecting a Thomistic orthodoxy on Ibn Sīnā. This puts the cart before the horse. Ibn Sīnā laid out the metaphysics that made possible Thomas' articulation of an orthodox position here. Merlan's reading ignores the arguments and the emphatic language of the philosopher and substitutes an enthusiasm Merlan disclaims[83] for the insistent clarity of Avicenna's text.[84] To substantiate his claim, Merlan relies on a remark in Ibn Sīnā's "Essay on Love": "The highest degree of approximation to It is the reception of its manifestation in its full reality, i.e., in the most perfect way possible, and this is what the Sufis call unification (*ittiḥād*)."[85] Merlan takes this to mean that "Avicenna within his system had a place for the 'ecstatic,' highly emotional union of Sufi mysticism and used the term *ittiḥād* to describe it." But this is to confuse use with mention. Ibn Sīnā is explaining the real nature of what the Sufis (misleadingly) call *ittiḥād*.[86] Like Fackenheim, Fakhry is misled by this remark, treating it as an exception to Avicenna's usual contentment with "conjunction" with the Active Intellect, "an emanation ten times removed from God." "Only once," Fakhry writes, "does Avicenna appear to abandon the language of conjunction (*ittiṣāl*) and to replace it by that of union (*ittiḥād*) – and that in a mystical treatise *On Love*."[87] But this notion is based on a misreading of Avicenna's words, and no apology for the context of the exposition is necessary. Ibn Sīnā does not abandon his carefully qualified theory at all.

More strictly translated, and including the opening lines that precede the passage Merlan quotes, Ibn Sīnā's words were, "We want to show in this chapter (*a*) that every being loves the Absolute Good with an innate love, (*b*) that the Absolute Good manifests Itself to all those that love it, although their receptivity to that epiphany and their contact (*ittiṣāl*) with it vary, and (*c*) that the highest degree of assimilation to it is in receiving its true epiphany (or manifestation), that is, as perfectly as possible. This is the meaning (*al-ma'nā*) of what the Sufis call union (*ittiḥād*)," or, more literally, "this is what the Sufis intend by the word 'union.'"[88]

Characteristically, Ibn Sīnā analyzes a religious idea for its philosophically workable content. Since maintenance of the integrity of the Absolute or Necessary Being is a value in his philosophy secured by his most rigorous arguments, those demarcating contingent from necessary being, it is not surprising that the outcome of his analysis should coincide with the commitment of orthodoxy to preserving the

Divine from pantheistic reduction. Ibn Sīnā fully recognizes that the manifestation or epiphany accessible to any being (animate or inanimate, rational or irrational) will depend on the recipient's capacity. So the manifestation is not identical with the Absolute Good, but is a true (not "real") expression of Him, as perfect as the specific limitations of each being allow. The qualification clearly echoes Plato's "insofar as in us lies" (*Theaetetus* 176B), a concession to the limits and the boundaries of humanity.

The classic danger of pantheism is its liability to equivocation: Is nature enlarged and elevated to the sanctity of God, or is God reduced to the fragility of nature? In *ḥulūlī* or immanentist varieties of Sufism in Islam that spring not only from ecstatic emotion but from the incarnationist penchant of charismatic Shī'ism, as in other experiments with pantheism, both sides of the equivocation are essayed, often simultaneously. Any false inferences that result are laid off against the traditional paradoxicality of the ineffable and ineffability of the mystical. Symptomatic of the dialectic between the alternative extremes, the one which elevates the self to the absoluteness of God and the other which debases God to the fragility of the self, are the mood swings of constriction and expansion that call forth the Sufi discipline of the *ṭarīqas* as a means of their direction and control.

Ibn Sīnā forestalls the oscillation not with a spiritual regimen but with the discipline of metaphysics, blocking the equivocation that is its source conceptually if not emotively. He interposes a two-fold safeguard: He sets the Active Intellect firmly between the mind and God, and he preempts the identification of even the Active Intellect with the human mind, insisting that the very fact of consciousness, which gnosis should heighten, guarantees our discrete identity and thus precludes the loss of individuality in the wholeness of *any* hypostasis.[89]

Despite his many criticisms of the philosopher, al-Ghazālī adopts Ibn Sīnā's solution here, even to the point of relying on the Neoplatonic device of an intermediary between man and what he knows. In the *Kitāb al-Maḍnūn al-Ṣaghīr*, or "Esoteric Minor," al-Ghazālī links a problematic *ḥadīth* based on the Biblical thesis that God created man in his own image with what we might call the Delphic *ḥadīth*, arguing that the man who knows himself knows God *because* of the inner kinship between man and God. The basis of that kinship, he explains elsewhere, is the human soul.[90] It is this that makes man a microcosm, ruled by the soul as the world is ruled by God. In the *Niche for Lamps*, glossing the celebrated Light verse of the *Qur'ān*, a key topos for

Neoplatonic fusions of Islamic and Greek thought, al-Ghazālī is most explicit in his Avicennism. There, as Altmann explains, he distinguishes God in His transcendence from his Presence (*ḥaḍra*; cf. the Hebrew *shekhinah*), a hypostasis variously called *al-Raḥmān*, the Merciful (commonly taken as an epithet of God Himself), or *al-Muta'* (He who must be obeyed).

Altmann recognizes the functional equivalence of such figures to the Philonic *logos* yet wonders along with W.H.T. Gairdner, the translator of the *Niche for Lamps*, whether the sensitivity shown here to the immanentist type of pantheism represented by the crucified Muslim mystic al-Ḥallāj does not mean "that al-Ghazālī considered, albeit for a fleeting moment and with great hesitation, the possibility of understanding the *ḥadīth* about man being in the image of God, and, obviously also the *ḥadīth* about self-knowledge, in terms of an ultimate identity."[91] I suspect that Ibn Ṭufayl caught al-Ghazālī's intent more precisely when he read him as carefully skirting the heretical enthusiasms of such pantheistically inclined Sufis as al-Ḥallāj or al-Bistāmī while not abjuring the access of the mind to the divine that the Neoplatonic theory of assimilation could afford. As Ibn Ṭufayl wrote of al-Ghazālī on just this issue, "his was a mind refined by learning and education."[92] The refinement here is what al-Ghazālī learned from Ibn Sīnā, and through him from the Neoplatonic tradition.[93] This was the learning that allowed al-Ghazālī the freedom he exploited in reaching out for God without fear of absolute absorption and without the appetitive ambition to *become* God: The mind does not become God but comes into intellectual contact or contiguity with the Active Intellect, a hypostasis, to be sure, but the bearer of the form in which human likeness to the divine is made most vivid.

Pablo Neruda, in a poetic line of confessional power, writes, "I closed my eyes and foundered in the core of my own substance." When Avicenna takes flight in his Flying Man thought experiment, closing his eyes to the world and even to the fact of his own embodiment, has he foundered, rather than found the core of his own substance, as he had hoped? Clearly, he does not situate or indeed existentiate the self in its dialectical interaction with a physical, let alone a social environment, as many a philosopher and phenomenologist might have wished him to do. Indeed, he does not ground the substantiality or ontic and active primacy of the human rational soul in any other thing, epistemically – not even in the delicate balance of its dependence on and independence of his God, as he is so careful to do ontically with all finite things, finding their very being in their contingency. The human rational soul, whose act is consciousness, finds itself in a proto-Cartesian (or post-Philoponean) act of self-affirmation. Yet even the immortality which self-consciousness seems to Ibn Sīnā to bespeak does not take its claims beyond the realm of the contingent and dependent. Ontically the dialectic of the Necessary and the contingent remains, providing the discipline that will preserve the mystic gnosis of Avicenna from the antinomian excesses of pantheistic immanentism with as clear and calm an authority as that by which it allows Descartes to keep the skirts of the same rational soul from trailing in the muddiness of materiality and catching in the wheels of physicality to submerge consciousness itself among the objects which never will be subjects in the pure and perfect sense that Avicenna, like Descartes, speaks of.

Clearly Avicenna does not choose to lay emphasis upon the material and indeed social conditions of the birth of consciousness. And in one way this is a flaw. Indeed (and like Descartes) he accepts the gift of clarity of consciousness from God without making awareness of its imparting an *intrinsic* condition of its possession. This he does despite the fact that an awareness of that conditionedness, with all that it entails by way of ontogeny, phylogeny, cosmogony, evolutionary ecology, politics, and familial support, is the mediate and immediate condition of any adequate understanding of the miracle of consciousness. He does it despite his own recognition theologically, and even biologically or sociologically, that no comprehensive grasp of the true nature of consciousness is possible in such purely abstract terms. The self of the Floating Man argument is an abstract and abstractive entity, in much the way that the self of the Cartesian *cogito* is an abstract and abstractive entity, as Descartes himself acknowledged.[94] That is, it is a fiction, as Ibn Sīnā's references to it as part of a hypothetical stipulation repeatedly call to mind. And yet, that abstractive fiction does serve a purpose, Avicenna's purpose of reminding us insistently of the Primacy of individual consciousness, not ontically, and still less historically, but epistemically, creatively, as a prime mover in the realm of thought. For, regardless of how consciousness comes to be (and Ibn Sīnā would be the last philosopher to imagine that it was eternal, unconditioned, or ahistorical), once it exists the mind does act. And, as Ibn Sīnā shows us, its most distinctive act as consciousness is to differentiate itself from all that it is not, even from all that its own existence presupposes. Without the primal recognition of the fundamental datum of consciousness, there would be no intersubjectivity to engage with, no physicality other than that of mere things, no act of creation that could be acknowledged.

NOTES

1 See Michael Marmura, "Avicenna on Primary Concepts in the *Metaphysics* of his *al-Shifā'*," in R.M. Savory and D.A. Agius, eds, *Logos Islamikos . . . in honorem G.M. Wickens* (Montreal: Pontifical Institute of Medieval Studies, 1984) 219–39.

2 See Nelson Goodman, *Fact, Fiction and Forecast* (London: Athlone, 1954) and C.I. Lewis' reduction of scientific laws to solipsistic *yet predictive* statements about hypothetical observations in *An Analysis of Knowledge and Valuation* (La Salle: Open Court, 1950).

3 Ibn Ṭufayl, *Ḥayy Ibn Yaqẓān*, tr. Goodman (New York: Twayne, 1972; repr., Los Angeles: Gee Tee Bee, 1991) 100; cf. Oliver Leaman, *An Introduction to Medieval Islamic Philosophy* (London: Cambridge University Press, 1985) 91.

4 Herbert Davidson, "Alfarabi and Avicenna on the Active Intellect," *Viator* 3 (1972) 153: "The reason why Alfarabi took variant positions in different texts can only be conjectured, but the tone of his writings is suggestive. *Al-Madīna al-Fāḍila, al-Siyāsat al-Madaniyya*, the *Philosophy of Aristotle*, and the *Risāla fī al-'Aql* all read like matter-of-fact summaries of familiar positions – and yet the positions differ. It is therefore tempting to understand the differences as a result of Alfarabi's working from different oral and written sources at different times. . . .The position of the Commentary on the *Nicomachean Ethics* would then have been taken by Alfarabi when his reading of Alexander finally convinced him of the impossibility of any true immortality of the human intellect."

5 See my *On Justice* (New Haven: Yale University Press, 1991) 214–20.

6 See Ibn Sīnā, *Najāt, De Anima* XII–XIII, tr. Rahman, as *Avicenna's Psychology* (Oxford: Oxford University Press, 1952); repr., Westport: Hyperion, 1981) 56–63; cf. "The Afterlife," in Arberry, ed., *Avicenna on Theology*, 64–76; *Shifā' De Anima* V 2–4, ed. Rahman (London: Oxford University Press, 1959) 209–34.

7 Al-Ghazālī, *TF*, 1, ed. M. Bouyges, 2nd edn (Beirut: Catholic Press, 1930) 55; *TT*, ed. M. Bouyges, 25, translated by Simon Van Den Bergh as *L'Incohérence de l'Incohérence* (London: Luzac, 1954) 13.

8 Al-Ghazālī writes:

> And if it is said the truth is Plato's view that the soul is eternal and indeed one, divided only when embodied but reunited when sundered from those bodies and returned to its Source, we answer: This is still uglier and more absurd, and more fittingly held contrary to rational necessity. For we argue that the soul of Zayd is either identical with that of 'Amr, or different from it. But it cannot be identical, since each is conscious of his own identity (*yash'uru bi-nafsihi*) and knows that it is not that of anyone else. If they were identical, the knowledge which is constitutive in the identity of each and which enters into every relation that they are party to would also be identical.

TF, 55 = *TT*, Bouyges 28, tr. Van Den Bergh, 15. Thérèse Druart asks (in a private communication) whether the two men would be one if their knowledge were identical. But in the Avicennan theory of individual identity, on which al-Ghazālī builds here, the uniqueness of individual knowledge is guaranteed by the uniqueness of our individual histories. This is what is constitutive in the formation of human identity according to Ibn Sīnā. But, even if two men had the same histories (say, in different, unconnected worlds), they would be two and not one; their minds would be distinct, although the proof would be a little less obvious than the marker Ibn Sīnā uses. The discreteness of our knowledge is a sufficient proof, not a necessary condition, of our separateness.

9 See Philoponus, *De Anima*, in *Commentaria in Aristotelem Graeca*, 15 (1897), 465, where the equation of self-consciousness with the rational ego (*to prosektikon*) is ascribed to "modern" interpreters of Aristotle (*hoi neoteroi*). In adopting this view, Philoponus emphasizes the everpresent *I, ego* that accompanies all our experiences. As Rahman points out in *Avicenna's Psychology* 103–4, even "Aristotle, although . . . he maintained the unity of the soul in experience, he failed to formulate the idea of an individual central ego, on account of his general doctrine that soul in itself, being form, is universal and is individualized only through matter." Symptomatic of Aristotle's difficulty here, and compounding the problem, as Rahman observes, was Aristotle's attribution of self-consciousness "to a sensual principle."

10 The Floating Man argument is discussed below in section 2, pp. 149–63.

11 In particular, see the *Meno* and the *Theaetetus*.

12 *Najāt, De Anima*, tr. Rahman, 36.

13 *Najāt, De Anima*, tr. Rahman, 30.

14 *Posterior Analytics* II 19, 100a 4–14. G.R.G. Mure renders: "until the original formation has been restored." But the argument thrusts powerfully *against* Platonic *anamnesis*. (Jonathan Barnes reads *aklen* for *archen*, to give the sense: "until a position of strength is reached." But this seems unnecessary to me.) A company regroups when it finds *any* workable battle order, not necessarily a preestablished one, as though the scene were a parade-ground rather than a battlefield. True Aristotle privileges certain patterns, but these are ordered by nature and our situation, not by freestanding Ideas.

15 *Nicomachaean Ethics* V 10, 1037b 30; and see Martin Ostwald's note *ad loc*. in his translation (Indianapolis: Bobbs-Merrill, 1962). Such rules are still in use; some made of (vinyl covered) lead, others of articulated links. They are illustrated in the better tool catalogues.

16 See G.E.L. Owen, "Tithenai ta Phainomena," in J.M.E. Moravcsik, *Aristotle: A Collection of Critical Essays* (Garden City, NY: Doubleday, 1967) 167–91; first published in French in *Symposium Aristotelicum* (Louvain, 1961) 83–103.

17 Ibn Sīnā, *Shifā'*, *De Anima* V 5, ed. Rahman, 234–5.

18 See the *Najāt*, *De Anima* VII–X, tr. Rahman, 38–54.

19 Ibn Sīnā, *Shifā'*, *De Anima* V 2, ed. Rahman, 216.

20 Ibn Sīnā, *Shifā'*, *De Anima* V 2, ed. Rahman, 215.

21 Ibn Sīnā, *Shifā'*, *De Anima* V 2, ed. Rahman, 216. See S. Landauer, "Die Psychologie des Ibn Sīnā," *ZDMG* 29 (1876) 370–1.

22 *Danesh Nameh*, tr. Achena and Massé, *Le Livre de Science* 1 (Paris: Les Belles Lettres) 111. Scammony, *Convolvulus scammonia*, is a morning glory the resin of whose roots is a powerful cathartic.

23 *Shifā'*, *Burhān* 9, ed. A.A. Afifi (Cairo, 1956) 93–8, 222–4; cf. N. Heer, "Ibn Sīnā's Justification of the Use of Induction in Demonstration," presented at the A. O.

S. Western Branch, Seattle, 26 October 1990.

24 Ibn Sīnā develops his argument here at some length in view of the notion of certain *mutakallimūn* that consciousness or knowledge was located in a single, geometrically indivisible atom.

25 Ibn Sīnā, *Shifā'*, *De Anima* V 2, ed. Rahman, 209–13.

26 Fazlur Rahman writes (*Avicenna's Psychology*, 98–9) that Ibn Sīnā's "elaborate argument" to prove that imagination is a physical faculty has, "so far as I know, no Greek source. It most probably emanates from Avicenna himself." The thesis that imagination is a physical faculty is found in al-Fārābī, *'Arā ahli 'l-Madīnati 'l-Fāḍila*, ed. and tr. R. Walzer (Oxford: Oxford University Press, 1985) 165 l. 9; 211–27. The endeavor to place such faculties as imagination anatomically stems from Galenic medicine. Galen offers evidence, for example, from the disabilities caused by lesions in specific parts of the brain, as to the locations of the motive and sensitive powers; see *De plac. Hippocrat. et Plat.* vii 3 and Van Den Bergh's discussion in *TT* 2.189, n. 334.10, commenting on al-Ghazālī's summary of the Avicennan faculty psychology.

27 See Ibn Sīnā *Shifā'*, *De Anima*, ed. Rahman, 209 ff., 247–8; *Najāt* (Cairo, 1938) 174 ff.; *Ishārāt*, ed. J. Forget (Leiden, 1892) 129–30; tr. A.-M. Goichon (Paris: Vrin, 1951) 330–5.

28 See Noam Chomsky, "Linguistics and Philosophy," in Sidney Hook, ed., *Language and Philosophy* (New York: New York University Press, 1969) 60–94, reprinted in Stephen P. Stich, *Innate Ideas* (Berkeley: University of California Press, 1975) and Charles D. Laughlin and Eugene G. D'Aquili, *Biogenetic Structuralism* (New York: Columbia University Press, 1974).

29 A surprising number of writers continue to ascribe a rigid determinism to Ibn Sīnā, which is drawn not from his writings but from the seminal critique of his views so forcefully laid out by al-Ghazālī and widely echoed by others. For Ibn Sīnā's (intellectualist) account of divine volition, see Achena and Massé, 1.202–5; cf. 1.169–73, 178–85.

30 See Achena and Massé, 1.193–4.

31 See Ibn Sīnā, *Shifā'*, *Ilāhiyyāt*, ed. Anawati and Zayed, 413.

32 Ibn Sīnā, *Najāt*, *De Anima*, X–XII; *Shifā'*, *De Anima*, V 2.

33 *Qur'ān* 8:17. The verse is taken traditionally to refer to Muḥammad's casting dust in the eyes of the foe at the start of the Battle of Badr; but, as Watt remarks, the word *ramayta* "almost certainly refers to the shooting of arrows"; W. Montgomery Watt, *Companion to the Qur'ān* (London: Allen & Unwin, 1967), and *Muḥammad at Medinah* (Oxford: Clarendon Press, 1962) 312–13. As Watt puts it, the *Qur'ān* takes divine sovereignty and human responsibility to be "complementary"; see *Qur'ān* 2:5–6, 6:125, 7:92–9, 10:99, 18:28, 20:84, 76:29. The *Qur'ān* itself does not work out (or at least does not spell out) the basis of this complementarity – thus the *scriptural* relevance of work like Ibn Sīnā's here. But Ibn Sīnā's underlying assumption, that we act by powers imparted by God, is clearly representative of one line of Qur'ānic exegesis, that of the Mu'tazilites. Cf. Watt, *Free Will and Predestination in Early Islam* (London: Luzac, 1948) and *The Formative Period of Islamic Thought* (Edinburgh: Edinburgh University Press, 1973).

34 Aristotle, *Eudemian Ethics* VII 1248a 20–37. The text goes on to ascribe veridical dreams and special insights and intuitions to those who are well attuned to the divine.

35 See *Danesh Nameh*, Achena and Massé 2.66–77, and *Compendium of the Soul*, excerpts and discussion in Dimitri Gutas, *Avicenna and the Aristotelian Tradition* (Leiden: Brill, 1988) 16–21, 161–76.

36 Ikhwān al-Ṣafā', *Rasā'il* 1.392: "You should know that the inquiry involved in the study of logic involves finding out how the soul grasps the notions of beings as they really are, via the senses, and how ideas are kindled in the thought of the soul by the mind, which is called inspiration (*waḥy*) and revelation (*ilhām*)."

37 Ibn Sīnā, *Shifā', De Anima* I 1.

38 Cf. Alexander of Aphrodisias, *De Anima* 1.9–15, tr. Athanasios P. Fotinis (Washington: University Press of America, 1979) 6–11; esp. 1.12, p. 8: "every being owes to its form not only the particular mode of its existence, but also the differences which distinguish it from other things. Nor is this all: the different ways in which bodies act and are acted upon also result from their forms. For corporeal existents act and are acted upon inasmuch as they are bodies, but the specific ways in which they act and are affected result from form."

39 Al-Ghazālī, *TF* 17, Bouyges, 2nd edn, 196.

40 For Maimonides' elaboration of al-Ghazālī's equation of Neoplatonic principles with the traditional symbolism of angels, see my "Maimonidean Naturalism," in Goodman, ed., *Neoplatonism and Jewish Thought* (Albany: SUNY Press, 1992). In the light of al-Ghazālī's critique, Maimonides' elaboration gives appropriate emphasis to the voluntary character of the "angels'" acts.

41 *TF*, Bouyges, 2nd edn, 197.

42 Ibn Sīnā, *Shifā', De Anima* I 1, ed. Rahman, 4–5.

43 *De Intellectus Emendatione Tractatus*, ed. Carl Gebhardt (Heidelberg: Carl Winter, 1972, 1st edn, 1925), 2.10 ll. 17–19, regarding apprehensions of the third kind: "when we infer the cause from the effect, or when something is inferred from some universal, which some property always accompanies." Spinoza himself applies the principle to the mind-body problem: "once we clearly apprehend that we sense such a body and no other, I say that we clearly conclude from this that the soul is united to that body, this union being the cause of the sense we have of the body. But what this sense and this union are in themselves we cannot understand from that fact." Gebhardt 2.11 ll. 4–8.

44 Ibn Sīnā, *Shifā', De Anima* V 2.

45 Ibn Qayyim al-Jawziyya, *Kitāb al-Rūḥ* (The Book of the Spirit) (Hyderabad, 1963) 310. For Ibn Qayyim al-Jawziyya's reactionary romanticism, see my "The Sacred and the Secular: Rival Themes in Arabic Literature," Halmos Lecture (Tel Aviv: Tel Aviv University, 1988) 30.

46 Alexander of Aphrodisias, *De Anima* 1.19–30; see Fotinis' commentary, 163–72.

47 See Roger Arnaldez, "Un précédent avicennien du 'Cogito' cartésien?" *Annales islamologiques* 11 (1972) 341–9; Thérèse Druart, in her edited volume, *Arabic Philosophy and the West: Continuity and Interaction* (Washington: Center for Contemporary Arab Studies, 1988) 31. As I put it in an early article: "What Avicenna must do, using the perspicacity with which the mind locates middle terms, is to determine how it is that consciousness demands substantiality. The answer, of course, is in terms of subjectivity." See my "A Note on Avicenna's Theory of the Substantiality of the Soul," *Philosophical Forum* N.S. 1 (1969) 551. But the argument which serves to awaken us to the fact of our self-awareness is not to be confused with that very self-awareness; nor is the perspicacity which shows us that subjectivity is the middle term linking consciousness with

substantiality to be confused with the intuition of our own existence.

48 Druart rightly noted my ignoring (in the 1969 article just cited) of the epistemic load of the term Avicenna used for the introspection called for. But to gloss the term as "reminiscence" in my view goes too far. The appeal is not to Platonic *anamnesis*. Rather, *tadhkīr* here means a calling to mind, as Druart puts it, "some kind of process of self-reflection . . ." She overstresses her point when she adds, "that uncovers something already present but hidden." Perhaps because she is seeking a content-bearing intuition, she is surprised at the direction Ibn Sīnā's argument actually takes. She writes (p. 32): "Yet Avicenna seems to switch from this process of self-reflection to a purely hypothetical and imaginary situation, a thought experiment." On the contrary, the thought experiment *is* the *tanbīh*, cue or animadversion, that will arouse *tadhkīr*, recognition, of Avicenna's elemental thesis about our consciousness, that it is always self-present, since (*pace* Kant) it would be so even in the absence of any sensory inputs. What we are reminded of is not some piece of innate knowledge, clinging to the mind, as it were from a different and distant life; but rather, of our constantly present self-consciousness, which is so much with us that we can readily fail to notice it unless it is called to our attention. Michael Marmura, "Avicenna's 'Flying Man' in Context," *Monist* 69 (1986) 383–95, explains that, although Avicenna cannot accommodate Platonic *anamnesis*, "he does not reject the view that the soul, by its very nature, has self-knowledge." The purpose of the Floating Man argument is to alert us and remind us (or awaken us) to the fact of our self-consciousness (386–7). Marmura finds it mildly paradoxical that Avicenna wants to remind us of what the philosopher claims we always know. But Avicenna is quite consistent in holding that self-consciousness is always ours, even if we are not always thinking about the fact that we have it, and even though we may never have thought before about the precise implications which Ibn Sīnā believes that fact has. Self-consciousness, I would argue, is never actually hidden, but it is only rarely what we are paying closest attention to. In the language of phenomenology we can say that self-consciousness is rarely "foregrounded." Marmura (383) finds a parallel for Ibn Sīnā's argument in the *kalām* doctrine that our own existence is a fundamental given. See 'Abd al-Jabbār, *Sharḥ al-Uṣūl al-Khamsa*, ed. A.A. Uthman (Cairo, 1965) 50; al-Baqillānī, *K. al-Tamhīd*, ed. R.J. McCarthy (Beirut, 1957) 9–10. The assumption that something exists was a key premise of the *kalām* argument from contingency, and it was natural in that context, dialectically, to posit one's own existence; cf. Maimonides' exposition of *kalām* argumentation in *Guide to the Perplexed* I 74, methods 1 and 2.

49 *Shifā', De Anima*, I 1, ed. F. Rahman, 16. Avicenna says "if it were possible for him . . . to imagine," because he holds that in fact imagination does depend on our embodiment. And without sensation, imagination becomes problematic.

50 See my discussion in *Philosophical Forum* N.S. 1 (1969) 551 and in my preface to Ibn Ṭufayl's *Ḥayy Ibn Yaqẓān* (New York: Twayne, 1972; repr., Los Angeles, 1991). In the latter I argued that Descartes' *cogito* responds to Ibn Sīnā's argument, which "transformed Plato's almost axiomatic identification of thought with being into a cogent argument for the substantiality of the soul, based neither on the external evidence of the senses nor on *a priori* deduction, but rather on an introspective test which anyone might successfully perform," p. vii. I also noted the connection of the Floating Man argument to Ibn Ṭufayl's

thought experiment with an isolated human being in *Ḥayy Ibn Yaqẓān*. The connection with Descartes was made much earlier. See Étienne Gilson, "Les sources gréco-arabes de l'augustinisme avicennisant," *Archives d'histoire littéraire et doctrinale du Moyen Age*, 3.41; Ján Bakoš, *Psychologie d'Ibn Sīnā d'après son oeuvre aš-šifā'* 2 (Prague: Czechoslovak Academy of Sciences, 1956) 195, n. 58: "This is the celebrated 'Cogito ergo sum' of Avicenna. One cannot say that Avicenna here follows the doctrine of Plato or of any of the Neoplatonists on the soul . . ."

51 Ibn Sīnā, *Shifā'*, *De Anima*, I 1, ed. Rahman, 16.

52 Ibn Sīnā, *Shifā'*, *De Anima* V 7. He repeats the argument again in the *K. al-Ishārāt wa 'l-Tanbīhāt*, ed. J. Forget, 119; tr. A.-M. Goichon, 303–8, where the emphasis is on the claim that the immediacy of self-knowledge argues against the materiality of the soul, or its dependency upon anything material.

53 Ibn Sīnā, *Shifā'*, *De Anima* I 1, ed. Rahman, 15.

54 See S. Kripke, "Identity and Necessity," (1971) in S.P. Schwartz, ed., *Naming, Necessity, and Natural Kinds* (1977) and David Wiggins, *Sameness and Substance* (Cambridge: Harvard University Press, 1980).

55 *K. al-Ishārāt wa 'l-Tanbīhāt* III 1, ed. S. Dunya, 2.319–24. The reflections quoted here are labeled *tanbīhāt* in the text, animadversions, the same designation originally applied by Ibn Sīnā to the Floating Man argument in the *Shifā'* and used in a generic sense in the title of the work and throughout its contents.

56 In the Refutation of Idealism, *Critique of Pure Reason*, tr. N. Kemp Smith (New York: St. Martin's, 1965; 1929) 245–7.

57 See *Shifā'*, *De Anima* V 4–5; *Ilāhiyyāt* IX 7, X 1; and especially, *Al-Risālatu 'l-Aḍḥawiyya fī 'l-Ma'ād*, Italian translation by Francesca Lucchetta, as *Epistola sulla vita futura* (Padua, 1969); cf. *Ishārāt*, ed. J. Forget as *Le Livre des théorèmes et des avertissements* (Leiden, 1892) 120; translated by A.-M. Goichon, as *Livre des Directives et Remarques* (Paris: Vrin, 1951) 309. Robert Hall writes: "The idea itself which Ibn Sīnā had formed of personal salvation was simply that an individual's intellect could be developed during the person's lifetime to the point that it would survive the death of his body and become a part, still self-identical [i.e., discrete], of a celestial intellect"; see "A Decisive Example of the Influence of Psychological Doctrines in Islamic Science and Culture: Some Relationships between Ibn Sīnā's Psychology and other Branches of his Thought and Islamic Teachings," *Journal of the History of Arabic Science* 3 (1979) 51. By invoking Neoplatonic notions of the quasi-independent existence of all intellectual realities, Ibn Ṭufayl makes a heroic effort to rationalize Ibn Sīnā's doctrine that the soul both retains its individuality and is assimilated to the timelessness of the celestial intelligences; see *Ḥayy Ibn Yaqẓān*, tr. Goodman, 154.

58 See my "Rāzī's Myth of the Fall of the Soul," in G. Hourani, ed., *Essays on Islamic Philosophy and Science* (Albany: SUNY Press, 1975) 25–40; "Rāzī's Psychology," *Philosophical Forum* 4 (1972) 26–48.

59 See my "A Note on Avicenna's Theory of the Substantiality of the Soul," *Philosophical Forum* N.S. 1 (1969) 547–54.

60 *Najāt*, *De Anima*, tr. Rahman, 58–9.

61 *Najāt*, *De Anima*, tr. Rahman, 41–50.

62 *Najāt*, *De Anima*, tr. Rahman, 51–4. In the *Incoherence of the Philosophers* al-Ghazālī counts (and rebuts) ten arguments in Ibn Sīnā for the incorporeality of the human soul and two for its immortality. See *TF*, 206–34. See the discussions in

M. Marmura, "Ghazali and the Avicennan Proof from Personal Identity for an Immaterial Self," in *A Straight Path . . . Studies in Honor of Arthur Hyman* (Washington: Catholic University of America Press, 1988); T. Druart, "Imagination and the Soul-Body Problem in Arabic Philosophy," in Anna-Theresa Tymieniecka, ed., *Soul and Body in Husserlian Phenomenology* (Dordrecht: Reidel, 1983) 327–42.

63 Cf. Ibn Sīnā, *Najāt*, *De Anima* XI, tr. Rahman, 54–6.

64 Goodman, "A Note on Avicenna's Theory of the Substantiality of the Soul."

65 See Fazlur Rahman's important note to the *De Anima* of the *Najāt*, 111–15, and Ibn Sīnā's ch. 15, on the unity of the soul, 64–8.

66 *Shifā'*, *De Anima* V 4.

67 Hall, 51; cf. Gerald Verbeke, "L'Immortalité de l'âme dans le *De Anima* d'Avicenne," *Pensamiento* 25 (1969) 271–90.

68 Plato, *Alcibiades I*, 127e, 132b; cf. *Epinomis* 988, *Philebus* 48c, *Charmides* 164d; Aristotle, *Metaphysics* Alpha 2, 982b 22 ff. See Alexander Altmann, *Studies in Religious Philosophy and Mysticism* (Ithaca: Cornell University Press, 1969), and Werner Jaeger, *Aristotle*, tr. R. Robinson (Oxford: Oxford University Press, 1948, 1962) 164–6:

> In his *Life of Socrates* Aristoxenus the Peripatetic related that an Indian, meeting Socrates in Athens, asked him about his philosophy. When Socrates answered that he was attempting to understand human life, the Indian represented to him the hopelessness of such an undertaking, since man cannot know himself until he knows God. This sounds apocryphal, but it is simply the legendary formulation of the view, universal in the later Academy and summed up in the *Epinomis* as a program for religious reform, that in future Oriental astralism and theology would have to be combined with the Delphic religion of Hellas . . . the way to this combination is mysticism . . . it is impossible to understand Aristotle's influence on posterity unless we realize that he breathed this atmosphere for many years, and that his metaphysics is rooted in it . . . . The establishment of the worship of the stars, which are confined to no land or nation but shine on all the peoples of the earth, and of the transcendental God who is enthroned above them, inaugurates the era of religious and philosophic universalism.

69 See S. Landauer, "Die Psychologie des Ibn Sīnā," *ZDMG* 29 (1875) 340–1, 374–5.

70 See my "The Sacred and the Secular: Rival Themes in Arabic Literature," Halmos Lecture, Tel Aviv University, 1988.

71 See, e.g., al-Ṭabarī as cited in Franz Rosenthal, "On the Knowledge of Plato's Philosophy in the Islamic World," *Islamic Culture* 14 (1940) 410.

72 See Ibn Sīnā, *Aḥwāl al-Nafs* (Cairo, 1952) 130.

73 Alexander of Aphrodisias, *De Anima liber cum mantissa*, ed. I. Bruns in *Supplementum Aristotelicum II* (Berlin, 1887) 84–91; cf. Fotinis, 109; see Merlan, *Monopsychism, Mysticism and Metaconsciousness* (The Hague: Nijhoff, 1963) 14–16.

74 Merlan, 21–2. Ibn Ṭufayl criticizes as a fallacy the inference from the identity of the mind with its object to the identity of the mind with God; see *Ḥayy Ibn Yaqẓān*, tr. Goodman, 150. The fallacy is treated as a delusion symptomatic of the would be mystic's continued dependence on matter and reliance on its categories: Just as a giddy ascent into the empyrean and swooping return to earth might leave one clutching for the seeming solidity of some material anchor, so

the departure of the mind from the material conditions of its consciousness, when incomplete (as any mystic state must remain while we are embodied), leaves us grasping for the solidity of the familiar and still untranscended categories of sameness and difference – categories whose roots are physical and whose application beyond the physical realm is inevitably fallacious.

75 Jaeger, citing *Metaphysics* Alpha 2, 983a 5–11, understands Aristotle in the same sense that Merlan finds in Plato: "*cognitio dei* is conceivable only if it is God Himself knowing himself . . . . The self is the *Nus*, which is said to 'come in from without' and to be 'the divine in us'; and it is through *Nus* that the knowledge of God enters into us." Yet, "Aristotle never emphasizes God's unity with human *Nus* more than His transcendence." Here, as in the conception of motion and movers, we see not so much an ambiguity on Aristotle's part, to be resolved by Ibn Sīnā, but a natural expression of the pagan overdetermination of effects, which requires sorting out on Ibn Sīnā's part, in the interests of a chaste and sober monotheism. Of the confusions latent in Jaeger's notion that an *externally* derived Nous is actually *our own*, and that we ourselves are thus the divinity that visits the self, I say nothing.

76 M. Fakhry, "The Contemplative Ideal in Islamic Philosophy: Aristotle and Avicenna," *JHP* 14 (1976) 139–40; cf. Fakhry's "Three Varieties of Mysticism in Islam," *International Journal for Philosophy of Religion* 2 (1971) 198.

77 Compare the treatment of Augustine, who was well aware of the linkage between self-knowledge and knowledge of God but declined to parse it, writing instead: "I could not find myself: How much less then could I find You" (*Confessions* V ii 2; cf. III, vi 11, X vi 9, viii 15). And see Peter Brown, *Augustine of Hippo* (London: Faber, 1967) 168.

78 See *Enneads* V 1, ed. and tr. A.H. Armstrong (Cambridge: Harvard University Press, 1984).

79 *Enneads* V 3.17, VI 9.11. Al-Kindī reflects Plotinus' usage when he speaks of the human soul actually *touching* (*bāsharat*) the hypostatic (first) Intellect; see *Rasā'il al-Kindī*, ed. M. Abu Rida (Cairo, 1950) 155, 356. *Ittiṣāl* is a subtler expression for the same idea, less connotative of physical contact.

80 For the importance of *ḥads*, rational intuition, in Ibn Sīnā's theory of knowledge, see Gutas, *Avicenna and the Aristotelian Tradition* (Leiden: Brill, 1988) 19 n. 15, 49 n. 22, 50 n. 1, 55–6, 62, 159–76. The concept goes beyond the Aristotelian (*Posterior Analytics* I 34, 89b, 10), constructivist conceptualization of intelligence as perspicacity (*anchinoia*) with which Van Den Bergh equates it, *TT* 2.173 n. 313.9, and to which al-Ghazālī seeks to reduce it, *TF*, ed. Bouyges, 192 = *TT* ed. Bouyges, 513; tr. Van Den Bergh, 313. Still less is it, as Van Den Bergh suggests, to be equated with "the conjecturing power," *TT* 2.181 n. 324.3. As Gutas notes (201 n. 6), *anchinoia* is a species of *eustochia* (penetration), namely the sagacity of those who excel in hitting the mark with respect to middle terms. The word that *ḥads* renders is *eustochia*, in the sense of insight or discernment, not *anchinoia*. Ibn Sīnā, as his epistemology requires, assigns a far more Platonic sense to intuition than Aristotle does. Al-Ghazālī's remark that "rational insight (*al-quwwatu 'l-'aqliyya*) reduces to *ḥads*, which is speed in moving from known to known," is explicitly reductive and comes in the context of a heated polemic against Ibn Sīnā's spiritualism and intellectualism. Van Den Bergh suppresses al-Ghazālī's words "reduces to" in his translation. In his ethical, spiritualizing writings al-Ghazālī makes an intellectual virtue out of insight which requires

no proof (a mark of intuition); he also insists that practical wisdom is not just cleverness in finding means to ends, the pragmatic counterpart of the speculative search for and success in finding middle terms, insisting, as does Aristotle himself, that to be called wisdom in a practical sense such insight must choose the right ends as well as the right means.

81 *Avicenna on Prayer* (*Risāla fī Māhiyyati 'l-Ṣalāt*), ed. M.A.F. Mehren (Leiden: Brill, 1894) 32–4; cf. Arberry's translation in *Avicenna on Theology* (London: Murray, 1951; repr., Westport: Hyperion, n.d.) 53–4.

82 *Kitāb al-Ishārāt wa 'l-Tanbīhāt*, ed. S. Dunya (Cairo: Dār al-Ma'ārif, 1958) 3.698–708; Goichon, tr., 442–8; and see her notes.

83 Merlan, 25.

84 See W. Kutsch, ed., *Ein arabisches Buchstück aus Porphyrios (?)*, in *Mélanges de l'Université Saint Joseph* 31 (1954) 268; *K. al-Shifā'* Psychology, ed. and tr. Jan Bákoš (Prague: Nakladatelstvi Ceskoslovenske Akademie Ved, 1956) 235–46 = 169–77; Goichon, *La Distinction de l'essence et de l'existence d'après Ibn Sīnā* (Paris, 1937) 87, n. 1; 316–28; cf. *Monopsychism, Mysticism and Metaconsciousness*, 25–9.

85 Emile Fackenheim, tr., *Medieval Studies* 7 (1945) 225.

86 Even when Ibn Sīnā wants to refer to the sustained communion that he understands as the essence of the mystical state at its fullest he still does not use the term *ittiḥād*, but speaks of "keeping company" with the Active Intellect, as distinguished from "surface contact," as Barry Kogan aptly renders *ittiṣāl* in that context. See *Shifā'*, *Ilāhiyyāt*, ed. Anawati and Zayed, 425; *De Anima*, ed. Rahman, 240; *Ishārāt*, tr. Goichon, 331 n. 5.

87 M. Fakhry, "The Contemplative Ideal," 141.

88 Ed. Mehren, 22.

89 In *Ishārāt* IX 20 (Goichon 498; Dunya 4.841), Ibn Sīnā writes "One who chooses gnosis for its own sake is a dualist in effect [for preferring something other than God as the ultimate object of his quest]. But one who finds gnosis as though that were not what he was seeking, has in fact found what he was looking for. He has plunged into the very depths of Attainment (*wuṣūl*)." My friend Nicholas Heer writes (private communication, 27 August 1991), "In the ninth Namat of the *Ishārāt* Ibn Sīnā talks about *wuṣūl* as well as *ittiṣāl*. In connection with *wuṣūl* Ibn Sīnā clearly has God in mind, not the Active Intellect. Again, however, he says nothing about *ittiḥād*." *Wuṣūl*, another cognate of *ittiṣāl*, seems to me to be used here with similar intent to the *muwāṣila* of the Essay on Prayer, cited above, which I rendered in terms of "linkage." As Heer explains, rightly it seems to me: "Ibn Sīnā seems to believe it possible for the soul to 'reach' God Himself, without, however becoming united with Him." Addressing the Sufi theme of *fanā'*, Heer adds: "Ibn Sīnā also seems to be saying that the soul can lose consciousness of its own identity, but does not go so far as to say that it actually does lose its own identity in God." As Heer recognizes, Ibn Sīnā's use of the Sufi language of "attainment" or "arrival" to describe successful achievement of the mystic's goal does not commit him to the dissolution of individual subjecthood, and indeed is couched, dialectically, in a rejection of the intoxicated Sufis' apparent predilection for mystic experience as though it were an end in itself. The proper end, of course, is God. But one cannot enjoy communion with God if either the self or God has lost its identity in the very act of consummation.

90 Al-Ghazālī, *Iḥyā' 'Ulūm al-Dīn*, IV (Cairo, 1933) 263; *K. al-Imlā'* (Cairo, 1927); *Al-Maqṣad al-asnā* (Cairo, 1905) 17–27; Farid Jabre, *La Notion de la Ma'rifa chez*

Ghazali (Beirut, 1958) 86–108, and appendices 11–12.

91 Alexander Altmann, *Studies in Religious Philosophy and Mysticism* 11–12.

92 Ibn Ṭufayl, *Ḥayy Ibn Yaqẓān*, tr. Goodman, 96. The chastity of erotic mysticism in the Jewish Kabbalah is itself in part a byproduct of Ibn Sīnā's metaphysically chaste approach, as I explain in further detail in my "Crosspollinations: Philosophically Fruitful Interactions between Jewish and Islamic Philosophy," in Jacob Lassner, ed., *The Jews of Islam* (Detroit: Wayne State University Press, forthcoming). Kabbalism, as Zwi Werblowsky explains, summing up the findings of Gershom Scholem, "employs erotic mysticism only in describing the relations of the Divine to itself, not of man to God." It "does not aspire to mystical union with the Divine . . . but to mystical communion or *devekut*." The term *devekut*, usually rendered as 'cleaving' (sc. to God) and often interpreted in terms of meditative exercise or concentration, is an appropriate rendering of *ittiṣāl*. See R.J. Zwi Werblowsky, *Joseph Karo: Lawyer and Mystic* (Philadelphia: Jewish Publication Society, 1977) 133; G. Scholem, *Major Trends in Jewish Mysticism* (New York: Schocken, 1971; first edn, 1941) 235 and s.v. *devekut*, and "*Devekut* or Communion with God," in Scholem's *The Messianic Idea in Judaism and Other Essays in Jewish Spirituality* (New York: Schocken, 1971; based on lectures given at Hebrew Union College, 1949 and first published in *Review of Religion* 14, 1949/50).

93 Indeed, Plotinus himself, as an immanentist, can afford to be equivocal on the soul's "unity" with the divine. In *Enneads* IV 4.2 he writes: "But does the soul when it is in the intelligible world experience this 'first one thing and then another' . . .? No, when it is purely and simply in the intelligible world it has itself too the characteristic of unchangeability. For it is really all the things it is: since when it is in that region, it must come to unity with Intellect, by the fact that it has turned to it, for when it is turned, it has nothing between, but comes to Intellect and accords itself to it, and by that accord is united to it, without being destroyed, but both of them are one and also two." Plotinus' final qualification here is the basis of Ibn Ṭufayl's proposed compromise between the individualism of Ibn Sīnā and al-Ghazālī on the one hand and monopsychism on the other. The idea that in a transcendent world, beyond materiality, the earthly categories of sameness and difference no longer apply is Ibn Ṭufayl's way of gently tipping monotheism in the direction of Sufi monism so as to appropriate Plotinus' teaching here. What is striking in Ibn Sīnā is that he will none of this. Even in the height of ecstasy, even in immortality, individuality is preserved.

94 See Descartes' letter to Princess Elisabeth of June 28, 1643, tr. in John J. Blom, *Descartes: His Moral Philosophy and Psychology* (New York: New York University Press, 1978) 112–16.

4

LOGIC, PERSUASION, AND POETRY

Looking back over the history of Arabic and Islamic arts and letters, the great fourteenth-century social theorist Ibn Khaldūn explains that it was because Aristotle made logic a systematic science and placed it properly at the head of all philosophical studies that Muslims called him the First Teacher. Al-Fārābī, Ibn Sīnā, and Ibn Rushd commented on and developed Aristotle's achievement. They expanded the scope and power of Aristotelian logic and assimilated the methods of Greek logic to the language and usages of Arabic learning.[1] In its early days logic was seen clearly as a foreign import, and it was even debated whether Greek logic was applicable to Arabic usages or anchored so firmly to its Greek origins as to be relative to the dead culture of an extinct (!) race.[2] The early Arabic writers on the Greek sciences who were committed to the enterprise of philosophy saw logic essentially as a matter of following the Organon of Aristotle, even to the extent of identifying the sub-disciplines of logic with the titles of the constituent books of the Organon: Introduction (Porphyry's *Isagoge*), Categories, Hermeneutics (*De Interpretatione*), Syllogistic (*Prior Analytics*), Apodictics (*Posterior Analytics*), Dialectics (*Topics*), Sophistics (*De Sophisticis Elenchis*), Rhetoric (*Rhetorica*), and Poetics (*Poetica*). But Avicenna made logic an independent study, no longer tightly bound to the Aristotelian texts but capable of expansion and development on its own in the Islamic context. The outcome was fraught with significance.

Ibn Khaldūn notes a sea change in Islamic theology with the spread and naturalization of Avicenna's logical methods. In the early days of Islam, as Ibn Khaldūn puts it, religion was a matter of habit and culture, a matter of practice, inner piety, and unaffected charity. There was little that would pass for theory. The *Qur'ān* and the traditions were the recourse for whatever understanding and elaboration folk required, but doctrine was a foundation of practice for the devout, not an end in itself. The early Muslims avoided the quest for ultimate causes beyond the familiar givens of experience. They even, quite rightly, suppressed the search for comprehension of proximate causes, seeing that such inquiries breed only confusion, frustration, and, ultimately, perdition. It is enough to know what the *Qur'ān* teaches, that God is the Cause of causes, inviolate, inexplicable, and unique.[3]

But the excessive and incoherent literalism of some readers of Qur'anic anthropomorphisms, the desire of some Muslims to systematize and organize a doctrinal theology, the extreme purism of the Mu'tazilites, in trying to do away with all divine attributes (lest the most corporeal attributions of the *Qur'ān* be taken literally; and, we may add, lest Christians seize upon any plurality in the attributes of God as a warrant for trinitarianism) necessitated the development of an authentically Islamic theology. The expounding of such an authentically Islamic *kalām* was the achievement of al-Ash'arī, who moderated the excesses of the conflicting views, synthesized and rationalized the beliefs that underlie true Islamic piety, and formally articulated the doctrines of an orthodox creed.

To facilitate their work, the theologians of the *kalām* devised arguments and indeed elaborate systems of postulates, both exegetical and cosmological, which they grounded in a curious and distinctive informal logic of their own, a logic that seemed adequate for their frequent public disputations and written debates, yet one that was never reduced to system. That logic, as Ibn Khaldūn assays it, was flawed, misleading, and *ad hoc.* It lacked the powerful Aristotelian method of the categorical syllogism and the rigorous tests that Aristotelians applied to such syllogisms. But even had such tools been available to *mutakallimūn* like the Ash'arītes, they would have been rejected, Ibn Khaldūn argues, for their association with the impious beliefs of the Philosophers, if not because they were so obviously inadequate to the purpose of justifying the articles of faith.[4]

All the same, once the methods of logic had been laid out by the philosophers of Islam, particularly by al-Fārābī and Ibn Sīnā, and once Ibn Sīnā had disengaged philosophical logic from its textual matrix, its methods became impossible to ignore. As al-Ghazālī wrote:

> Nothing in logic touches religion one way or the other. On the contrary, logic is merely the study of the methods of proof and reasoning, the requirements for premises in a demonstration[5]

> and the manner in which they are to be combined, or the requirements for a sound definition, and the manner in which it is ordered. Knowledge is either a conception, which is known through a definition, or a judgment, which is known by demonstration. There is nothing here which needs to be denied.[6]

Al-Ghazālī reassures his reader that the general idea of such a methodology is acknowledged by the accredited theologians and theorists of the faith. He urges that the logic of the philosophers differs only in terminology and degree of elaboration and systematic classification. He then gives the example of a perfectly innocuous seeming syllogism that reaches its conclusion simply by locating a specific class under the genus in which it falls. He says nothing of the differences between the logic of the Philosophers and that of the earlier theologians of the *kalām*, and he glosses over the fact that the Philosophers' elaborate system of classification is rooted in an ontology and epistemology strikingly at variance with traditionalist Islamic notions.

In point of fact, as we learn from Ibn Khaldūn, al-Ghazālī was the first Ash'arite to accept and make use of Aristotelian logic. This was the logic he had learned from his study of Avicenna. In his hands that logic became the entryway to Islam of a muted naturalism that finds its place even in the heart of al-Ghazālī's celebrated critique of causality. For if the properties of the genus must belong to every member of its species, then *some* causal relations at least will be matters of logical necessity. Thus, confronting the charge that Ash'arite occasionalism plays havoc with our ability to know and predict the events of our everyday world, al-Ghazālī responds:

> The answer is that the absurd is not within God's power. And what is absurd is the simultaneous affirmation and denial of the same thing, or the *affirmation of the specific while denying the more general*, or the affirmation of two things while denying one of them. But what does not reduce to such a case is not an absurdity and therefore is within God's power.[7]

My italics mark al-Ghazālī's admission of an important role for logic in delimiting the possibilities of nature, even with regard to God's absolute power. His example:

> It is impossible for a non-living being to have knowledge implanted in it, for by "non-living being" we understand one that has no awareness. If knowledge were imparted to it, it

would be absurd to call it non-living in the sense we understood; and if it had no awareness, then to call what it acquires knowledge, although it apprehends nothing by it, again would be absurd. So such a notion is a bald absurdity.[8]

Al-Ghazālī does argue that God could *change* the nature of a substrate to make possible a miracle. If God wanted to impart knowledge to a corpse, He would first render it alive.[9] But al-Ghazālī's concession to naturalism is not nugatory, even though it allows miracles. For he has accepted the dependence, indeed the logical dependence, of one form upon another. Correspondingly, he accepts the Neoplatonic metaphysics of emanation in place of the atomism of the *kalām*, which the work of Ibn Sīnā had discredited. The traditional Ash'arite view had made *every* event dependent on the immediate act of God. It is true that al-Ghazālī's concessions to the emanationism of Avicenna do not follow the Philosophers in their tendency to *equate* ontological with logical dependence, as though the relationship of effect to cause in the scale of being that leads down into nature from the spiritual/intellectual "Principles" of things were simply a matter of necessary implication. It is for the sake of the voluntarism it fosters that al-Ghazālī retains the traditional language of "angels" rather than "Intellects" as the mediating principles between the archetypal and the natural worlds. But al-Ghazālī clearly understands that the recognition that "this is not that and that is not this" does not entail the truth of occasionalism but rather, leaves room for a causal nexus, albeit on a (theistically) voluntaristic rather than logicist basis. Formal causes, and thus at least some natural causes, are necessary to their effects, even if formal causes are never self-sufficient, for reasons which Avicenna himself made very clear.

Our present interest, however, is not to belabor the extent of al-Ghazālī's somewhat cautious naturalism, but rather to point out that his complete rethinking of the operations both of nature and of miracles rests on his acceptance of the Aristotelian logical scheme taught by Ibn Sīnā. He has accepted the view that substances are to be classified conceptually and that the properties of the more general must be found in the more specific. With that view comes a new metaphysics distinct from, even if still influenced by the metaphysics of the *kalām*. God's acts are now mediated by intellectual principles, even though it is insisted that those principles remain under volitional control.[10]

The impact of al-Ghazālī's methodological concession is emblematic of the general impact of Ibn Sīnā's setting forth of the Aristotelian logic of the Philosophers as an independent science. Once Ash'arism was transformed into a systematic theology by such writers as al-Baqillānī and al-Juwaynī, Ibn Khaldūn writes, Muslim theologians, beginning with al-Ghazālī, found it necessary to separate the methods of the Philosophers from their doctrines, and to adopt the former, even while rebutting the latter. In the process, it became necessary for them to reject much of the edifice that had once been the *kalām*. Aristotelian logic had never been intended as a metaphysically or cosmologically neutral system. Through the work of the reformed, post-Ghazālī Ash'arites, the powerful metaphysics embedded in the logic of Aristotle became Islamic and transformed Islamic theology from within, just as it had transformed the Ash'arism of al-Ghazālī. The new Ash'arite theologians, following the lead of al-Ghazālī and Fakhr al-Dīn al-Rāzī and accepting the logic of Aristotle and Avicenna, now found that Aristotelian logic rendered obsolete not only the dialectic of the *kalām*, but also the occasionalism and atomism, the doctrine of the void, the denial that one "accident could sustain (or depend on) another", and the denial that any atom could endure longer than a single instant – all dogmas which the earlier Ash'arites had regarded as basic givens, "second only to the articles of the faith in their authority." Henceforward, discussions of theology became almost inextricably entwined with philosophy.[11]

1 AVICENNA'S PROPOSITIONAL LOGIC

Propositional logic was not an area much developed by Aristotle. It was pioneered by Theophrastus and extensively developed by the Stoics, partly as a riposte to the work of Aristotle. Ibn Sīnā seems to have mastered the subject from Galen's logical works, but his innovations also reflect his own intuitive approach. They aim to rescue propositional logic from the grip of the *kalām*, whose practitioners had found in it a passport to modes of thinking that seemed from a Peripatetic standpoint fundamentally anti-scientific. Propositional logic was an area of special sensitivity for two reasons: First, its development among the Stoics and their Megarian predecessors represented a serious challenge to the authority and indeed the competence of Aristotelian class logic as a rigorous formalization of the modes of sound inference. Second, *kalām* reliance on hypothetical reasoning undermined the naturalism which the categorical syllogisms of the

Peripatetics were meant to shore up.

The Stoics, who grew to critical stature as philosophers under pressure from the Skeptics, were uncomfortable with the idea of categorical truth claims. Their more empiric, skeptically chastened canons of knowledge and their tendency toward nominalism about Platonic ideas gave them grounds for preferring empiric "signs" and symptoms to the necessary and sufficient criteria that were the stock in trade not only of Plato's dialectic but also of Aristotle's science. The propositional calculus that the Stoics developed, following the lead of the Megarians Diodorus Cronus and his pupil Philo of Megara, was designed to make room for the tentative and problematic. The "undemonstrated" or axiomatic syllogisms which afforded the schemata of Stoic logic, e.g., "If the first, then the second, but the first; therefore the second," could accommodate not only truisms like "If it is day, then it is light; it is day; therefore it is light," but also more problematic, evidentiary claims like "Where there's smoke there's fire." The object was not to intuit implications in pure ideas, as in the thought of Plato, since for the Stoics there were no such ideas but only words and notions.[12] Nor was the idea to progress, as in Aristotelian syllogistic, from one necessary and universal truth to another or to seek to discover necessary and universal patterns, by induction, in the particularities of sense experience. For such notions still harbored an ontologically disciplined but epistemologically unrepentant Platonism.[13] Rather, the Stoic plan was to allow for probabilistic and suggestive reasoning, following marks and evidence, as the Stoics put it. There were necessary truths in Stoicism, to be sure. Indeed a principal complaint against the Stoics was that their doctrine of *heimarmene* or destiny made all truths necessary in the end. But Stoic necessities were not an expression of the intrinsic or imparted natures of things and their kinds but of the general condition of the world, the whole concatenated system of interlocking and interactive causes which the Stoics called *sympatheia.* Possibility, impossibility, and necessity are explained in Stoic logic not in terms of essences or natures but in terms of external circumstances, which a finite individual can never know comprehensively.[14] Peripatetics may pursue necessary and certain knowledge, but the Stoic sage is content to live his life in accordance with moral certainties: "A reasonable proposition is one which has, at the outset, more chance of being true than not, e.g., 'I shall be alive tomorrow.'"[15] Logic can afford us higher certainties, but only by way of "inclusion."[16] Science, in the Stoic view, is not to be enshrined above such ordinary inferences. But room was to be left for hints and guesses, even signals, signs, and omens from the gods.[17]

The Stoic approach was neither wholly apologetic nor wholly defensive in posture. But it was aggressively anti-Aristotelian. Recognizing what most modern logicians would later insist upon as the primitiveness of propositional logic, Stoic logicians attacked the Aristotelian syllogism as parasitic upon their own propositional calculus: Was not "All men are mortal; Socrates is a man; therefore Socrates is mortal" no more than a special case of the first undemonstrated syllogism? The criticism put Peripatetics in a particularly awkward spot. For to allow that a syllogism in Barbara rested surreptitiously on the Stoic hypothetical syllogism was to render the Aristotelian syllogism redundant and thus fallacious, making it prejudge the same truth it was intended to discover to us. It was, moreover, to excise the very nerve of Aristotle's syllogism by ignoring the relations among the predicative terms within the categorical propositions of the syllogism. These terms and their relations, in the eyes of all faithful and scientific Aristotelians, were the crucial basis of all sound reasoning. For syllogisms were not merely formal exercises about hypothetical posits; they were the living nerve and sinew of Aristotelian science.[18]

Aristotle argues at the outset of the *Posterior Analytics* that the only way to solve Plato's puzzle in the *Meno*, that either knowledge is never acquired or it is only of what we already know, is to hold that the premises in a valid syllogism do not contain the conclusion the way the Trojan horse contained the Greeks but rather affirm a concept, or, more strictly, a relationship among concepts that allows us to infer the predication proposed in the conclusion. That is, they contain the conclusion "in a way," i.e., virtually; "but in another way not," i.e., not explicitly or concretely. Otherwise the syllogism would not be a method of discovery but only a method of exposition and there would be no learning but only trivial deduction from a priori concepts, as in Plato, or from complete enumerations, as in some naive form of radical empiricism.[19] What Aristotle is referring to is what modern epistemologists call ampliative reasoning. By blocking or bracketing access to the semantic content of predicative terms, the Stoic propositional calculus crippled the Aristotelian basis for such reasoning. It rendered the syllogism materially opaque in a way that would be deadly for the sciences, where Aristotle saw the reasoning at work that formal logic only sketched abstractly. In Stoic propositional logic, any proposition could be dealt with, but none had a materially privileged status over others.

The problem was exacerbated by the work of the *kalām*. Most Muslim *mutakallimūn* simply discarded the idea of natural kinds, but they retained the Stoic theory of signs and a rather free-form (deformed, degenerate, or *ad hoc*) version of Stoic hypothetical reasoning. Al-Ash'arī, for example, eager to vindicate the absolute dependence of salvation upon grace, denies that any inferences can be made from the moral character of a sinner to his ultimate fate, despite even the seemingly categorical condemnations of God Himself in the *Qur'ān*:

> One cannot determine that God's words "and the profligate shall surely burn in Hellfire" (*Qur'ān* 82: 14) or "Lo, they who devour [the property of orphans do but swallow fire into their bellies; they shall burn in the flames of Hell]" (*Qur'ān* 4: 10) apply to all or some. . . . The poet Zuhayr said, "Who is not profuse in flattery will be rent by fangs and trodden underfoot."[20] But not everyone who fails to use flattery suffers that fate. He also said, "Who does not wrong others will be wronged by them." But not everyone who does not wrong others is wronged by them.[21]

Al-Ash'arī intentionally ignores the pre-Islamic poet's irony and detachment as single mindedly as he ignores the earnestness and categorical emphasis of the *Qur'ān*'s condemnation.[22] He presses an entirely fanciful ambiguity in the Qur'anic text, arguing solely from the omission of an explicit quantifier for the claim that such blanket condemnations cannot be taken universally, regardless of what the text may seem to say, or what theological adversaries may make of them.[23]

Al-Ash'arī's appeal to the ancient poet seeks to establish the classical Arabic usage, and so to show that the syntactical form found in the *Qur'ān*: "He/they/one who . . . is . . ." is not to be taken as the universal premise necessary to a syllogism in Barbara: "All . . . are . . ." But despite the appeal to the poetic prooftext, what is determinative for al-Ash'arī here is neither external evidence nor internal exegesis of the Qur'anic language itself, but theological doctrine, and in particular, revulsion against the ultimately Khārijite heresy that a mere mortal can know by character and overt actions (and so may investigate and must punish) those whom God has condemned to burn in Hell. To allow class logic into the discussion would be to risk the point, to make God's grace seem predictable, indeed determinable by human standards, on the basis of human actions.

With conditional logic, by contrast, another condition can always be stipulated. The epistemology becomes like that of our contemporary philosophers of science who argue from the underdetermination of theories by evidence that no crucial experiment can ever be performed and that no theory is ever conclusively confirmed.[24] Thus, arguing against free will and the Mu'tazilite claim that human beings act by their own powers, al-Ash'arī seeks to demonstrate that our actions depend not on our limbs but on a power imparted to us directly by God:

> If the limb does not exist, the power will not exist. But it is the lack of the power that makes appropriation of the act impossible, not the lack of the limb. If the limb were non-existent but the power were present, appropriation of the act would take place. Indeed, if appropriation were impossible only because of the lack of the limb, then having the limb would mean appropriating the act.[25]

Note the form of the argument. It is typical of the *kalām* method. Indeed it presupposes a corresponding Mu'tazilite argument that is taken to make a limb the sufficient condition of an act. Such a reading makes a strawman of the Mu'tazilite, but it clearly reflects, albeit in caricature, the hypothetical syllogism that an opposing *mutakallim* would have used. Al-Ash'arī's theory of action, with its Stoic-influenced notion of inner appropriation, is far more sophisticated than the Mu'tazilite attempt to equate capacities for action with possession of one's unimpaired limbs and organs. But the reliance on hypothetical logic is much the same.

The very argument that al-Ghazālī affirmed, that a non-living being cannot act voluntarily because it is non-living, is rejected by al-Ash'arī, the founder of the orthodox school to which al-Ghazālī adheres. Al-Ash'arī uses an only slightly more complex hypothetical (and *ad hoc*) syllogism to defend his view. Addressing the question whether lack of life entails lack of action, he answers:

> Yes, because when life does not exist, power does not exist. It is on account of the lack of power that appropriation is impossible, not on account of the lack of life. Do you not see that life can be present along with powerlessness, so that a man appropriates no action. Thus it is known that appropriation does not fail for lack of life and does not occur because of life.[26]

The point is not that the dead can act, as some radical occasionalists in the *kalām* held, a view which al-Ash'arī evidently found extreme.[27] Rather, the inaction of the dead is from lack of power. That is a seemingly trivial claim; but what matters to al-Ash'arī is what he believes follows by analogy, that life itself imparts no power: We do not act because we are alive (or to be alive would be the same as action and we would constantly be "appropriating" all sorts of acts including opposing acts); rather, we act through a Godgiven power of action, which covers and indeed determines only one particular "appropriation" and one particular act, which *eo ipso immediately takes place.*

The logic of al-Ash'arī is a logic of immediacy. Indeed, its Stoic and Megarian roots make it a logic of timelessness. Its submersion of predicates within the opacity of the propositional terms of a hypothetical syllogism is no accident but is symptomatic of the original Megarian reaction against Aristotle's theory of predicates and potentiality. For, as al-Ash'arī's use of the scheme makes clear, Ash'arite propositional logic takes aim specifically at the Aristotelian theories of bivalent volitions and future contingency, the very naturalism about inanimate causes and voluntarism about human choices that were licensed by Aristotle's theory of predication.

To philosophers like al-Fārābī and Ibn Sīnā the motives of the Ash'arite theologians (and *a fortiori* of their more radical occasionalist predecessors) were crystal clear. Natural kinds, like the essences on which their stability would depend, presented loci of independent (or quasi-independent) powers within nature. If all events and all reasonings about events must wait on the immediate grace of God, we may make inferences from Godgiven signs and analogies, but there will be no categorical judgments and none of the certainty of the Aristotelian apodeictic. *Kalām* logic, then, will never pretend to state a priori what can or cannot happen in the world. Rather, it must work from hypotheticals: "Given this, our expectation would be that." Typically, to cite a Mu'tazilite argument: "Given God's goodness, it is inadmissible to claim that God would fail to create the *Qur'ān.*"[28] Quantification, a crucial reference point for Aristotle in drawing any line between demonstration and sophistry,[29] falls out of account, not because it is forgotten but because there is no class to quantify over if the talk is about God; whereas in a world radically dependent on discrete and ultimately arbitrary acts of grace, little, perhaps nothing, remains for the critical "always" and "never" to govern. Every event is now thought of historically rather than generically or specifically. That is, every event is now thought of not in terms of its essential likeness to others but in terms of its uniqueness.

Like the Stoics, albeit for somewhat different reasons, most *mutakallimūn* are chary of attempts to say precisely what the nature of the world must be. Their preference (which their penchant for hypothetical reasoning enshrines) is for arguing *dialectically* from assumptions which may come from scripture or its interpretation in tradition and may tell us things about the created world which no amount of observation could possibly confirm. Indeed, tradition and revelation may make known facts to us which a priori reasoning would most likely deny – as even al-Ghazālī and Maimonides himself are quick to point out. A priori reasoning, they argue, if informed only by rigidity and a superficial acquaintance with the familiar course of natural events, would readily deny the possibility of fire, or of the birth of human beings from women.

In *kalām* there will be no science of being as such, beyond recognition of its radical contingency and the consequences dialectically derived from that fact. Yet, by the same token, there is no proposition that cannot be entertained, and no conclusion that lies beyond question. Hypothetical logic was the natural expression of the world's utter contingency, just as the categorical logic of the Aristotelian syllogism, deriving necessary and universal conclusions by valid inferences from necessary and universal premises, based on rational induction of the eternal essences of natural kinds, was a natural reflection of the Aristotelian eternalism, rationalism, and naturalism.

By al-Fārābī's time the situation seemed, to a committed Aristotelian and a naturalist, to be all but completely out of hand. The rise of Ash'arism, with its rationalizations of theistic subjectivism, particular providence, and prophetic miracles, and its submersion of human volition under the mask of the (ultimately Stoic) doctrine that we do not "create" but only "appropriate" our acts and choices, was a manifest danger, against which philosophy in general and logic in particular were engaged in deadly combat, a combat in which both sides recognized the prowess of their adversaries, but in which philosophy stood at a distinct disadvantage, since its logical armamentum, although powerful, required greater skill to operate and offered far fewer comforts to allies, auxiliaries, or even mercenary confederates. Dialectical theology (*kalām*), al-Fārābī wrote, with its commitment to the defense of received dogmas and its latent or patent fears of independent thinking, was the natural enemy of philosophy.[30] Doctrines like the widespread but false claim that divine omniscience obviates human choice are "very, very dangerous for people to believe," and must be cleared away by logical analysis.[31]

Directing his attention specifically to the logic used by theologians, al-Fārābī finds much that is salvageable, especially, he says, if one applies the rule of charity (*musāmaḥa*) and treats some theological arguments as enthymemes, typically deploying a special, back-handed version of *reductio ad absurdum.* In this last form of argument, as al-Fārābī analyzed it, *mutakallimūn* laid on the table a pair of premises, one of which was understood to be true, and then deduced a materially false conclusion from them. The outcome was the exposure of the falsity of the premise not yet known to be false, since it was taken to be the source of the acknowledged false outcome. Such arguments, al-Fārābī explains, are in principle reducible to sound, syllogistic reasoning. They are in fact examples of the familiar sort of argument in which we say such things as, "If Hitler was a military genius, then I'm a monkey's uncle," to use Copi's example.

Al-Fārābī has no difficulty in formalizing such suasions, and in general he is rather pleased with his ability to discern valid formal structures behind the cut and thrust of *kalām* dialectic. Indeed one of the manuscripts of the work containing his discussion of these arguments bears the subtitle "*In which he extracted* (kharraja) *the Arguments of the mutakallimūn and the Analogies of the Jurists as Syllogisms conforming to the Doctrines of the Ancients.* Al-Fārābī himself described analogy (*nuqla*, cf. the Greek *metabasis*) as "the syllogism of the *kalām*," and again had no difficulty in extracting the intended logical form. But, naturally, in many specific cases of theological reasoning he found that the necessary reduction required supplying premises which were not known or not admitted on all sides. The most characteristic arguments of the *kalām* were thus dialectical in the classical sense - understandable, perhaps tolerable in their context, but often lacking in rigor. *Kalām* inductive arguments, for example, often fail by the incompleteness of the surveys they employ, or the inconclusiveness of the predications they assume. Arguments from analogy, a favorite of the *kalām*, although useful within limits, too easily mistake irrelevant for relevant similarities. All these forms - enthymeme, reductio, induction, and analogy - can increase our knowledge. But the standard against which all are judged and found deficient is the apodeictic syllogism. Any of the lesser forms, used incautiously, can yield false conclusions and misconceptions in place of knowledge. Failure to quantify properly or to follow the contours of proper classes, that is, species, or to keep in mind that what one knows about the particular need not apply to the more general can all lead to error or worse. Ibn Sīnā explains the point patiently in his Persian work: When you say "Men move," or "Men write," without making clear whether you mean some or all men, the propositions are indeterminate and need a quantifier (*sūr*) like "all" or "some" to render them determinate.[32]

As Gyekye makes clear, al-Fārābī's intent in his discussion of *kalām* dialectic is to assay, and in some measure to rein in the argumentation of the *kalām*. But his critique is sober, appropriately tolerant and modest, not wishing to restrain informal reasoning by standards of rigor that would seem excessively rigid or out of place. Echoing Aristotle's sentiment of the *Nicomachaean Ethics* that it is a mistake to bring greater precision to a discourse than is warranted by the subject matter, al-Fārābī argues that theology and rhetoric allow room for inexact and sometimes unexacting arguments.[33] His treatment of the hypothetical or conditional syllogism, the mainstay of the *kalām*, is unambitious, conventional, and unthreatening.[34] On the whole he seems convinced that the problem presented by the *kalām* is not in their use of a specific kind of reasoning but simply in their penchant for certain fallacies, which any inquirer of good will and good sense would avoid once their formal error had been exposed.

Ibn Sīnā goes further, using his Galenic background to take over for Aristotelian philosophy the hypothetical syllogism. He makes a point, as he does so, of revitalizing the predicative terms as well as the syntactic operators of that syllogism, a hallmark of his approach to logic we have observed even from his youth. The effect is to corral the achievement of the Stoics but reinstate the dependence of all reasoning on the recognition of classes, their properties, and essential or accidental relations.

Ibn Sīnā recognizes the distinctiveness of the propositional syllogism, rejecting the illusion that conditional syllogisms can be made the formal equivalents of categorical ones: "Conditional propositions are deduced from pure or mixed conditional syllogisms, but never, as you know, from predicative syllogisms."[35] Yet, in the true spirit of Aristotelian syllogistic, Ibn Sīnā finds a place for quantification even in propositional logic, prefacing many conditionals by an *always* or a *never*. Indeed he develops an elaborate system of modal logic based on quantifying the Stoics' temporal interpretation of modality.[36] He knows that hypothetical propositions deal in clauses rather than subjects and predicates:

> One difference between the antecedent and consequent on the one hand and the subject and predicate on the other is that a subject and predicate can be single terms, but an antecedent and

> consequent can never be.... Another difference between the antecedent and consequent of a conditional syllogism and the subject and predicate of a categorical one is that it is possible to ask about a subject-predicate proposition whether the predicate belongs to the subject or not. For example, when someone says "Zayd is alive," you may inquire whether or not he is. But when someone pronounces a conditional, you cannot ask whether the consequent "belongs to" the subject.[37]

Here Ibn Sīnā highlights the centrality of predication in Aristotelian class logic and shows how that relation is masked in the propositional calculus. Yet he maintains that "Every conditional or disjunctive proposition ... is reducible to categoricals," since it makes no difference whether one says "All men are mortal" or (in his own interpretation of the modal judgment *Every man must die*): "At some time during one's existence 'dying' is predictable of every man." As he puts it in the *Danesh Nameh*, "The antecedent and the consequent in conditional judgments have the same relation as the subject and predicate in categorical sentences."[38]

In addressing a given set of facts or principles, Ibn Sīnā argues, there are corresponding hypothetical and categorical syllogisms that are equivalent in force (*fī quwwa*). The observation is of particular relevance to hypothetical syllogisms with multiple premises that state different things about the same subject. It is here that the material equivalence of the two forms of argument will be most obvious. Indeed, the case is of practical relevance: The compound antecedent can be a series of clauses which link with the consequent to form a single proposition describing the diverse attributes of what proves to be a single subject, "as when you say, 'If this man has a chronic fever, a hard cough, labored breathing, shooting pains, and a rasping pulse, he has pleurisy.'"[39] The same signs or symptoms, as Stoic doctrines of experience would call them, can be treated as the matter of an Aristotelian induction, leading to the framing of a generalization suitable for use in a scientific, categorical syllogism, and leading to a theory of the nature of the disease. And that, in the case of pleurisy, was precisely the direction in which Ibn Sīnā's medical work had led, as we know from his pathbreaking clinical description of pleurisy in the *Qānūn.*

Among conditionals Ibn Sīnā distinguishes "connective" from disjunctive arguments, remarking on the oddity that we call some statements conditional when they do not state conditions at all but rather *exclude* connections among states of affairs. The "connective" conditional, of course, aims to state an implication or consequence ("If the sun has risen, then it is day" or "If a man has a fever, his pulse will be elevated"); whereas the disjunctive addresses alternation or "opposition" ("Either this will occur, or that will"; "His pulse is not elevated, so he does not have a fever" – this being an inference from the premise connecting pulse with fever: "Either his pulse is elevated, or he does not have a fever").

Both "conjunctive" and disjunctive conditionals have a truth value, and Ibn Sīnā knows that the truth value of the whole depends on that of its constituent clauses – that is, the truth values they would have if they were independent clauses and actually made claims about the world. But because he thinks that the component clauses of conditionals do not actually have truth values of their own, Ibn Sīnā does not elaborate the idea of truth functional logic most familiar to us. In his view the truth value of all conditional sentences depends ultimately on their correspondence to the world. Since his primary interest is in sound arguments rather than merely valid schemata, his focus, even with a conditional syllogism, is on the true premises that compose it. And these resolve ultimately to true predications.

Logic in Ibn Sīnā's view is about truth and the means of finding it, and truth is not about words but about the world. In the *Najāt* he says that logic is, "an instrument common to all the sciences. It is a method of discovering the unknown from the known." In the *Danesh Nameh* he says that logic is the method of discovering the unknown from the known as well as the scale in which claims to knowledge must be weighed.[40] Fleshing out his material and intuitive as opposed to formalistic approach, he argues in the logic of the *Danesh Nameh Alā'ī* that the definition of man as "rational animal" tells us nothing until we have some idea what "rational" and "animal" mean.[41] Psychologically, pedagogically, even epistemologically the argument seems unanswerable. For why would one accept an abstract schema as valid if one did not first intuit the soundness of its material instances? And how could one apprehend that soundness without first comprehending the material relations among its terms – ultimately, subjects and predicates.[42] The reasoning seems to resonate with our knowledge of Avicenna's first awakening to logic as a discipline. But although only minimally tutored, that first discovery of the intuitive basis of logic was not unsupported. Peripatetics traditionally saw themselves as realists in logic and disparaged the Stoics as formalists, whose logic dealt with words.[43]

It is an expression of his realism that Ibn Sīnā maintains that the elements of conditional propositions, although generally expressed in sentential form, are not propositions in themselves but only, as we might put it, proposition-functors. "If *p*" and "then *q*" are not sentences at all in his view. Embedded in a complex conditional, they make no claim about the world. As he puts it,

> The antecedent, "If the sun rises" and the consequent, "then it is day," seem to be but are not bona fide propositions. The presence of the word "if" precludes the antecedent from being a proposition. "If the sun rises" is neither true nor false. And the consequent, "then it is day" is also neither true nor false. Similarly in our example of a disjunctive: The expression "Either this number is even," is not a proposition, because of the word "either." Nor is the alternative, "or it is odd," because of the word "or."[44]

The completeness or incompleteness of a judgment, after all, is not simply a matter of how many words it contains. *Adding* "either" to one term of a disjunction renders what was a complete judgment incomplete. The word "even" by itself might express a complete judgment, for example when it is given as the answer to a question. But the addition of "or" renders the thought incomplete. It now affirms nothing, has no truth value.

Even in languages (or idioms) which mark no distinction morphologically between an independent clause and the protasis or apodosis of a conditional sentence, the distinction remains critical between a dependent clause and an independent proposition: The notional content of *If it is day*, however the thought may be expressed, has no truth value of its own, although "It is day" does have one. It could just as well be expressed: *It being day. . . .* The same is true for the apodosis, *then it is light*, a thought we might express in the fragment, *there would be light . . .* or even *the appearance of light* – a manner of expression that does somewhat more to preserve the non-propositional content or sentential incompleteness of what follows from the antecedent.

Leibniz, who was familiar with the tradition Ibn Sīnā represents, takes a similar position. As Hidé Ishiguro puts it,

> A conditional proposition is not considered by Leibniz primarily as a complex proposition or a complex of propositions as contrasted with a simple proposition. He contrasted it with a pure proposition. In other words, it is a conditional assertion of

the consequent, as opposed to a pure or unqualified assertion of the consequent. We might say that we are committing ourselves to the consequent only if the antecedent obtains. As Leibniz writes to Foucher, "All hypothetical propositions assert what will or will not be, given that some fact or its contrary holds."[45]

The contrast is not between a simple proposition and a complex proposition, but between a qualified and an unqualified proposition.

The approach is appealing intuitively. As Ishiguro remarks, "a judge giving a suspended sentence can be described as giving a sentence in a certain qualified manner," – i.e., not at all, unless certain conditions are met.[46] As she explains, Leibniz' legal training may have informed his perspective here. He wrote his baccalaureate dissertation on the logic of conditionals in law and incorporated his early findings in two papers completed at age twenty-three in 1669, directing his attention, including his analysis of probability, to the likelihood of the consequent.[47] Ibn Sīnā's approach may also reflect his legal training. For clearly a contract that involves conditions is no contract unless those conditions are met, and the sanctions of a penal law have no actual application unless someone has committed the crime it forbids.

Frege addresses the same issue when he treats each element of a truth-functional assertion as "a mere complex of ideas . . ., '*the circumstance that*'."[48] What its being day implies is "its being light" – not anyone's commitment to the belief or affirmation of the proposition that it is light. In Ibn Sīnā's view, the only fully fledged truth value in conditionals is found in the conditional sentence as a whole, not in its elements taken as elements. Modern logicians acknowledge this when they point out that a conditional asserts the implication of its consequent by its antecedent but does not assert the antecedent or the consequent themselves. Indeed, as Ibn Sīnā points out, the clauses of some conditionals do not even obliquely affirm their propositional contents. For when we say "If Zayd is writing then his hand is moving," we make no claim of fact as to what Zayd is doing.[49]

We can appreciate some of what is at stake here for Ibn Sīnā if we consider the modern interest in what has been called the logic of relevance. Ishiguro writes,

> Leibniz realizes that in making a conditional assertion of the consequent one is also indicating a certain specific connection between the truth of the antecedent and the consequent. Leibniz calls this a conditionality (*conditionalitas*). It is a link (*junctura*), which is as it were the form of the inference we make.

> The antecedent and the consequent can be considered as the truths that are linked.[50]

Avicenna calls this linkage "harmony"[51] and sees it as a positive counterpart to the incompatibility on which rests the soundness of syllogisms that appeal to a disjunction, i.e., syllogisms whose nerve is an exclusive *or*.

What links propositions in the relevant way, as Leibniz knows, are predicates, that is, the characteristics of things. Our familiar propositional logic, however, because its terms are facts and neither things nor characteristics of things, is so devised as to suppress direct reference to the characteristics of things, or the relationships among those characteristics, except as relationships among opaque, atomic facts. Small wonder that our logicians have so much difficulty with relations like causality. Hume's argument that *a* does not entail *b* seems unanswerable in such a framework. Indeed, al-Ghazālī argued in the same way against the emanative naturalism of the Neoplatonic Aristotelians of his day: "This is not that, and that is not this; the affirmation of the one does not imply that of the other, and the denial of the one does not imply denial of the other."[52] A kind of logical atomism here dissolved the logicism, intellectualism, and emanative holism of the Philosophers, and with it, their very conception of the causal nexus, leaving room for al-Ghazālī's volitional recasting.

Addressing our contemporary scandal in logic, the inadequacy of our formal schematisms to map many of the reasonings we normally and habitually employ, John Passmore remarks that mathematical logicians "have often granted that we should not normally try to persuade people, for example, that *q* follows from *p* by telling them that *p* is false." Today's formal logicians, he explains, generally feel prepared to live with some anomalies, if they can give us a logic "which is clear, precise, adequate for deriving theorems from axioms and free of any confusing talk about 'meaning.'"[53] Ibn Sīnā was more tolerant of notions like that of meaning, but far more demanding of logic. He wanted a logic that would serve as a proper tool of science and discovery. He would have welcomed the work of such investigators as Anderson and Belnap, who hold, as Passmore puts it, that for one statement to entail another they have to have something to do with one another.[54]

Appraising the paradox of material implication (that a false assumption implies *everything*), and other comparable embarrassments of twentieth-century formal logic, such as the corresponding paradox of strict implication (a contradiction implies any proposition whatever), Passmore paraphrases Richard Routley, *Relevant Logic and its Rivals* (1982), as arguing that a classical, Russellian logician "behaves like an engineer who has invented a device to lift water from a stream. It is so badly designed that it spills most of its freight. Instead of trying to improve the device he devotes his energy to 'constructing ingenious arguments to prove that . . . there is nothing wrong with wasting water' or that the device has 'beautiful, clean, simple lines' which it would go totally against his engineering intuitions to modify." Avicenna's hybrid quantified and modal propositional logic would probably not win any beauty contests. But it is a logic of relevance that restores the centrality of predication, which lies at the root of most of our claims about facts.

Avicenna's approach to the logic of relevance is ingenious. He notes the difference between *or* and *if . . . then* that we express by saying that the former relation is commutative and the latter is not – i.e., that order makes no difference in disjunctions but makes all the difference in the world in the assertion of implications.[55] But he remarks another difference that typical systems of formal logic do not take account of or acknowledge. He argues that implications may connect subjects that are regarded as related or unrelated causally. They may deal with matters whose connectedness they assume to be wholly coincidental. To do so is not mere idle fantisizing, but often useful, since facts that we do not *assume* to be causally related may have some remote causal connection, say through some common causal factor. (We can say that facts which we do not know to be related may be found to be so, but should not be assumed to be related, say, while we are studying them.) But the exclusive *or*, taken strictly, Ibn Sīnā argues, never has a corresponding use, affirming that exactly one of two facts must hold although regarding those facts as having only a chance relation. For the exclusive *or* requires that one of the elements of a disjunct must be false and the other true; and allowing arbitrary alternations would allow the implication of false conclusions by true premises.[56] The non-existent, Ibn Sīnā argues, may be impossible *per se.* If so, its non-existence needs no necessary connection with the causes of what actually exists, and the heuristic value of arbitrary implications that we find so useful normally in the framing of causal hypotheses becomes irrelevant and would become misleading if a counterpart were sought for it in disjunctive reasoning.[57]

Semantical analysis is important to Ibn Sīnā at two levels with regard to hypotheticals and disjunctives: (*a*) He wants to insist upon the dependence of the truth value of the entire conditional (and any syllogisms it may be used to form) upon the categorical relations of the terms in its constituent clauses. This intensionality, Ibn Sīnā's avoidance of a purely formalistic propositional calculus, and his commitment to a logic of relevance arise for reasons that our discussion of Stoicism and the *kalām* should render obvious. Too abstract a treatment of propositions will license all sorts of *ad hoc* schemata based on arbitrary or alleged posits, and it will submerge the class relations among predicates, which underlie all sound scientific reasoning. (*b*) Ibn Sīnā wants to do justice to the varieties of relations among predicative terms (as understood with the aid of the sciences) by assigning an appropriate semantical loading to the syntactical operators of the hypothetical itself, i.e., what our logic calls the truth functional connectives.

(*a*) Naturally, the analysis of subject and predicate relations on which conditionals will depend for their validity can itself be reduced to formal terms. That is the purpose of the classical Aristotelian syllogistic. But *relative to the propositional relations of a sentential logic* the relations among subjects and predicates are a material rather than a formal consideration. By creating a propositional logic whose sentences are exploded into quantified categoricals or conditionals which are themselves expressed in subject–predicate form, Ibn Sīnā achieves the same result in propositional logic as he does in class logic when he insists upon the constant relevance of the material reference of categorical terms: He renders the logical form itself transparent and makes judgment responsive to the known facts about nature. The effect is not to elevate causal relations to matters of logical necessity but to undo the formalism by which *kalām* had seemed to render every formally coherent judgment a live option or a viable hypothesis. *Kalām* arguments can then be analyzed as appeals to analogy, presumptive connections, inductions (often incomplete), and other less than apodeictic forms.

We can see the profit of Ibn Sīnā's approach in the realism he employs in the analysis of conditionals whose elements are false. Here he finds little interest in formal analysis for its own sake and avoids the paradoxical claim that all hypotheticals with a false antecedent are valid. Instead he argues that *s*, "If man is not an animal, then he is not sensitive" is true; whereas *t*, 'If man is a creature that caws, then a raven is a creature that talks" is false. For *s*, Ibn Sīnā insists, expresses a valid inference, even though both its antecedent and its consequent (taken propositionally) are false. But *t* expresses no real relation of implication and cannot be treated even as a matter of coincidence between two intrinsically unrelated facts. The structural symmetry of the predicates *talks* and *caws* in *t* pretends to warrant their transposition. Such structural interchange is a staple of myth and fable, as Levi-Strauss showed exhaustively. It calls to mind the sort of *ad hoc* formal schematisms that render typical *kalām* arguments suspect, al-Ash'arī's "If appropriation were impossible only because of the lack of the limb, then having the limb would mean appropriating the act." When we evaluate in earnest and without a *parti pris*, Ibn Sīnā concludes, the determinant of our very reading of the two arguments *s* and *t* is the relation among the *predicative* terms of their constitutive clauses and the resultant correspondence or failure of correspondence to the world of the propositions intended in those clauses.

(*b*) We can see the same effect in Ibn Sīnā's analysis of what we since Frege have called truth functional connectives. The heart of his approach is to focus on that aspect of these connectives that we would call their semantics. Just as in mathematics diverse formal relations can be used to map quantitative relations in nature (e.g., multiplication can be used to express the relation between linear dimensions and area but also to express the relationship between, say rates of travel, distances, and travel times), so in logic the formal connectives can be assigned diverse tasks and may need diverse interpretations expressive of the relations we seek to schematize by their means.

Naturally Ibn Sīnā distinguishes the exclusive from the non-exclusive "or"; he also differentiates a special case of the exclusive "or" that means "not both" but allows that both of the disjuncts be false. This is the operator (one of the two) that Sheffer found was adequate for the construction of all other truth functional connectives. But Ibn Sīnā does not note any special importance for it. He does not see his task as one of reducing all logical relations to a single, simplest formal usage. Rather, his goal is faithfully and flexibly to reflect the variety of natural relations to which the syntax of natural languages is sensitive. Thus he elaborates his point by contextualizing and illustrating the ambiguities and suggestive connotations of the various disjunctives in use rather than abstracting and formalizing their most distinctive characteristics.

Ibn Sīnā's semantical interests are vividly exemplified in the asymmetry he proposes between "or" and "if . . . then." The reason disjunctive propositions are never matters of purely coincidental exclusion is clearly pragmatic: We may assert causal or purely coincidental connections between two facts, but would never, Ibn Sīnā claims, assert a merely coincidental exclusion of one fact by another. To affirm such an exclusion, he argues, would be tantamount to affirming a causal relation. Ibn Sīnā drives home the point by arguing that non-facts do not require a cause, since what is impossible might be impossible in itself and need no external explanation. As an example, he chooses the void, which all good Aristotelians held to be a self-evident and intrinsic impossibility. If we allowed disjunctions between assertions that are not causally related, then the true disjunction "Either man exists or there is a void" might require the existence of the void should man suddenly become extinct. Since there is no use or application for such disjunctions in the first place, Ibn Sīnā follows what he takes to be the usages of natural language in excluding them.

Positive connections, Ibn Sīnā argues, can be matters of implication or matters of coincidence: "When we assume the rising of the sun, this implies, both in fact and in thought that it is day."[58] We might be tempted to say that the inference is analytic. But the point for Avicenna is that thought or language or usage takes the relation to be analytic, by way of reflecting the causal relation between daylight and the sun in nature: "Either because what is implied is the cause of the existence of the second . . . or because it is an inseparable effect . . . or a correlate . . . or because both are effects of the same cause . . . as thunder and lightning are effects of the movement of the wind in the clouds . . . or for other reasons." Alternatively, there may be causal connections that link facts without our knowledge, or without our paying attention to the linkages. For (to use Avicenna's example) there are causal conditions that link together the fact that there are horses with the fact that there are men, but we may reason about the proposition that "Whenever there are horses there are men" without making use of any such assumption in our reasoning. Or, in the case of pure coincidences, there may be connections or concomitances that are accidental or factitious and without causal significance.

To express the protean varieties of necessary or contingent, natural, logical, or accidental relations among states of affairs, Ibn Sīnā proposes his own material interpretations of the truth functional connectives. His proposals in this regard, like most formalizations, do not conform precisely to the usages of the natural language he uses, but they do express a real sensitivity to the varieties of application which these connectives may be called upon to serve. He points out, for example, that one does not say, "Given that the resurrection comes, mankind will be judged," as though the final judgment followed analytically from the resurrection of the dead; for (it is assumed) God's act of judgment is dependent on His will. Accordingly, we say "When the resurrection comes . . ." The antecedent states the occasion, not the cause, and still less the sufficient condition of the consequent. In English we often use "if" and "when" to make the protasis of a conditional seem problematic or presumptive. In like manner Latin (and English too, when we use subjunctives carefully) distinguishes "future less vivid" from more positive conditions: "The new institute will . . ." versus "The proposed rules would . . .". Avicenna regards it as critical here, as always, to distinguish mere concomitance from causal (or logical) relations of necessity, and purely circumstantial from inferential connections.

By the same token, he is very interested in relations of mutual implication, the relation our logicians symbolize by the expression *iff*, as in "*p* iff *q*". Shehaby labels this "the same as the equivalence described by modern logicians," and reports that Ibn Sīnā's discussion of this relation "is probably the first time the concept of equivalence is mentioned in the history of logic."[59] But Cicero records the Stoic use of the biconditional in *De Finibus*, when the Stoics seek to show the equivalence of virtue and the good by arguing that "whatever is good is praiseworthy; whatever is praiseworthy is morally right (or virtuous, *honestum*)";[60] for it was a given that whatever is morally right is good. And again in the "citadel" of Stoic theology, "If there are gods there is divination, and if there is divination there are gods." Here, at least, the Stoics did not assign an overt equivalence between the two propositions. But the Stoic heritage of monism did foster the notion of the equivalence of all truths, precisely on the grounds that all had the same truth conditions.[61] In this circumstance, only a Fregean distinction between sense and reference could have provided the appropriate fix, since monism would demand in the end that all distinctions are subjective.

Ibn Sīnā's sensitivity to the semantic values of sentences as well as terms, his characteristic unwillingness to render logic opaque to the material content of the predicative notions that we will marshal into arguments, allows him to avoid the presumption of those modern logicians who suppose that when two sentences have the same truth conditions they are in fact equivalent sentences. This view, we can say, is either a cause or an effect, or an inseparable concomitant (the two perhaps both stemming from the same unseen cause) of operationalism and instrumentalism, among other tendentious applications of the authority of modern logic. For when a positivist equates the meaning of a sentence with its means of verification, or when an anti-realist cashes out the message of a factual claim in terms of hypothetical measurements and experiments, both are assuming that whatever is true if and only if *p* must be *p*. Both are ignoring the paradox of seeking to warrant *p* by *p*.

Ibn Sīnā clearly understood that we cannot equate two propositions merely because they are true at the same time, or under the same conditions – unless we are so expansive in defining what we take to be conditions as to include any factor that might influence the sense of one proposition or the other. In the self-contained and insulated hothouse of an artificial language, it may in certain circumstances be quite permissible to allow free substitutions of propositions that imply each other. But if logic is to retain any claim of application to a world not of its own devising, it must recognize not only intensional but extensional differences among propositions that may have the same truth conditions. This often ignored but elemental necessity is particularly important for worlds in which there are necessary universal truths, i.e., for any world that would count as natural in an Aristotelian sense. For, in all such worlds, the truth conditions of all natural laws are identical, although these laws themselves are not the same but state quite different (even if sometimes related) principles about different states of affairs. It may even be true (as the Stoics supposed) that *sub specie aeternitatis* all truths imply all other truths. But, if this taken to imply their equivalence, such knowledge obviates the very notion of particular causal relations, from which (via the idea of *sympatheia*) it seems to spring. The Stoic doctrine that all truths imply each other is in fact an expression of Stoic monism and must be laid aside or bracketed if we are to retain any possibility of differentiating specific relations (the horizontal ones) from the alleged universal necessity and the general hum of circumstance (*heimarmene*).

The logic devised for monism will not be of much use in a pluralistic universe, as Aristotle made clear, before there were any Stoics, when he argued that the Platonic tactic of ascribing all causation to the Good contributes little to the scientific interest in specific causes. To put the matter in terms more acceptable to Avicenna, which is to say, more suitable for reconciling the thought of Plato with that of Aristotle, the ascription of all effects to a single cause can in no way obviate the ascription of each to its particular, proximate cause.

Ibn Sīnā's treatment of the logic of judgment allows us either to assume and treat as canonical causal relations among states of affairs, or to avoid such assumptions. By avoiding the assumption that the truth functional connectives are univocally related to matters of causality, essences, or analytic truths, Ibn Sīnā's approach escapes both the conundrums of the Stoic pan-analytic delusion, which treats every fact as a necessary and sufficient condition of every other, and the aporia of the logical atomism known to us from Hume and his successors, but known to Ibn Sīnā himself from the work of the *kalām*.

In Ibn Sīnā's treatment there is room for causality, but its operation is not simply imposed upon the structure of logic. As he puts it, "the consequent is not a definition of the antecedent."[62] Avicenna's ability to escape the logicism that would later trap Ibn Rushd, while still avoiding the accidentalism of the *kalām* is, of course, an expression of his conception of the relative contingency of all events in nature, dependent on their causes, but capable of treatment in abstraction from the supposition of those causes.

Averroes will ultimately insist that all causal relations are logical relations, on the grounds that all events are expressions of the essences of things. The claim will damage the authority of philosophy beyond measure in Islamic lands. For it is obvious, as the critique of rationalist philosophy by al-Ghazālī had made clear, that there is no logical contradiction in denying a causal judgment and no self-evidence in affirming one. Averroes is reduced to charging his adversaries with stupidity or stubborness for their failure to see that causes are the logical counterparts of their effects. His response to al-Ghazālī will fare better and survive longer in the west than in the lands of Islamic rule and culture, in part because the secular forces gaining strength in the west just as the works of Averroes/Aristotle are being translated will offer a warmer welcome to science and scientism, logic and logicism, than did the theologically charged political environment of Islam. But, in the end, Averroistic bluster will not get past Hume, when he reformulates the old empiricist, nominalist, traditionalist objections against logicist and intellectualist accounts of causality.

What this means is that Ibn Sīnā's logic has a special relevance for us, in our post-Humean philosophical environment, if we are not simply to fall back on customs and habits of the mind, as Hume and the early Ash'arites would have us do, or to go on simply bluffing our way along, not in the style of Averroes but in the style of the post-Kuhn, post-Feyerabend philosophy of science, which knows no warrant for causal judgments but treats scientific method simply as the familiar or marketable or likeable voodoo of the scientific priesthood. For Ibn Sīnā, despite his rationalism and intellectualism, is committed to no such logicism as that of Ibn Rushd. Indeed his rationalism and intellectualism are welcome dialectically if not materially in our present circumstance, in that they reveal the separability of a rationalist account of causality from the logicist determinism of an Ibn Rushd. Ibn Sīnā's guiding conception, that the same event may be contingent in itself and necessary only in relation to its causes, allows him, as we have seen, to abstract from the givenness of those causes and look at any event as contingent. His logic enshrines that insight rather than attempting to use the internal necessity of formal implications to jack up the contingent facticity of nature into a formalistic necessitarianism buttressed by a specious logicism.

The irony of Avicenna's achievement in logic is that in appropriating propositional logic and assimilating it to the scientific mode of thought that Aristotelianism represented, he found it necessary to break away from the confining boundaries of the approach traditional among his predecessors, no longer simply following the contours of the Aristotelian texts. His very originality and independence made his work itself authoritative. He emancipated logic, transforming it into a non-Greek, non-foreign, widely accepted, and widely used organon that no longer made any necessary reference to the ideas or the works of Aristotle, but that was, in the hands of others, routinized beyond recognition when compared with his own constantly questioning, philosophical approach.

As Ibn Sīnā's influence spread and his modified Aristotelian approach to logic was internalized in the Islamic sciences, even the Islamic rejection of Greek metaphysics was muted, as we have seen. Logic and metaphysics together were adapted to Islamic legal and theological discussions. But the logic now employed was not a living organism but a hidebound technique, just as the metaphysics was, increasingly, an epistemologically unstable blend of speculative theology, dogmatic cosmology, and traditional symbolism.

In the work of later logicians, the outcomes of the Aristotelian/Avicennan approach were boiled down to practical essentials. The doctrine of the *Categories* was dropped from the standard syllabus, reportedly because its content seemed tangential to the daily work of logic. Ibn Sīnā himself had rightly seen that the *Categories* pertains to metaphysics more than logic. But, as a result, he deemphasized the nexus between logic and metaphysics which the *Categories* of Aristotle enshrines. Outlining the contours of logic for his students in the *Shifā'*, he wrote:

> There is no need to study terms within logic insofar as they designate real or mental entities, particulars or universals. For the terms indicative of particulars hold no interest for science; and the terms signifying the highest genera, which are customarily called predicaments, *kategorias*, and to which a treatise is devoted at the outset of the Logic, do not properly belong to logic. . . . The categories belong to metaphysics insofar as they address themselves to being, to psychology insofar as they are mental notions, and to language insofar as they involve the proper use of terms. We must only note, however, that the study of the categories can serve us in the formulation of definitions. For in defining some object, we refer back to its category or highest genus . . . relation, substance, quantity, quality . . .[63]

Pedagogically, in logic, as in medicine, Ibn Sīnā's impulse was to simplify. Indeed, this impulse, and the pressure of demand that came from his students were diametrically opposed to the quest for differences, subtleties, and complexities that is the great theme of his method as a philosopher. From the outlook of his students, and all the more so of their successors, the subject matter of the *Categories* was too abstruse and theoretical, too metaphysical, too philosophical in a word, for the uses that logic as a tool was now called upon to serve.

Other segments of the corpus were merged and rearranged, the *Posterior Analytics, Topics, Sophisticis Elenchis, Rhetoric,* and *Poetics* were sharply downgraded in prominence, disappearing after Ibn Sīnā's time, as discrete sub-disciplines of logic. Philosophical logic lost its connection with the logic of formal inference in the disciplines. And Ibn Khaldūn could finally report that his contemporaries had lost interest almost altogether in primary studies of logic and had reached the point of simply relying on textbooks and compendia like those of Fakhr al-Dīn al-Rāzī and al-Khūnajī. "The books of the ancients are avoided," he writes, "as if they had never existed, although they are replete with the fruits of logic and highly beneficial."[64] In emancipating logic from the *Organon* of Aristotle, Avicenna had found room to make genuinely insightful contributions, proudly reporting, new forms of syllogistic argument, "unknown until now, which I myself discovered."[65] But, in the hands of lesser thinkers, logic was not selfeuthanatized, but simply routinized, as it always becomes for those who see in it a mere technique of argument and exposition, insulated from philosophic wonder and inquiry, rather than a minefield that demands the most thoughtful and creative placement of our philosophical footpaths.

2 AVICENNA ON THE ART OF PERSUASION

Aristotle is kinder to rhetoric than Plato, who calls it (among other things) a bastard and imposter knack of flattering deception.[66] Like Abe Lincoln, Aristotle did not suppose that would-be persuaders can fool all the people all the time. His greater confidence in the people, or at least his greater realism about human variability, may reflect the softening influence of the time that passed between the death of Socrates and his own maturity. Athenian democracy did not still hold the odor of horror that it did for Plato, who kept the memory of the death of Socrates at the hands of that democracy alive so long and preserved the shock of its wrongness so well that his readers even now can scarcely believe that this martyrdom was the work of the same Athens that Pericles hailed as the school of Hellas. Unlike Plato, Aristotle does not think that one must enter the realm of mathematics before gaining access to the truth. He prefers the plain analogy of the barn door, which is so broad that no one misses it altogether, no matter how hard it may prove to strike any one part of it with precision (*Metaphysics a* 993b 3–5). With the death of Alexander and the fall of Antipater, Aristotle himself was brought within range of Socrates' fate; but, as he sidestepped it by self-exile, he could glance at it longwise and philosophically and disavow any intention of sharing it. It was clear enough what the people were, and if a man did not live by their good opinion there was no need to die for it. The people could be persuaded – if not here and now, then later, or elsewhere.

Having more confidence in people in general than Socrates did, and less need for one people in particular, Aristotle has less fear of rhetoric than Plato does. He knows that students learn and that even audiences remember. Indeed, his first job at the Academy was to teach rhetoric (and the dissolution of sophistries) to Plato's students, as a kind of counterforce to the oratorical teachings of Isocrates. And when Aristotle came to write down the content of those lectures, he recorded the worldly but principled advice that, if a speaker hopes to persuade and to continue to persuade, he ought not to compromise his credibility – counsel that even a sophist or a student of sophists would be well advised to take seriously: "It is not true," Aristotle writes, "as some writers assume in their treatises on rhetoric, that personal goodness revealed by the speaker contributes nothing to his power of persuasion; on the contrary, his character may almost be called the most effective means of persuasion he possesses."[67]

Aristotle would not have been dismayed at the assimilation of his Rhetoric to the *Organon* by the later school tradition, since he regarded rhetoric as an application of dialectic and saw its arguments as enthymemes that were not degenerate or deficient apodeictic proofs, but rather the very matter from which more formal proofs are made. For Ibn Sīnā rhetoric is the art of persuading the populace and is as suited to the purpose as formal proof is to the conviction of specialists and the intellectually adept. It need not eliminate all doubt but may rest with probabilities. The *Qur'ān* itself, he urges, finds a role for both philosophical and popular persuasion, along with dialectical, argumentative appeals.

Glossing *Qur'ān* 16: 125, Ibn Sīnā writes,

> The Book, which bears no falsehood before or behind it, the revelation of the Allwise and Allpowerful speaks in much the same sense: *Call men unto the path of thy Lord* [God instructs His prophet] – that is, the true religion – *with wisdom* – that is, by way of proof [*burhān*, apodeictic demonstration, taken here as philosophical, since "wisdom," is the common term for philosophy] – that is, for those who can handle it – *and with fair persuasion* – that is, rhetoric, for those who cannot manage philosophic rigor; *and engage them in argument with whatever is best* – that is, by appeal to the commonly accepted standards of what is praiseworthy and commendable. It mentions dialectic after the other two arts because they are devoted to finding what is beneficial, whereas dialectic is used for criticism. First we must know what is beneficial; only then do we engage in controversy or polemic with those who are committed to opposing it."[68]

The proper role of rhetoric is to deal with particulars. Its discourse needs to know whether or not particular things exist, or will exist, or have existed in the past, whether a certain act is just or unjust, beneficial or harmful, virtuous or vicious. These are not matters of proof – as though we could establish apodeictically whether or not the Cubs will win the World Series. But they are matters on which conviction is possible.[69] One can offer arguments, and arguments which are of greater or lesser power and merit, in convincing people, say, that capital punishment, abortion, or euthanasia is wrong, or that public speech is more worthy of protection than private sensibilities. Or that Billie Sol Estes or Oliver North is or is not a dangerous criminal.

Some matters of benefit and harm are such that everyone knows them; others require special expertise before a rhetorician should tackle them.[70] One need only think of some health and environmental issues today. Everyone knows that pollution is dangerous and can be deadly, but not everyone knows what pollution is, what causes it, how close to critical levels it may have come. For this we rely on experts. But when experts arrogate to themselves the role of arbiters of value and begin to pronounce for or against the value of wilderness, say, as an end in itself, they are treading on the common ground that belongs to all of us. Their predictions about the effects of tetraethyl lead or chloro-fluorocarbons are necessary to any sound policy. But their predilections for the spotted owl over the snail darter, taken as value judgments, have no more authority than anyone else's. Rhetoric must state the case for the spotted owl *vis-à-vis* the jobs of loggers. Synthetic thinking will seek a means by which both can be preserved. But science does not state the value to be assigned to either.

Some acts, Ibn Sīnā writes, are declared blameworthy or praiseworthy by the universally known and commonly accepted religious law. For example, the law regards it as a virtue to protect victims of wrongdoing from harm. More specific, positive ordinances make it a virtue to fast and to perform the Pilgrimage. But other actions are not so clearly classified and require argument, in terms of setting rules or policies in areas not regulated by the law, or in terms of adjudicating particular cases and evaluating individual circumstances.[71] This realm of argument is the real heart of the rhetorician's concern, not the superficial issues normally dealt with in handbooks of rhetoric, whose object is simply the devices and techniques by which a speaker may induce his audience to hear him out and predispose them to hear his arguments with favor. Rather the heart of the matter is argument itself, specifically the sort of argument that leaves its major premise unstated, that is, the enthymeme (*al-ḍamīr*).

If the mere external tricks of orators were the real basis of rhetoric, Avicenna writes, then hermeneutics would be an art, and disputation would be another. Indeed there would be not just one art of quarreling and disputing, but several, an art of major quarrels and another of market wrangles. But in fact, there is an art of rhetoric, which is to say, a standard to which rhetoric may (and must) appeal, and the basis of that art, the name of that standard, is enthymeme. The externalities that are the cynosure of rhetorical handbooks are no more than gimmicks (*mu'addāt*) by which a speaker may embellish his discourse.[72] As Aristotle said in addressing the same issue: "The means of persuasion alone come properly within the art; other things are merely additions" (*Rhetoric* I 2, 1354a, 13–14).

Postmodern readers may be surprised to be told that there is a common formal basis for rhetoric, although the material standards and the moral and cultural contexts to which speakers appeal may vary. But they may not be displeased to see that a philosopher who denies that the form of judgment in rhetoric is culture-bound or "local" also denies that hermeneutics (*al-tafsīr*) is an art in the strong Aristotelian sense that requires an art to rest upon the epistemic footings of some science. For hermeneutics, Ibn Sīnā is implying, *is* local, dependent on the particularities and peculiarities of usage and custom. In a way, he seems here to recognize the well-known postmodern problem of the hermeneutic circle. But he does not think that the dependence of hermeneutics on local standards and usages is globally damaging to discourse, and the reason is epistemic: Discourse can and will be local, following the usages of natural languages, which will have their local idioms and their local experts, as al-Fārābī explained in his *Book of Letters*.[73] But logic will not be local but universal, drawing its categories ultimately from the Active Intellect. And rhetoric, despite its formal incompleteness, belongs to logic, not to literature or the grammar of the idiomatic. It is not a matter, simply, of eloquence.

I can illustrate Ibn Sīnā's point from the empirical studies of my anthropologist friend Jack Bilmes, who worked with Thai villagers on the matter of the rhetoric of public policy. Jack offered a small sum of money, about $150, to the village for some public project, provided that the people could agree on how the money would be spent. His interest was in observing the procedures and particularly the modes of discourse they employed in determining how to spend it. A number of projects were proposed. Some villagers advocated a rest house for wayfarers; others, electrification of the village; others, a farmers' marketing and warehousing association; others, a loudspeaker system with batteries or a generator, to enhance the village festivals; still others, the purchase of traditional musical instruments, which it was hoped some of the young people would learn to play. All of the proposals would produce some benefit materially or in prestige and self-respect, and the advocates stressed the expected benefits when they spoke for their preferred projects. They also modified their expressions of preferences in terms of their expectations about others' choices, saying, for example, that one project would be too expensive in the long run to command much support, or that they did not want to be dissenters.

The villagers tended to ascribe one another's preferences to the perceived interests of the individual chooser or the group that he belonged to. But in advocating their own choices they couched their arguments in more general terms, involving profit to the village as a whole or broad based points of principle.[74] We may see in this move toward the general a natural human willingness to dissemble one's true motives, or the healthy push of social pressure toward intersubjectivity and thus in the direction of morality. Doubtless there was a mixture of self-serving and genuine public spiritedness in the responses. But even the desire to mask selfish with unselfish motives is not entirely unwholesome.

The arguments offered by the villagers were always enthymemes. Not that they were fallacious. But no one needs or wants to be told why good health, say, is advantageous, or why prosperity or prestige, or even proper reverence toward the gods is desirable or worthwhile. The particularities involved in any given choice, of course, are dependent on local knowledge: One who does not know that the prestige of festival dance performances can enhance village prosperity would not understand all of the reasoning behind some proposals. One who did not understand what electricity can be used for would miss even more. But the idea that persuasion rests on an appeal to benefits and is convincing when the hearers are convinced that one benefit (or detriment) outweighs the rest is not a local but a universal matter. Only a formal system that took no cognizance of interests would be incapable of detecting the kinds of persuasive merit that all the competing schemes appealed to. The givenness of the values appealed to is not an automatic or an a priori matter. Nor is it a trivial or easy matter to adjudicate among them, ordering priorities to reach a single outcome. The fact that the choosers were all members of a single, fairly small, fairly well integrated, traditional, and rather homogeneous community did not make their choices uniform or trivial. One could not read off a preference from a simple list of the values they all shared. Nor was there anything like a one-to-one correspondence between what they said and what, on other grounds, seemed to motivate them.

A hermeneuticist would have to be very open and sensitive to individual and shared values and differences about values before venturing to interpret anyone's motives. Arab village men, when asked to state their preferences, between a television and a higher wall for privacy, tend to say they want the wall. But, like the rest of us, they do not always spend their money in the same way as they answer questionnaires.[75] Which is to say that hermeneutics is an art in our sense, not in Aristotle's or Avicenna's. But rhetoric is an art in Avicenna's and in Aristotle's sense. As Aristotle says, "Rhetoric may be defined as the power of observing in any given case the available means of persuasion. . . . First we must ascertain what are the kinds of things, good or bad, about which the deliberative orator offers counsel. . . ."[76] Knowing these, the art of consists in ordering an appeal to them, just as the art of politics consists in maximizing the attainment of all the goods they serve.

3 AVICENNA'S POETICS

Among the most difficult texts for Arabic translators and interpreters of Greek philosophy was Aristotle's *Poetics*. Most of the specific poetic forms mentioned there are not found in Arabic. Drama, the main subject of the surviving text, was not an established form of Arabic literary culture, and theater as Greeks knew it was unknown to Muslims in Ibn Sīnā's time.[77] Thus even the relevance of a work like the *Poetics* seemed limited in the extreme, at least at first blush. The great Nestorian translator Ḥunayn ibn Isḥāq knew Greek well enough to recite from Homer in his youth. But, although he found time to translate over a hundred works of Galen, he never translated Homer. Theophilus ibn Tūma of al-Ruhā' (d. 785) did translate portions of the *Iliad*, but the translation was rarely copied and little read. It left no impression on Arabic literature and was not preserved. The Homeric world, had a Muslim thinker read of it, would have seemed not only exotic but primitive and foreign to the interests that motivated philosophical reflection.

Yet the commitment of Arabic scholarship to the extraction of all that was worthwhile from the works of Aristotle did not stop short of the *Poetics*. Around 932 Abū Bishr Mattā (d. 940), the Nestorian Christian philosopher and logician whose work laid the foundation that enabled al-Fārābī to establish himself as a Muslim logician, translated the *Poetics* into Arabic from the Syriac version (c. 900) of Ḥunayn's son Isḥāq. This was the same Abū Bishr who defended philosophical logic at the court of the Abbasid *wazīr* Ibn al-Furāt against the grammarian al-Sīrāfī's charges that its standards were relative to the Greek language and had no universal application. The Monophysite Christian philosopher, copyist, and bibliophile Yaḥyā ibn 'Ādī (893–974), a disciple of Abū Bishr's and the principal disciple of al-Fārābī, reportedly translated the *Poetics* as well, improving on his master's version. Abū Bishr's translation, extant in a Paris manuscript, is described by Zimmermann as "notably unsuccessful." It is the superior version of Yaḥyā that Ibn Sīnā seems to have used in writing his commentary around 1020.[78] For all of these men, the two Christian translators and the two Muslim philosophers, the initial interest of the *Poetics* stemmed from its placement within logic.

The inclusion of the *Poetics* within the *Organon* was quite natural for a tradition that saw that Aristotle's writings discuss not only apodeictic but fallacious, dialectical, rhetorical, and sophistical arguments. Aristotle himself had assigned persuasive primacy to the dialectical, since no one would engage in formal reasoning if not persuaded of its usefulness, and since the most basic law of logic, the prohibition against contradiction, cannot be proved apodeictically – without circularity – but is defended *dialectically* by the recognition that one who rejects it can affirm nothing. Inclusion of the *Rhetoric* and *Poetics* in the Aristotelian *Organon* is traced by Rescher at least as far back as Simplicius and is doubtless much older.[79] It clearly gave the work a relevance far beyond its immediate cultural horizon at the time of its composition.

For Muslims of philosophic outlook the *Poetics* offered a standpoint for the sympathetic but still critical understanding of the *Qur'ān* as a kind of poetry. It was, in fact, the very poetry that Plato had prescribed in answer to the dilemma of the Cave: A philosopher has both a moral responsibility and an intellectual need to report what he has learned. But the attempt to relate unfamiliar truths to an uncomprehending audience leads most often to misunderstanding and can lead to the philosopher's death, as Plato well knew. Indirection was the most viable solution. One must convey the abstruse truths of philosophy to the unphilosophical populace by way of symbols, myths, "true lies," which will suggest what more explicit language cannot, or what it would not dare affirm more bluntly. Imagination can clothe the truth in vivid similitudes, to use the term (*amthāl*; cf. the Hebrew, *mashal*) that Muḥammad himself seems to have adopted from the ancient practice of the Hebrew prophets. But only a trained and well-exercised intellect can capture the truth itself in its conceptual nakedness.

The philosophers' use of the *Poetics*, a cornerstone of al-Fārābī's thinking, required a retreat to the most generic conception of poetry. The pointed and specific literary teachings of Aristotle's work, perhaps predictably, were most often lost on a non-Greek audience in any case. Thus al-Kindī, the first important Muslim philosopher, was drawn to the *Poetics* as an explication of the logic of discourse about character. He reportedly wrote super-commentaries on Alexander of Aphrodisias' treatments of the *Poetics* and the *Rhetoric*; and he even wrote an outline of the *Poetics* long before its translation by Abū Bishr. In his sketch of Aristotle's *Organon*[80] al-Kindī assimilates comedy to panegyric and tragedy to the dirge and the lampoon, hewing not only to the familiar genres of Arabic poetry but to a literal reading or over-reading of Aristotle's account of the moral purposes of poetry.[81]

Abū Bishr Mattā, for similar reasons, rendered the Greek terms for tragedy and comedy as "encomium" and "satire" or "lampoon" – an assimilation to ancient Arabic genres that is understandable in view of Aristotle's remarks about the nobility of character and baseness of manners portrayed in the two dramatic forms.[82] That is, the confusion is understandable in an author who had no firsthand knowledge of the genres under discussion. The distinctiveness of the Greek genres is understandably submerged, and what was a defense on Aristotle's part against Plato's complex but spirited attack on the moral seriousness and commitment of poetry now becomes a matter of definition.

Al-Khwarizmī, again not the ninth century deviser of algebra, from whose name the word algorithm is taken, but the tenth century author of *The Keys to the Sciences*, an early lexicon of technical usages in the Arabic religious and literary sciences and the new foreign sciences, which we mentioned in our first chapter, shows even greater distance than al-Kindī from the specific genres of Greek literary art. Yet he does grapple with the perennial question of literary engagement. He argues that imaginative representation in poetry involves "the excitation of the mind of a hearer toward pursuit of a thing or flight from it, without one's being literally convinced of it. . . . It is said that I portray a thing when I induce its representation in your mind . . . a representation or imitation or portrayal of me are all forms of knowledge. The proof is that I recognize the object. It is because it is recognizable to me that I am convinced."[83] Here al-Khwarizmī uses the Stoic model of motivation or assent as grounded in pursuit and avoidance to gloss Aristotle's elusive references to pity and fear and to vindicate the cognitive content of the emotive assent that poetry in general and dramatic poetry in particular seek to attain. The distinctive means of portrayal employed in the theater seem, understandably, to remain just beyond his reach, and he can only mention the terms for crisis and complication without giving definitions for them. Yet what he finds in the *Poetics* is a matter of practical usefulness to one who might seek to understand how it is that representations which we know are fictional can move us and even make us change course or alter our outlook in life. The key is our recognition of the objects and situations represented – not that we are deceived about there being a representation, but rather that we are able to recognize what is represented *through* the representation, and so are enabled, and indeed emotionally compelled to respond to it.

Al-Fārābī finds in poetry not only the metric of prosody, which rests upon the distinctive features of a given language[84] but also an "imaginative syllogism," based essentially on our identification with the situations represented and corresponding to the illusory syllogism of sophistic, the enthymeme of rhetoric, the dialectical syllogism grounded in commonly accepted notions, and the scientific syllogism of apoedictic reasoning. Combining the ideas of "imaginative representation/assent" and encomium/lampoon, he argues that poetry puts an evaluative spin on things, representing them as better or worse, more beautiful or ugly, than they really are. The object is to move the audience by emotive rather than intellectual means.[85]

Admirers of the autonomy of poetry may agree with Dahiyat that such a scheme "does result inevitably in pushing poetry down to a rather humble status when it is contrasted with the demonstrative science which is allegedly productive of logical truth and certitude." But one would have to qualify the claim that "poetry is 'placed' at the very bottom of the logical hierarchy"[86] – for surely it lands above sophistry and its deceptions. The question that al-Fārābī, like al-Khwarizmī, wants to answer is how it is possible for poetry to convey truths by indirect means. When we look to al-Fārābī's account of religion in general and of the *Qur'ān* in particular, we find that the role of poetry is not subordinate at all, but central.

The highest and most praiseworthy form of poetry, he writes, "aims at the improvement of the powers of reason, guiding its thought processes and its actions toward our wellbeing. Poetry fosters the imaginative representation of things divine and excellent and promotes the graphic envisioning of the virtues and their attractiveness, and the foulness and baseness of evils and deficiencies." Poetry may moderate our tendencies to anger, pride, cruelty, insolence, vainglory, power madness, gluttony, and the like. And it may shore up our human slackness and allow us to master pity or fear, anxiety, grief, shame, luxury, or softness. Some genres of poetry (like the melodic modes described by Plato in the *Republic*) may have just the opposite of these effects.[87] But that is only the measure of the seriousness of its task. Although poetry is put to work here and not left autonomous, its role and its responsibilities are hardly trivial.

Moreover, al-Fārābī does not reduce the *means* of poetry to the merely didactic, as though it were a form of sermonizing, since poetry grips us in ways that merely hortatory words cannot. Those who think that poetry is demeaned by being made the imaginative guide of life and thought should ask themselves (before criticizing al-Fārābī) whether they have assigned poetry, or the arts in general any higher role than that of providing amusement, titillation, entertainment – or, perhaps, advertising. For it is clear that one who holds that poetry, for example, should shock us from our presumed complacency has yet to ask whether such shock value is an end in itself or a means to an end. If it is an end in itself, as claims for the absolute autonomy of art would make it, then poetry is sheerly a matter of titillation. If it is for the sake of some higher vision, then al-Fārābī's claims as to the mission of poetry in our moral and intellectual lives are in effect accepted, and the question that Islamic philosophy inherits, as to the means by which the virtual or imaginative assent of the mind can yield cognitive outcomes remains an interesting one.

It is here that al-Fārābī's conception of an "imaginative syllogism" becomes important. The theory is that representation in general and symbolic or metaphorical representation in particular (where metaphor serves as a paradigm of all poetic devices) invokes an implicit or tacit comparison, a "virtual analogy," and by so doing, evokes a tacit reasoning process. Representation, for al-Fārābī, is the proximate goal of poetry; the aim is not to deceive but to evoke images. These, like the accounts given by propositions, may be faithful or unfaithful to what they represent. Taken literally, their claims are false, just as the image in a mirror is not literally the object it represents before our eyes. But when poetic statements are expanded by a proper semeiology to spell out the virtual analogies they indirectly state, we can readily see, even in the language of prose, that the claims of poets may well be sound: Images may be apt or remote as well as graceful or awkward.[88] Indeed they may become the very stuff of prophecy.[89]

Al-Fārābī's theory of the poetic syllogism is the point of departure for Ibn Sīnā's poetics. Writing in summary form in the Logic of the *Danesh Nameh*, Ibn Sīnā speaks of certain givens as imaginative rather than factual. Their virtuality does not diminish their power:

> These are premises that stimulate the soul to a lively desire or loathing for some thing. One might be well aware that these premises are false, but if someone says, "What you are eating puts the bile in motion," even when it is honey and you know perfectly well that this is false, it is only natural to be disgusted and want no more. Thus both true and seemingly true opinions can form the givens of imagination.[90]

Such emotive appeals, regardless whether they are true or false, form the basis of the poetic syllogism. The reasoning invoked need involve no actual affirmation, yet it can produce a powerful psychic commitment or aversion.[91] Just as in al-Khwarizmī, it is because the givens are recognizable that their representation has the intended effect.

Parting company with Aristotle's emphasis on dramatic poetry, Ibn Sīnā reverts to his own experience and the varieties of poetry that he knows best, in an effort to penetrate the workings of our engagement by poetry, so as to work out the nature of the assent it does evoke. He is aware that dramatic poetry involves the playing of a role, but he assimilates its effectiveness to that of the symbolic, via the Aristotelian notion of gesture and presentation, features of "the player's art" (*hypocrisis*). Perhaps the Iranian tradition of the passion play makes him a bit more at home with the idea of role playing than some of his predecessors were.[92] But the undeveloped state of the form does not tempt him into elaborate discussions of the willing suspension of disbelief. Instead, he takes the more familiar and by his time richly studied and practiced realm of lyrical poetry as his paradigm and singles out the use of imaginative imagery as its most salient feature: Poetry produces its emotive effect through the representation of objects in imaginative images. In this sense it speaks to us hypothetically rather than categorically, calling old age "the evening of life," to cite a favorite example that Ibn Sīnā draws from Aristotle. The image represents a virtual syllogism by way of an implicit analogy – as if one had said, "If life were a day, old age would be its evening." On a human level, by reference to human experience, values, expectations, longings, and desires, the claim is true, the argument is sound, and not only sound but poignant, perhaps in part because the shortness of a day suggests the brevity of life, and the periods into which the passage of a day falls suggest the natural and inevitable sequence and cessation of the periods into which life too will fall.

Although imagery of the kind that Ibn Sīnā singles out is indirect (the very word for figurative usage in general in Arabic is *majāz*, license; metaphor specifically is *isti'āra*, literally, "borrowing"),[93] human responses to imagery (because of its personal and evocative pull on the emotions) are immediate, "unreflective," and spiritual (*nafsanī*) rather than mediate and mental (*fikrī*).[94] The reasoning process is implicit in the mind of the poet rather than explicit in the mind of the audience. Thus hearers need not supply an argument, as they do, for example, in listening to rhetoric, by Aristotle's account; we may be affected without overt mental engagement. The logic of metaphor, in other words, speaks directly to the heart – or, as Ibn Sīnā put it, it works directly on the imagination.

If one says "Honey is vomited bile," the characterization may be true on a literal level, but the intended effect is to produce aversion through the connotative impact of the classification, for bile is generally thought of as something disgusting. If one calls the face of the beloved a moon, the intended effect is to evoke the idea of beauty, through the comparison with the beauty of the moon. Literally the description is false, but figuratively the poet intends it to be true: In beauty the face of the beloved is claimed to be like the beauty of the moon.

Yet not every metaphor is true or apt, even on a figurative level. When a poet says (to quote Avicenna's own example), "The rose is a mule's anus with dung in its midst," he does not intend the description to be apt but only to evoke disgust. The evocative power of the image overpowers any claim upon verisimilitude: "It is as if one were trying to say, 'Everything which is . . . of such a description is filthy and unclean [so the rose too is filthy and unclean].' Although the utterance has the form of a syllogism (that is, if its premises are granted, its conclusion follows), the speaker does not intend any argument for the soundness of his claim but only to disgust the soul by the image that is applied."[95]

Appeal to such imagery, more for effect than for the truth that poetry can express, is not as rare as Avicenna's extreme example might suggest. Consider, for instance, the way Fitzgerald's Omar Khayyam links blood with roses, and the way decadent romantics in general can hardly avoid linking love with death, spring with death, eros with violence and death. Love, one might observe, is not the object of their interest. Avicenna purposely chooses an extreme example, because he wants to minimize even the appearance that a truth (rather than an emotive response) was intended. He thus isolates the emotive and evocative from the analytical dimension of poetic discourse. In great poetry these dimensions reinforce one another rather than competing. But in weak poetry they do compete. And our love for poetry in general should not obscure to us the fact that, if poetry can utter truths at all, then some poetry can lie.

Rhyme in Arabic poetry is *de rigueur.* It was quite unknown in the poetry that formed Aristotle's subject matter, so its prominence in Arabic was a matter of note for Ibn Sīnā. Indeed rhyme is unknown in most of the old literatures of the world, and it may well have come into European literatures through influences from the Arabic, first in the Byzantine and later in the Andalusian contacts of Arabic and European cultures. As Ibn Sīnā notes, meter is much more widely used in the world's diverse literatures. Yet neither rhyme nor meter, he argues, are of the essence of poetry, and poetry is certainly possible without them. Indeed, mere versification does not make a discourse poetry. That will depend on the evocative use of images.[96]

Matters of form like rhyme or meter are relevant at all because imaginative assent arises directly from what is said, whereas literal conviction focuses on the content and abstracts away from the manner of expression. It is for this reason that sound is relevant in poetry, as well as sense, and that poets pay such close attention to those elements of communication that "resonate between sound and sense."[97] Virtuosity in the use of language and images is what brings delight and marvel to poetic art. And these, we can say, are of the essence, although the aim is imaginative assent and thus communication of a special kind. For the effectiveness of poetry depends on the poignancy and immediacy of language – not on its being the most direct or literal way of denominating an object, but its immediacy to the emotions in gaining assent to the aptness of its images, which is to say, the fittingness and penetration of its claims.

Applying his standard of poetry, Ibn Sīnā argues that, say, the fables of Bidpai, those Aesopian, mildly satirical tales that were translated into Arabic via the Persian version of a Sanskrit original and gained popularity among the administrative or "secretarial" classes in Islamic societies, would not be poetry even if they were set to verse, because they "seek to state opinions resultant from the experiences of non-existent beings." The judgment may seem a little harsh. The point is not simply that the tales are untrue because the witty jackals Kalīla and Dimna or the King of the Mice are imaginary creatures. That would be a difficulty for any imaginative writing. But here the trouble is in finding an application for the Aristotelian hypothetical, "What would such a person do in such a situation?" How can questions of character or authenticity be answered when the device of animal fable has been used to make the figures of a fiction no more than mouthpieces for specific attitudes? Here the power of fiction has been vitiated by the trivialization of the thought experiment. We can inquire into the authenticity of Dostoevsky's or Cervantes' or even Homer's representation of the human condition and (crucially) we can be moved by the plight of an Oedipus or the wonderings of a Prince Andre or Pierre Bezuhoff, even though we know these personages are fictional – indeed our aesthetic response is heightened by that knowledge. *War and Peace* or *Crime and Punishment* would clearly qualify as poetry by Avicenna's standards. But the scrapes of Mickey Mouse and Donald Duck, or the cheap schematics of Fievel's troubles in the animated melodrama *An American Tale* do not qualify as poetry by Ibn Sīnā's standards, and even the anthropomorphisms of the portrayal do not help. Hans Christian Andersen's stories of the Nightingale or the Mermaid, or the Little Match Girl, or the Ugly Duckling, or even the Tin Soldier, the Christmas tree, the snails in the garden, or the pyrotechnic device, count as poetry by Ibn Sīnā's standards, because they move us by bringing us to confront some element of our humanity (even when their nominal subject is an animal or plant or inanimate object). But mere schematics do not.

Fable here is to poetry as cartooning is to painting: The mere denomination of the occasion for an emotion is not the same as the evocation of that emotion, just as the mere schematic suggestion of a surface or a face is not the same as the representation of that surface or that face. Skill and effort, virtuosity and commitment are required, just as in verse (no matter how heartfelt) art is needed to make the difference between greeting card doggerel and poetry. We know that we have poetry when we are moved, and what will move us in this case is what leads us, through images and delight in their special kind of truth, to a clearer or more vivid apprehension of what we call the human experience or the human condition, but what Ibn Sīnā calls simply matters of humanity (*al-insāniyyāt*).

Is this approach an example of a persuasive definition? Clearly there is a valuative content in terms like "poetry" or "painting" that allows a certain standard of merit to be applied before such terms (like accolades) are to be applied. There is some merit in the Chinese idea of "rectification of names": A soldier is a person who will fight, not merely one who wears a uniform. A painter is not a mere dauber, and it must remain possible to say that some professed painters are impostors, even though it is not a charge that should be made loosely or just tossed around at any painter whose work one does not care for. Surely we need to leave room for saying something other than celebratory about art in any genre, and so one must not reserve the very name of artist to a tiny elect. Yet the fact remains that, if we define the aims of an art broadly and generically enough, it should prove possible not only for some to practice an art badly but also for others to try but fail to practice it at all – and for some applications of the name of an artistic mode to be misnomers.

No one is offended if it is pointed out that Rodin did not make mobiles, and no one supposes that to combine that claim with the further recognition that Calder did would be somehow to pretend that Calder was a greater sculptor than Rodin. By the same token, I doubt that the owners of the several hands who originated and adapted the fables of Bidpai would have been mortally offended to learn that what they did was not poetry. It remains perfectly possible, in a kind of metaphoric exuberance or bathos to say that Disney's early black and white animations of Mickey Mouse are pure poetry. One can even claim (and with practice some have found that they can do it with a straight face) that the figure of Mickey teaches us much about the human condition. But bear in mind that Ibn Sīnā's standards do not validate poetry insofar as it is didactic (as though authentic achievement in one genre could be vouched for only by the standards of another.) On the contrary, Mickey Mouse is rarely moving – although often entertaining, especially at first sight. The interest of the image of man as mouse or mouse as man is fairly rapidly exhausted, far more rapidly than the antics of the image itself. And that, I think, is the source of Avicenna's problem: Where poetry turns into play, it ceases to be poetry, not because poetry must be work but because play too easily loses focus and becomes an end in itself rather than a means of moving human hearts through the projection of artful images.

Because Ibn Sīnā focuses his discussion of poetics on genres he knows and derives his knowledge of Greek literature from philosophic sources, he presumes that Greek poetry "was generally intended for imitating actions" and "to encourage or forestall action," while Arabic poetry is more interested in persons and characters. Arabic poetry, he observes, does not seek simply to paint men better or worse than we are or to moralize, like the allegorical paintings of the Manichaeans, which illustrate the ugliness of anger and the beauty of compassion. Rather, it can be more disengaged, painting things, as it were, as they are, perhaps for the sheer pleasure of the representation.

Here Ibn Sīnā recaptures the conceptual sense of Aristotle's point about the mimetic character of art. At the same time he remembers that because representation situates us in relation to what is represented it is always potentially evaluative. Homer, for example, offers subtler effects than the merely rhetorical view of poetry allows for, situating the mind with respect to a rich and often elevated world. The limitations of Ibn Sīnā's knowledge of Greek literature suggest a contrast to him in this regard between Greek and Arabic poetry. As Dahiyat puts it, Ibn Sīnā sees Greek poetry as "more engaged" than Arabic poetry. This judgment of Ibn Sīnā's is an artifact of Aristotle's apologetic claims *vis-à-vis* Ibn Sīnā's own knowledge of the character of Arabic poetry.[98] But it is notable that Ibn Sīnā does not adopt a moralistic stance toward poetry or even attempt to call the Arab poets "back" to their Platonic or Farabian mission. He does not even give preference to such poetry as belonging to a higher type. Nor does he locate the more disengaged sort of poetry exclusively among the Arabs or chauvinistically celebrate its "purity." Finally, he does not portray the tension between engagement and aesthetic distance in art as a starkly demanding *either/or*. Rather, his model suggests that some level of engagement is necessary if we are to be moved by art, and some degree of detachment is necessary if we are not simply to be deceived by it and so not moved at all. The subtlest effects, he suggests, and from a poetic point of view the highest aesthetically, are not those in which what is evil is simply shown to be evil and what is good simply shown to be good, but those in which artistic virtuosity, the poet's skillful use of words, portrays our world to us in new ways, ways that reveal truths about that world which we might not otherwise have apprehended.

NOTES

1 Ibn Khaldūn, *Muqaddimah*, VI 22, tr. Rosenthal, 3 (New York: Pantheon, 1958) 139–42.

2 See D.S. Margoliouth, "The Discussion between Abū Bishr Mattā and Abū Sa'īd al-Sīrāfī on the Merits of Logic and Grammar," *JRAS* (1905) 79–129.

3 Ibn Khaldūn, *Muqaddimah* VI 14, tr. Rosenthal, 3.34–45.

4 *Muqaddimah*, tr. Rosenthal, 3.45–51.

5 E.g., that the premises of a scientific demonstration must be universal, necessary, and primary.

6 Al-Ghazālī, *Al-Munqidh min al-Ḍalāl*, ed. F. Jabre (Beirut: UNESCO, 1959) 22.

7 Al-Ghazālī, *Tahāfut al-Falāsifa*, ed. M. Bouyges, 2nd edn (Beirut: Catholic Press, 1962).

8 *TF*, op. cit. Al-Ghazālī's argument in brief: Knowledge entails awareness, and awareness entails life: It is absurd to speak of a non-living being's receiving knowledge, since conscious beings are a subclass of living beings.

9 *TF* 205, n 30 = *TT* 536 l. 21 - 537 l. 2.

10 See "Maimonidean Naturalism" in my *Neoplatonism and Jewish Thought* (Albany: SUNY Press, 1992) for Maimonides' careful following of al-Ghazālī's lead on this issue.

11 Ibn Khaldūn, *Muqaddimah* VI 14, 22, tr. Rosenthal, 3.51–5, 143–5. As we learn from his friend Ibn al-Khaṭīb, Ibn Khaldūn was the author of a royally commissioned work on logic, an abridgement of the *Muḥaṣṣal* of Fakhr al-Dīn al-Rāẓī and abridgements of many of the works of Ibn Rushd. See Rosenthal, xliv.

12 See Diogenes Laertius, *Lives of the Eminent Philosophers* VII 60: "A notion is a mental presentation (*phantasma*) which, although it is not a reality (*on*) or a quality (*poion*), is treated as though it were (*hosanei*) a reality or a quality." Since Stoic *lekta* are terms rather than mere words or empty signs, and since the Stoic *ennoema* does have reality as an object of thought, one can call the Stoics conceptualists rather than nominalists in the full sense. But Stoic notions lack the constancy and uniformity that Aristotelian conceptual forms bring with them as a legacy of Platonism: Peripatetic conceptualism is an epistemic realism, where Stoic conceptualism, granted its mentalism, lacks the immanent essences that give intelligibility (and eternity) to Aristotelian natural kinds. Stoicism treats ideas as mere notional abstractions.

13 See Aristotle, *Peri Ideon* in Daniel Frank, *The Arguments from the Sciences in Aristotle's* Peri Ideon (New York: Peter Lang, 1984) 13–16. Aristotle, ap. Alexander of Aphrodisias, Commentary on the *Metaphysics* (79.15–80.6), argues that Platonic arguments for the reality of the Forms based on the existence of scientific knowledge, "do not prove the point at issue, namely that there are Forms, but prove that there are things besides individual and sensible things. By no means does it follow that these are Forms. For, besides the individuals there are the universals (*ta koina*), with which we say the sciences are concerned." Aristotle is a realist here, with regard to species, and universals in general; Plato's argument from the sciences *is* taken to require the reality of *some* object of knowledge — if not the Forms, as Plato supposed, then the (immutable) species which are the true locus of the intelligible forms resident in things.

14 Diogenes Laertius VII 75.

15 Diogenes Laertius VII 76.

16 See Sextus Empiricus, *Outlines of Pyrrhonism* II 110–12; cf. Diogenes Laertius VII 71. Note that Stoic inferences, as materially applied, always involve an assumption about the nature of the world, e.g.: 'The world is such that if it is day it is light.' The soundness of the argument that rests on such a premise is never purely a matter of form; still less is it a matter of essences. The argument can become a certainty, but only by stipulating appropriate (causal or logical) relations among its (sentential) terms and reducing their relations to the appropriate undemonstrated schema.

17 See Cicero, *De Divinatione; De Natura Deorum*. Platonism too is oracular in its way, even in the highly Peripatetic recension of Avicenna, as we have seen. But Stoic divination is far more dependent on arbitrarily imparted significances; far less so on implicitly understood meanings and intrinsic essences - far more voluntaristic, we might say. The differences between Stoic augury and Neo-

platonic intuition seem to presage the entire dispute between medieval voluntarists and rationalists.

18 The Skeptics pressed the problem the Stoics posed; see my "Skepticism," *Review of Metaphysics* 36 (1983) 819–48. As for the expository and explanatory functions of the syllogism and the directionality of its use in discovery, my friend and colleague Jim Tiles explicates clearly: "The direction of discovery in Aristotle is . . . from conclusion to premises; in finding the middle term which permits a syllogism, we find the explanation for the conclusion, and the syllogism is a means of presenting (demonstrating) that bit of understanding" (personal communication, 18 August 1991). The "conclusion," of course is what is observed, the phenomenon to be explained; the middle term, assigned to a subject, *kath' auto*, properly and essentially, carries an explanatory force.

19 *Posterior Analytics* I 1. The alternative, Aristotle suggests, is to admit that we do not know "that every pair is even," since there are pairs that we have never thought about and so could not have judged (sc., not explicitly) as to their evenness.

20 The line is from the *Mu'allaqa* of the pre-Islamic poet Zuhayr, here appealed to as a standard of linguistic usage, and interpreted (according to the rule of charity) as voicing no patent absurdity.

21 Al-Ash'arī, *K. al-Luma'*, ed. and tr. R.J. McCarthy (Beirut: Catholic Press, 1952) articles 186–7 = Arabic 87–8, English 107–8.

22 Zuhayr, in fact, was a moralist among the poets of the pre-Islamic heroic age, the age traditionally characterized in Islamic historiography as the age of barbarism. His *Mu'allaqa*, one of the seven most honored classics of pre-Islamic poetry, was written when he was in his eighties and celebrates the generosity of two tribal princes who composed a fratricidal blood feud that had grown to a clan war, by paying a huge indemnity, although they themselves had shed no blood. Zuhayr "with the wisdom of the age, stands out as the mouthpiece of the pessimistic ethics of the desert," H.A.R. Gibb, *Arabic Literature* (Oxford: Clarendon Press, 1963) 22; R.A. Nicholson, *A Literary History of the Arabs* (Cambridge: Cambridge University Press, 1956; first edn, 1907) 116–19. Zuhayr's cynical remark about wrongdoing is an expression of his pessimism, not of his morals.

23 Maimonides, following Rabbinic precedent, regularly adopts the opposite technique, relying on the absence of a quantifier to generalize rabbinic dicta, transforming them into rules and axioms: e.g., 'The Torah speaks in human language' – sc., not just here, but in general.

24 To be sure, syllogistic certainty can equally be nibbled away by unbridled stipulations about the necessary criteria of class membership. But the hypothetical and categorical forms of expression are not completely symmetrical in this respect. For the essentialism that is showcased and rendered canonical in the Aristotelian syllogism is suppressed and rendered (at best) implicit when predicate terms become invisible in hypothetical reasoning.

25 *K. al-Luma'*, article 129 = Arabic 57, English 80.

26 *K. al-Luma'*, article 130 = Arabic 57, English 80.

27 See al-Ash'arī, *Maqālāt al-Islāmiyyīn*, ed. H. Ritter (Wiesbaden: Steiner, 1963) 605–6.

28 Mu'tazilite doctrine adapts this argument from the Stoic reasoning, that divine concern demands both special providence and the provision of auguries. Muslim orthodoxy went even further in the same direction. For, although

insisting that mortals have no authority by which to judge what would be seemly in God, it vehemently objected to the notion that the *Qur'ān* was created. The orthodox preferred to treat the *Qur'ān* as an uncreated hypostasis, thus unwittingly following in the footsteps of pagan anti-creationists, Christian trinitarians and Jewish exponents of the Torah as God's eternal wisdom. See A.J. Wensinck, *The Muslim Creed* (New York: Cass, 1965; first edn, 1932). All of these forerunners of the now orthodox Islamic idea of an eternal *Qur'ān* upheld the notion that God, as essentially a Creator, would not withhold the grace of His creative act – at least not from the sort of hypostasis that would be capable of receiving it eternally. But note the hypothetical form of the argument, still preserved from the Stoic appeal to divine *pronoia*: "If there are gods, there is divination; if there is divination there are gods." It is this proposition that Cicero labels as "the very citadel of the Stoics"; see *De Divinatione* I vi 10. One cannot place God within a genus and argue from acquaintance with what others of His kind would do; here one must argue hypothetically. Ash'arites object to the Mu'tazilite attempt to box in God's choices by making inferences from divine perfection. But they employ the same *form* of argument themselves when they argue that 'Given God's sovereignty, it is impermissible to say that God commits any wrongdoing or injustice to His creatures.'

29 See Aristotle, *Prior Analytics*, I 27, 43b 12–15; *Posterior Analytics* I 5, 74a 27.

30 Al-Fārābī, *Book of Letters*, ed. Muhsin Mahdi (Beirut: Dar el-Machreq, 1969) 150–5. I understand that Professor Mahdi has a better ordered text in preparation and has circulated a preliminary version, but I have not been able to see this as of the present publication.

31 Al-Fārābī, *Sharḥ fī 'l-'Ibāra* (Commentary on *De Interpretatione*) 9, ed. Kutsch and Marrow, 98 l. 18; see my discussion in *Iyyun* 23 (1972) 100–12; in Hebrew with English summary.

32 *Danesh Nameh*, Achena and Massé *Le Livre de Science* 1 (Paris: Les Belles Lettres, 1986) 80–1.

33 Al-Fārābī, *K. al-Mukhtasar al-Saghīr fī 'l-Manṭiq 'alā ṭariq al-Mutakallimūn*, ed. M. Turker *Revue de la Faculté des langues, d'histoire et de géographie de l'Université d'Ankara* 16 (1958) 244–86, p. 282, citing *Nicomachaean Ethics*, 1094b, 1098a. Aristotle identifies ethics, politics and rhetoric as the areas requiring some imprecision; al-Fārābī's addition of *kalām* to the list suggests his general treatment of it as a mode of apologetic, thus assimilable to the realm of the prescriptive.

34 See Kwame Gyekye, "Al-Fārābī on the Logic of the Arguments of the Muslim Philosophical Theologians," *JHP* 27 (1989) 135–43; N. Rescher, tr., *Al-Fārābī's Short Commentary on Aristotle's Prior Analytics* (Pittsburgh: University of Pittsburgh Press, 1963).

35 Ibn Sīnā, *Shifā'*, *Qiyās*, translated by Nabil Shehaby as *The Propositional Logic of Avicenna* (Dordrecht: Reidel, 1973) 35.

36 See Shams Constantine Inati's translation of the Logic of Ibn Sīnā's *Ishārāt, Remarks and Admonitions: Part One – Logic* (Toronto: Pontifical Institute of Medieval Studies, 1984) 24.

37 *Danesh Nameh*, *Logic* tr. after Farhang Zabeeh, *Avicenna's Treatise on Logic*, Part One of *Danesh Nameh Alai* (The Hague: Nijhoff, 1971) 25.

38 Cf. *Danesh Nameh*, Achena and Massé, 1.92.

39 Nabil Shehaby, *The Propositional Logic of Avicenna* (a translation from *Al-Shifā: al-*

Qiyās) (Dordrecht: Reidel, 1973) 54–5.

40 See Zabeeh, 14–15; cf. *Ishārāt, Logic*, tr., Inati, 47.

41 See Zabeeh, 12 n. 2; 14.

42 Avicenna had a name for this process of penetrating to the inner meaning of an argument. He called the process of ascertaining the connections that hold together an argument *taḥqīq*, assaying; this was a matter, fundamentally, of discovering a middle term. He called the probing of the premises of an argument to lay bare the inner content of their terms (upon which the ultimate validity of the argument would rest) *taḥṣīl*, appraisal. He called philosophers who were penetrating in this way *muḥaṣṣilīn*, in the sense of "insightful." Cf. Dimitri Gutas, *Avicenna and the Aristotelian Tradition* (Leiden: Brill, 1988) 86 n. 1, 188–9.

43 See Shehaby, 14; Galen, *Institutio Logica*, tr. with commentary by J.S. Kieffer (Baltimore, 1964) 76. A notable instance of the realism embedded in the Peripatetic conceptualization of the role of logic is the Aristotelian doctrine, shared by Avicenna, of the existential import of affirmations. Ibn Sīnā takes "Zayd is sightless" to be an affirmation of the existence and blindness of Zayd, whereas "It is not the case that Zayd can see" is interpreted by Ibn Sīnā as compatible with the existence of no such person as Zayd. See Zabeeh, 22 and n. 11 and N. Rescher, "Existence in Arabic Logic and Philosophy," in Rescher's *Studies in Arabic Philosophy* (Pittsburgh: University of Pittsburgh Press, 1967) 73. Note however, that Ibn Sīnā does not regard his acceptance of the Aristotelian conception of existential import as conflicting with his doctrine that existence is a separate notion from essence, presumably because *affirmation* goes beyond mere conception in the same way that existence is understood to add a new fact not given in the mere conception of a subject.

44 Zabeeh, 25.

45 Hidé Ishiguro, *Leibniz's Philosophy of Logic and Language* (Cambridge: Cambridge University Press, 1990; first edn, 1972) 158.

46 Ishiguro, 157.

47 Ishiguro, 155.

48 G. Frege, *Begriffschrift* (1879), in P. Geach and M. Black, eds, *Translations from the Philosophical Writings of Gottlob Frege* (Oxford: Blackwell, 1960) 1–2.

49 Shehaby, 59.

50 Ishiguro, 158.

51 Zabeeh, 26; Achena and Massé render it "compatibility," but that is too weak to capture the claim Ibn Sīnā is making.

52 *TF* 195.

53 John Passmore, *Recent Philosophers* (LaSalle: Open Court, 1990) 7–8.

54 See Alan Ross Anderson and N.D. Belnap, *Entailment: The Logic of Relevance and Necessity* (Princeton: Princeton University Press, 1975); N.D. Belnap and J.M. Dunn, "Entailment and the Disjunctive Syllogism," in G. Fløistad, ed., *Contemporary Philosophy* 1 (The Hague: Nijhoff, 1981); and John Passmore's discussion in *Recent Philosophers* (London: Duckworth, 1985) 8–9.

55 Shehaby, 46.

56 Shehaby, 50.

57 My colleague Jim Tiles criticizes Ibn Sīnā here: "If there is any use for 'If *p* then *q*' which expresses only a coincidental connection between the two, why balk at coincidental exclusions? Any fallacies this permitted would have parallels in the

case of conditionals." I think this is correct, but it seems that Ibn Sīnā is more comfortable in allowing arbitrary stipulations about conditional claims than he is about disjunctive ones, despite his awareness of the convertibility of "conjunctive" and disjunctive conditionals: If *p* excludes *q*, Ibn Sīnā wants to be able to say why; whereas, if *p* entails *q* he is willing to allow that the relationship may be natural or purely stipulative. His point is that we cannot always assume that we need an explanation for the non-existence of something, since its *non-existence* may be necessary in the nature of the case. So (he seems to assume) we have no heuristic use for (arbitrary) disjunctions, as we do (in the play that precedes the framing of a hypothesis) for arbitrary hypotheticals.

58 Shehaby, 37.

59 Shehaby, 12, 27, n. 75.

60 See Cicero, *De Finibus* III viii 27.

61 Cf. Gerard Watson, *The Stoic Theory of Knowledge* (Belfast: The Queen's University, 1966) 55–7, 84.

62 Shehaby, 55.

63 Ibn Sīnā, *Shifā'*, quoted in Ibrahim Madkour, *L'Organon d'Aristote dans le Monde Arabe* (Paris: Vrin, 1969; first edn, 1934) 79–81; cf. 245.

64 *Muqaddimah*, VI 22, Rosenthal, 3.139–43 = Cairo ed. (n.d.) VI 27, 491–2; cf. Nicholas Rescher, *Studies in the History of Arabic Logic* (Pittsburgh: Pittsburgh University Press, 1963) 14–19.

65 *Danesh Nameh*, Achena and Massé, 1.102.

66 See Plato's *Gorgias* 459, 462–3, 500–2.

67 Aristotle, *Rhetoric* I 2, 1358a 11–13; and see Larry Arnhart, *Aristotle on Political Reasoning: A Commentary on the Rhetoric* (DeKalb: Northern Illinois University Press, 1986; first edn, 1981).

68 Ibn Sīnā, *Al-Shifā': La Logique VIII – Rhétorique (Al-Khaṭābah)*, ed. M. Salem (Cairo: Imprimerie Nationale, 1954) 1–6.

69 *Al-Khaṭābah*, 13–14.

70 *Al-Khaṭābah*, 15.

71 *Al-Khaṭābah*, 16–17.

72 *Al-Khaṭābah*, 18–19; *Najāt*, Rhetoric.

73 See Al-Fārābī's *K. al-Ḥurūf*, in Muhsin Mahdi, ed., *The Book of Letters* (Beirut: Dar el-Machreq, 1969) 137–47; see my discussion in *Sprachphilosophie*, 2.2.

74 Jack Bilmes, *Discourse and Behavior* (New York: Plenum, 1986) 22–5.

75 See Abner Cohen, *Arab Border-Villages in Israel* (Manchester: Manchester University Press, 1965).

76 Aristotle, *Rhetoric* I 2, 1355b 27; 4, 1359a 30.

77 Islamic Iran knew puppet plays and shadow plays, the mimicry of itinerant singers and dancers, and even a type of popular passion play; see note 92 below. But religious objections to the impersonation of living individuals prevented the development in Islamic lands of drama as we know it, until modern European influences led to the establishment of theaters and a tradition of dramatic writing in the mid-nineteenth century. As J.T.P. de Bruijn remarks, "The Greek theaters which existed in some places after the invasion of Alexander remained a foreign element and soon disappeared without having exerted a noticeable influence." *EI* 6.761b. Muslim students and faculty members at my own university effectively put a stop to a Religion Professor's dramatic impersonations of celebrated religious leaders by conveying a threat against his life

should he make good on his intention of including Muḥammad among those represented.

78 See Ismail Dahiyat, *Avicenna's Commentary on the* Poetics *of Aristotle: A Critical Study with an Annotated Translation* (Leiden: Brill, 1974); for al-Fārābī's relationship to Abū Bishr Mattā, see F.W. Zimmermann, *Al-Fārābī's Commentary and Short Treatise on Aristotle's* De Interpretatione (London: Oxford University Press, 1981) cv–cxvi; for the translation of the *Poetics*, J. Tkatsch, *Die arabische Übersetzung der Poetik des Aristoteles und die Grundlage der Kritik des griechischen Textes* (Vienna, 1928) 2 vols; Abū Bishr Mattā, *K. Arisṭuṭalis fī 'l-Shi'r*, ed. Shukri Ayyad (Cairo: Dār al-Kitāb, 1967); D.S. Margoliouth, *Annalecta Orientalia ad Poeticam Aristotelicam* (London, 1887) 1–78 and Margoliouth's *The Poetics of Aristotle* (London, 1911).

79 See N. Rescher, *Studies in the History of Arabic Logic* (Pittsburgh: University of Pittsburgh Press, 1963) 30.

80 Ed. Michelangelo Guidi and Richard Walzer, "Studi su al-Kindī: I - Uno scritto introduttivo allo studio di Aristotele," *Atti della Reale Accademia dei Lincei*, Memorie della classe di scienze morali, storiche e filologiche, Series 6, 6 (1940) 375–90.

81 See Rescher, 37.

82 See Aristotle, *Poetics* 1448a.

83 See Rescher, 75.

84 See al-Fārābī, *Iḥṣā' al-'Ulūm*, ed. Uthman Amin (Cairo, 1968) 68–9.

85 Al-Fārābī, 83–9.

86 Dahiyat, 18, 20.

87 Al-Fārābī, *Fuṣūl al-Madanī*, article 52, ed. D.M. Dunlop (Cambridge: Cambridge University Press, 1961) 135; cf. Dunlop's translation, 49.

88 Al-Fārābī, *The Canons of Poetry*, ed. and tr. A.J. Arberry, *Rivista degli Studi Orientali* 17 (1938) 267–78. Al-Fārābī calls the semeiologist "an expert on *rumūz*." Arberry renders *rumūz* "allusions." But this, as Dahiyat explains (p. 24), "is rather inaccurate: the word . . . has a much wider significance, — 'allegory,' 'symbol,' 'riddle,' or 'emblem,'" The reference is to any form of indirect signification. The expert al-Fārābī refers to is one who understands the significances that may be given to "emblems," "symbols," "allegories," and other figurative expressions.

89 See al-Fārābī, *K. Mabādi ārā ahli 'l-Madīnati 'l-Fāḍila*, ed. R. Walzer (Oxford: Clarendon Press, 1985) 218–27, 244–7, and Walzer's notes, pp. 416–17.

90 *Danesh Nameh*, Achena and Massé, 1.116.

91 Ibn Sīnā, *Ishārāt*, 81.

92 The Iranian passion play, a Shi'ite popular form based on the martyrdom of Hasan and Hussein, like the Persian miniature, manifests Iran's greater receptivity to the mimetic, as compared with Arabic culture. For the form, see *EI*, s.v. *Ta'zia*, and Matthew Arnold's classic essay, "A Persian Passion Play," in *Essays in Criticism* First Series, ed., Sister Thomas Marion Hoctor (Chicago: University of Chicago Press, 1964; the series was first published by Macmillan in 1865, but "A Persian Passion Play," delivered at Oxford in 1872, was added in 1875) 135–58.

93 The verb *ajāza* means to use poetic license; the adjective *majāzī* means figurative; the semantical root has to do with passage and permission, thus suggesting the indirection of imagery, which takes the license to encroach on neighboring senses. Metaphors are understood in terms of borrowing since they signify one

thing by way of terms that conventionally designate something else.

94 Ibn Sīnā, *Poetics* I 2, tr. Dahiyat, 61–2.

95 See Deborah Black, *Logic and Aristotle's* Rhetoric *and* Poetics *in Medieval Arabic Philosophy* (Leiden: Brill, 1990) 230.

96 Cf. Aristotle, *Poetics* 1, 1447b. See also the detailed account of the poetic syllogism in Selim Kemal, *The Poetics of Alfarabi and Avicenna* (Leiden: Brill, 1991).

97 Ibn Sīnā, *Poetics* I 4, 6; cf. Dahiyat, tr., 63–4.

98 Ibn Sīnā, *Poetics* II 10–13.

INDEX

Leibniz, G.W. continued
130; sufficient reason 52, 85
Lévi-Strauss, Claude 204
Locke, John 129–30
logic: Aristotelian 53, 93, 138, 188, 209; Avicennan 12, 198, 202–3, 208–10; Fārābian 195; Islamic acceptance 184–8; and metaphysics 69; predicate 196, 203; propositional 188–99; intensional, extensional 207; of relevance 202–3
logicism 94, 208–9
Logos 89–90, 168, 172

ma'ānī (*intentiones*) 145
Madkour, Ibrahim 113
Maḥmud of Ghaznā 4, 7, 8, 20, 22–4, 27, 29, 41, 46
Maimonides: ethics 62; God and nature 63, 79–80, 95, 119, 177; *Guide to the Perplexed* 167; *kalām* 53–4, 62, 89–90; possibility 84, 86, 92, 108–9, 194; soul 160
Majd al-Dawla 26–9
al-Makkī, Abū Ṭālib 90
malakūt 89–90, 167
Malcolm, Norman 76
al-Ma'mūn 4, 31
Ma'mūn b. Ma'mūn 23
Manicheans 3, 10, 225
Manṣūr b. Nūḥ 8, 10–11, 20–2
Marmura, Michael 87–8, 93, 178, 179
Mas'ūd of Ghaznā 23, 40–2
mathematics 12, 32–4, 146, 159, 211
matter 51, 55–8, 61, 63, 69, 72, 82, 89, 108, 128, 149; materialism 56, 66, 154
mawjūd 103, 107
Megarians 73, 113, 188, 193
melancholia 26
Merlan, Philip 164–5, 169–70
metaphor 220, 222
metaphysics 100–1, 194; of creation 67; of morals 62; *see also* being
metempsychosis 26, 128
meter 223
midrash 90
Mill, J. S. 129
mimesis 217–26
Miskawayh vii, 38, 62
monopsychism 126–9, 164–72
Morewedge, Parviz 73, 75
motion 115, 145, 149, 207
musāmaḥa 195
al-Muta' 91
mutability 55, 69, 76, 98
al-Mu'tasim 3
Mu'tazilites 21–3, 54, 229; action 62, 92, 176, 192–3; causality 34, 119; contingency 114
al-Muwaffaq 11
mysticism 72, 171; rational 39–40, 124, 165–7; *see also* Sufism

al-Narshakhī 10
Naṣr b. Aḥmad 8, 10
al-Nātilī 12–13
naturalism 54, 59, 78–80, 88–9, 92, 125–6, 149–53, 186–7
necessity: causal 63, 65–6, 74, 189; moral 54; relative 63–6, 80–1, 85, 88, 94, 115, 125, 143, 208
Neoplatonism 40, 56–62, 72–4, 80, 82–3, 91, 96–8, 123, 135, 150–3, 165, 171, 179, 187
Neruda, Pablo 172
Nestorians 3, 14
Newton, Isaac 150
Nīshāpūr 1, 2, 27
Niẓām al-Mulk 9, 12, 49
nominalism: modal 84–5, 94, 208; ontic 131, 137, 189, 227
Nūḥ b. Manṣūr 11, 16–17, 20
Nūḥ b. Naṣr 8, 10–12

occasionalism 23, 38, 50–4, 67, 144–5, 154, 162, 186–7
Oedipus 164, 224
Otherness 81

Pangloss 99
pantheism 40, 56, 96, 115, 128, 164–72
Paracelsus 34–5
Parmenides 55, 69, 165
Pascal, Blaise 13, 98–9
Passmore, John 201–2
Paul the Persian 30
Peirce, C. S. 75, 131